UNSUPERVISED
COWS

UNSUPERVISED COWS

A LIFE STORY

TIM LOWE

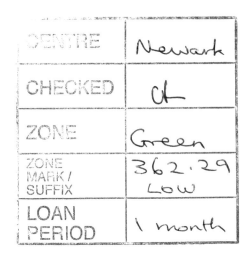

Copyright © 2011 by Tim Lowe.

Library of Congress Control Number:		2010918195
ISBN:	Hardcover	978-1-4568-2896-7
	Softcover	978-1-4568-2895-0
	Ebook	978-1-4568-2897-4

This book was printed in the United States of America.

To order additional copies of this book, contact:
Xlibris Corporation
1-888-795-4274
www.Xlibris.com
Orders@Xlibris.com
89204

CONTENTS

Prologue

The story title comes from my daughter, and after thinking about a title for a long time, my wife suggested "Unsupervised Cows." In life we are like unsupervised cows, never really thinking how our actions will affect our lives as well as the people who love and care for us every day.

According to who you talk to in my immediate family, the story of the unsupervised cows will vary. Here is the way I remember it.

On one of our many vacation trips, as I recall, we were on our way to Maryland to visit family and to see our nation's capital, Washington DC. My children were very young. Victoria was only four years old, and Timmy was at the wise old age of eight. As we toured the countryside, seeing how vast and fruitful America really was, we were blessed to be riding in the comfort of our Toyota Sequoia SUV, with the air-conditioning on and listening to some of my wife's favorite gospel music. We had plenty of time to talk with each other as we had left our busy work schedules behind. Our children always spoke freely, asking many questions about the things going on in their young lives. As we looked out of the windows, they asked us about the huge farms, industries, and how the landscape changed from Ohio to our destination.

We were on a ten-hour trip; and on that particular day, the Lord blessed us with a rainstorm, the rain sometimes increasing its intensity. I didn't mind because it cleaned some of the bugs off the windshield.

As my daughter Victoria peered out the window, she noticed a herd of cows standing in the heavy rainstorm on a hillside, next to a big barn and dairy farm. She said, "Look at those cows standing in the rain, just standing there. Dad, those cows need some supervision. Those are unsupervised cows. Don't they know it's raining?"

As soon as Timmy heard that, he began to break out in uncontrollable laughter, which made my wife and me laugh too. Victoria sat back in her seat, folding her arms with a look of disapproval because she didn't appreciate being laughed at. As the laughter increased, I saw tears rolling down her cheeks. Rhonda and I tried to explain to her that the rain and mud didn't really bother the cows, and they were perfectly content getting wet and muddy. To Victoria's credit, she actually had a valid point; and in her world, those cows did need a supervisor to tell them to get out of the rain. Many years later and after each of us telling the story of the unsupervised cows with much laughter, little did we know that this would be the title of my story.

Trying to find a title to a book about my life story, after some serious thought, I couldn't find anything that best described my life. As Rhonda and I put our heads together, she said, "Why don't you call it 'Unsupervised Cows'?"

I said, "Why would I call it that?" And I continued to search for a title, and I wondered why my wife would think that would be a good title. After a few days of thinking, I understood why that title fit; this was not a good title, but a great title.

In life we are like unsupervised cows not knowing when to come in out of the rain, and out of the mouth of a four-year-old baby girl, she had a thought that the cows needed a supervisor to lead them out of the rain. Sometimes people need other people to lead them in life; just like the cows, we don't have enough sense to come in out of the rain or doing what's right for us. We don't know when to stop doing drugs, drinking, and a host of other things that don't lead us down the right path in life. We are like unsupervised cows standing on the wet muddy hillside, waiting for something to happen. We need each other or a supervisor to guide us out of our path of self-destruction.

God is the answer. He is the supervisor, and he left us a guide (the Bible) to help us. He also gave us church with the help of preachers, who are the foremen who report to the supervisor, God, to lead the people or unsupervised cows out of the rain, into an environment that will shelter us from the evils of life. But just like the cows, we need some guidance to keep us out of the rain.

People and unsupervised cows have a lot in common; I was one of those unsupervised cows, not knowing when to come out of the rain. I didn't seek shelter and didn't even care how much it rained in my life, leading myself down a path of self-destruction. Life came at me like a blinding rainstorm, and I was with the herd standing in the rain, not knowing where to go. I lost my faith in the Lord, but through family and friends, God sent his supervisors with many messages and directions from the Bible to lead me out of the rain to protect myself.

After many years, I finally came out of the rain, and I am no longer an unsupervised cow. I seek shelter from the evils of the world through God and his mighty supervisors who lead me in out of the rain. I trust and have faith in the Lord, and each time a little rain falls, I ask for guidance to lead me from the cold rain that life brings.

This book is about the life of an unsupervised cow that didn't have sense enough to come in out of the rain. I was just one unsupervised cow, and there are too many unsupervised cows in the world. With the knowledge from experience, I hope that I can be one of God's supervisors to help lead you out of the rain and into the shelter of the Lord.

The Beginning

My mother told me I was born on the coldest day of the year and the first day of winter, according to the calendar, in a blinding snowstorm: December 21, 1960, in Cleveland, Ohio. I don't know if my father was even there. I was the second child born to my father, Fred Lowe, and my mother, Marietta Lowe. I am the second oldest of six children, the four children of Fred and Marietta and two more children to my stepfather John Fryer and my mother. All children were born caesarean, or C-section, which was one of many pains my mother suffered through life.

Living in Wickliffe, a suburb of Cleveland, Ohio, we were the only black family in a Catholic school system, Our Lady of Mt. Carmel. My aunts, uncles, and cousins also went to the same school. We didn't have a lot of money and would receive care packages throughout the year to help feed families that didn't have as much as others.

We were taught by nuns and priests with firm discipline and strong religion; although they did not understand that we were different than the rich well-to-do and the Italian children that went to the same school. Being black in Wickliffe was like living in the early sixties down south; even though we were in a Catholic school system, the children and their parents knew how to make you feel less than human. Racial injustice was alive and well.

By the time I was in kindergarten, I knew the word "nigger" very well. I was one who thought that there must be some harsh punishment for using such a word, so I became a great fighter. By the time I was in the fifth grade, I was known as one of the toughest kids in the school. My older brother, Bill, being the slim good-looking kid and a much more kindhearted child, was well received by many if not by all the kids in the school. I was known as the fat kid that could fight like hell. To the nuns and priests, I was trouble because I did not and still do not believe in turning the other cheek. Sometimes I would fight to help the weaker and smaller kids that would fall prey to the bullies and older kids. This was the way I would make friends that were actually scared of me because of my reputation. Basically I would never fight a kid that I thought I could beat up. I liked the challenge of the bigger and stronger kids, and I actually liked a good fight.

Learning was very difficult for me, being a fighter and trying to deal with all the things happening at home. To top it off, I was left-handed; and to the nuns, this was a curse. Later on in life, I considered being left-handed a blessing. The nuns would see me writing with my left hand and try to force me to write with my right hand; it was impossible, and I felt everything about me was different than any other student. Often, when I was caught writing with my left hand, the nuns would make me hold out my left hand and smack my hand with a ruler in hopes of correcting me, yelling at me to use my right hand. After getting my left hand smacked with a ruler more times than I care to remember, the nuns would finally give up, and I continued to use my left hand. At the time I was in grade school, the nuns believed being left-handed was a sign of the devil.

Later I would be taught by an old nun, who was probably seventy years old when I was in the fifth grade. She depended on me to carry her leather book bag to the convent, when all the other children would quickly run off after school. I actually enjoyed her company, and we were close friends. She would often invite me in the convent and talk to me. She believed I was a good kid despite all the trouble I would get into. Sister Reginald will be forever ingrained in my memory. She was the first teacher that ever believed in me. When I didn't have lunch, she would find a way to feed me and a host of other children that were hungry. She was actually a true saint, and everything that I was taught about a true Christian makes me believe that she is seated at the right hand of God in heaven.

Honor Thy Father
and Thy Mother

School was nothing compared to the demons my three siblings and I had to fight at home. My father liked to spend his free time beating the crap out of us and my mother. My father liked to drink and party and spend money we didn't have, and when my mother would question his actions, the fight was on. There would be days when everything was fine until he came home from work. First thing when he came home, he would expect to have his dinner served to him on a TV tray while he watched his television shows. He would take off his shoes with black dress socks; the entire house would reek of foot odor. He would then head for the shower and expect his dinner to be served to him without any interruptions from children, telephones, or anything else in the world.

My mother would try to talk to him about bills or school functions, and he would blow up, and many times would use his fists when he didn't have the answers. My sister would go to her room and hide; my brothers, Billy and Danny, would go to our room in the basement until my father would leave after he beat up my mother. After my father left the house, my mother would come and get us, and we would have a peaceful dinner.

My brother Billy—who was one year older than me and my sister, one year younger than me—actually had a true love for my father. My brother Danny is four years younger than I am, and later on in life, I found out that he had the same harsh feelings about our father. I can remember most, if not all, the beatings and abuse my mother took. I had no love, no respect, and no compassion for my father. As my mother told me, I was my father's greatest challenge. Everyone said, out of all my father's children, I was a carbon copy of him. I favored him, and he punished me for it. He would often say I was lazy, and he wanted me to be a fighter due to the fact that he wasn't, when it came to fighting men.

Actually my mother told me I was able to out-think him even at a young age; and he knew it, so he would always look for ways to punish or use his whipping brush to prove superiority. She told me that even as a child, I would not be broken. I was determined not to be anything like him. My brothers knew that if they wanted to start a fight, they would yell, "Freddy, Freddy, Freddy," at me. When I was growing up, I actually thought that I would beat my wife and abuse my children because I was just like him. I was actually scared for my future wife and children. I vowed never to get married in fear that I would change into the same kind of monster I was named after. Growing up, I tried to be everything he wasn't. If I thought it was something he would do, I would do just the opposite.

We had relatives on all five of the streets that blacks were allowed to live on in Wickliffe. Because we were Catholic, we had big families. My grandfather was the second oldest of twelve children; he had nine children, and all his sisters and brothers had many children. One of his sisters had fifteen children. We had over three hundred relatives in the city of Cleveland.

Some of the good times we had were when we had a big family get-together. We would all meet over one of the family members' house and party in the backyard, or inside in the winter months. There would be tons of food and drinks for everyone. I can remember my great-grandmother Margret Massey dancing with all the children. She was a little lady with a long gray ponytail that went down the length of her back. She would tell us stories of her childhood and how our family owned half the island of Martinique in the West Indies. She told us that our family had to flee the island when the British came to take the island. She also told us that our family gave our half of that island to the Catholic Church so the British couldn't clam it.

Some of my family members tracing the family tree tried to go back to the island for information about the family. They were told never to come to the island again; the people thought that they were there to claim our half of the island back from the Catholic Church. My mother's side of the family was West Indian with a slight touch of the Irish and Italian. My father's side of the family was Mexican and black. The world is truly one big melting pot.

All of my relatives on both sides of the family have light brown skin and wavy hair, or as darker-colored folk used to call us, high yellow, or red. I carry that trait very well; some of my cousins have red hair and blue or green eyes. My family is a mixture of many races and getting more mixed up every day. But to white people, they say we are black. I am proud to be called black; I am a light brown black man who is in love with my race. My family taught us to hold our heads high and be proud of what the Lord did some of his best work on. In our family, we were taught to love all the Lord's people. We are all equal in the eyes of the Lord.

Life wasn't all bad for us. We would often do things that would get one of us in trouble, which meant the rest of us would enjoy sidesplitting laughter, with tears rolling down our cheeks. Including my aunts and uncles next door, there was always a bunch of kids around. Their friends and all our friends meant that if you did something to promote laughter or make yourself the center of attention, there were plenty of people around to laugh at you.

My brothers and I would get haircuts in the backyard, and Danny was about four years old. We all had huge afros back then, and a local teenager would cut our hair. As I was getting my hair cut, the barber put the clippers down. When he turned around, Danny had cut a path about three inches wide and eight inches long right in the middle of his head. I believe he was the only kid that I ever saw with a reverse Mohawk. My mother took pictures, and Danny remained like that until his hair grew back. Everyone there laughed until they could laugh no more.

Well, I guess I will have to tell on myself too. I was about eight years old. My mother was talking on the phone and making chili; as she turned around, she saw me with some hot peppers in my hand. She screamed at me to put the hot peppers down. I looked at my brother Bill and shoved one of those hot peppers in my left nostril. Before I knew what was happening, I felt an intense burning sensation in my nose. I ran around the house screaming, "My nose is on fire, my nose is on fire!" I ran to the bathroom and grabbed a washrag, putting cold water on it and then on my nose. The washrag had some acne soap on it, which made my nose burn even more. My mother finally had to get off the phone and help me. My brothers and sister laughed for a week, and I had a burn on the left side of my nose for about a month.

When the winter months came, all the kids for miles around would go to the top of our street to sled ride. We had a monster hill that was on church property, and we would stay there all day. We would use whatever we could find to slide down the hill—cardboard boxes, garbage can tops. One day I found an old freezer door, and it made the best sled. Everyone wanted to use it. I would run up the hill and slide down as quickly as possible. Well, I had some old, slick-soled army boots on; and as I was running up the hill, I slipped on the freezer door. I broke my two front teeth and cut my upper and lower lip. Sliding back down the hill, I left a long trail of blood down the snow-white hill with the freezer door at the bottom.

About two weeks later, after my wounds healed, my mother took me to the dentist. Now I had two silver caps on my front teeth, and that provided a lot of entertainment for a lot of people. Now I was the fat kid with two silver teeth for all to see. I wore the two silver caps on my front teeth until I was eighteen years old and had a job with a dental plan to pay for normal-looking teeth. Some girls found it appealing, I didn't. One girl used to call me "silver mine." I just wanted to be left alone. If someone wanted to describe me, I would often hear, "Do you know the fat kid with the huge 'fro and silver teeth?" Most of my friends would never say anything. They knew it bothered me.

While growing up, we were banned from watching *The Three Stooges* because Danny would do what *The Three Stooges* would do. He would throw hammers and poke you in the eyes, bite you or slap you in the face, not knowing that these things could hurt you; it didn't hurt anybody on the television. There was also a show called *Ultraman* we couldn't watch because my sister had a dream that Ultraman climbed through her bedroom window one night. Bill would often stay up past his bedtime talking to some girl on the phone. He always had some little girlfriend, sometimes two or three. We nicknamed Bill the weasel because he would always find a way to con his way out of trouble. Many times we were shielded from bad things happening to us. Many times we thought that was the way every kid lived.

I can remember visiting cousins in the city of Cleveland. We were in the family station wagon; and my parents in the front seat, having their usual discussion about bills, money, and kids. The discussion became very heated, and at the next red light, my mother got out of the car and started walking. We were crying and pleading with my mother to get back in the car. My father was yelling and screaming at her and telling us to shut up.

No one was listening. I felt my mother was the only real thing that mattered in the world. We would be left to spend a living hell on earth with my father. Eventually she came to her senses and got back in the car. I don't know about my father, but as far as the children were concerned, we were in shock; my mother leaving us meant suffering beyond control every second of every day until we could take care of ourselves. I believe I was just seven years old at the time, and I was willing to find a way my siblings and me could stay together and live without my father.

I can't remember many happy times in my childhood. On Thanksgiving, when my father came home, my mother was making Thanksgiving dinner. I could hear the yelling starting, and as I entered the kitchen, I saw my father taking our turkey and wrapping it up with the tablecloth. My mother told us to help him. We gathered all the food and put it in the car.

My mother said, "I can't believe that you could take the food from their mouths."

My father's reply was, "I made the money that brought the food here, and I can take it away."

So he took our Thanksgiving dinner, loaded up in the car, and took off. That night our meal consisted of bologna sandwiches and chips. I didn't care. I was glad he was gone; our meal was in peace. My mother cried and provided the love children needed. Also once again, I felt we were safe from the evil ruler with the iron fist and fire in his eyes. I made a pact with myself that when I was strong enough, I would be the defender of my mother and the family. As well as I can remember, I was nine years old at the time.

My grandparents lived next door to us. My mother was the second oldest of the nine children my grandparents had. Mom would not go next door and ask for anything or bring her troubles to her father and mother's house. We would go next door to play with my aunts and uncles who were very close to the same age as we were. My grandfather, Louis Massey the first, was a real type of guy who didn't mind telling it the way he saw it; but we all loved him with every fiber in our souls.

My grandpa was one of the first black men to be promoted to foreman at his job at TRW, a plant that made airplane parts. He would often come home, and we would grab our fishing poles and head out to Lake Erie or some other body of water, to catch fish. I loved going to the Chagrin River when the salmon would spawn through the river. He would also take us to ball games and many other functions we couldn't afford.

Speaking of ball games, we had an almost automatic "in" when it came to Cleveland Indians baseball games. My great-uncle Luke worked at the TRW plant with my grandfather. In Luke's younger days, he played professional baseball for the Cleveland Indians in 1954. He was known as Luscious Luke Easter. My great-uncle Luke was a power hitter and first baseman. Luke Easter has a record that has never been broken to this day. He hit the longest home run ever hit in the Cleveland Stadium. When they tore the stadium down in 1998, no ball player had broken his record.

My grandfather would pile us into his car, my two brothers and I, and also two of my uncles. In total, including my grandfather, there were six of us. Grandpa Lew would take us to the Cleveland stadium; he always got a couple of tickets the day before the game from Uncle Luke at work. It really didn't matter where the seats were. When we got there, we would yell from where we were, "Uncle Luke, Uncle Luke!" He would see us and wave at all of us to come and sit next to him.

He would always sit in the second row right in front of home plate so he could talk to the ball players and watch the pitch. He would always have empty seats around him, and we would all climb into the seats around him. This would absolutely drive the ushers insane. They would come down and say, "Luke, these kids can't sit here."

Luke was no small fellow; he was about 6 feet, 6 inches and about 310 pounds, with a monstrously loud voice. Uncle Luke would stand up, reach into his pocket for some money, and say, "These are my babies, and I built this place. Nobody is going to tell me where my babies can sit. Now go get us some popcorn. You're disturbing the game." The ushers would come back with popcorn and pop and nothing more was said.

Uncle Luke would tell us what type of pitch the pitcher was throwing and what type of batter the guy at the plate was. He was always right, and I would sit on his lap not knowing how great he was and thinking this would last forever. He would call ball players over to meet us, and we would get all the stadium had to offer—bats, balls, hats, hot dogs, popcorn, peanuts, and pop.

One day at the ballpark, I saw Boog Powell stepping up to the plate. I kept yelling his name. Uncle Luke called him over to us before he stepped into the batter's box. Uncle Luke said, "Come on over here and meet my boy. Can't you hear him yelling at you?"

Boog was even bigger than my uncle. He came as close as he could, reaching over the netting behind home plate, and shook my hand. He looked over at Uncle Luke and said, "Luke, the whole stadium is yelling at me!"

Uncle Luke just smiled and said, "Hurry up and hit this home run and come back and talk to us." As the pitcher threw the third ball, big Boog hit a home run directly over center field, came back, and talked to us for ten minutes.

Every time I would go to see an Indians game, I would sit next to my uncle, and I would meet every Cleveland Indian that played. The managers and tons of people would come over and talk to Uncle Luke. He signed bats and balls and always made the person he was talking to feel special. Uncle Luke was never in a bad mood and was loved by all of Cleveland.

Uncle Luke was delivering money to the Cleveland Trust Bank for TRW in Euclid, and two men shot and killed him in the spring of 1979, my graduating year of high school. I received a call from my mother while I was at school. She told me to get my sister and come home. Mom told me not to tell my sister while we walked home. We were halfway home, and I couldn't hold back anymore. I told her. I thought I was going to have to carry her home.

When we got home, the story was on every channel, and the whole city was in mourning. The two criminals were apprehended. I'm not really sure, but I was told the two guys that shot Uncle Luke never made it to jail. They both had an untimely death somehow. What used to be known as Wood Hill Park is now Luke Easter Park, and every year the city of Cleveland has a big festival in his memory. I have never been to this festival, and I don't know if my cousins go.

Luke Easter had three children who were teenagers when my sister, brothers, and I were just babies. Uncle Luke lived in a big three-family house in Cleveland. My siblings and I would go over to Uncle Luke's house and spend the night a couple of days or maybe a week. My cousin Jerome would also join us. We would also go over my great-grandmother's house and stay or visit. She lived in an old house in a rough part of town in Cleveland. They treated us like gold, and we wouldn't want for anything. It was like a great big party, and we would run from one floor to the next.

My Aunt Thelma, Uncle Luke's wife, would cook and clean. She was a pleasant small-framed woman with a will of iron. She once stopped a robbery by chasing three young boys down the street until the police came. My uncle's children were all living at home. Little Luke was the oldest, a big ex-marine who worked out all the time and studied martial arts. He was tall and full of muscle and strong as an ox. Nana was a very beautiful girl and full of life. She was like a second mother to us. She would often babysit and kept us out of trouble. Gerald was the youngest. Everybody called him Bumpy, and he raced cars and was always in the backyard, working on one of his machines.

Life was good while we visited them, and we were away from all the evils of our home. Uncle Luke and his family loved my mother, and they knew what kind of a man my father was. The Easter family was related to my father.

For the most part of our childhood, we would stay close to my mother's side of the family, spending most of our days running from our house to my grandparent's house that lived next door, playing with our aunts and uncles. Grandma and Grandpa Massey would always have something going on. Some things weren't always good, but they always treated us well. My grandmother Gwendolyn Massey was a strict but loving woman. I would stand close by her side when she was cooking, and I believe this is where I developed some of my cooking skills. She was also a great lover of music; often when we entered the house, we would hear Johnny Mathis booming from her stereo. We would spend most of our time running from house to house especially when my parents couldn't see eye to eye.

My brothers and I would often go over to our grandparents' house to play with our Uncle Michael. He was a couple years younger than I was and closer in age with my younger brother Danny. He was also my mother's youngest brother and the baby of my grandparents' family. Michael would be my main running buddy as we shared a common goal to get high every second of the day. Danny and Michael would do battle almost every day, and we would stand and watch those two fight until my mother or grandfather would separate the two.

At one point, Danny and Michael would no longer run in the same circles because Michael would fall into the same trap as I did and got involved in smoking and drinking at the top of the street. Much later in life, Michael and I would separate, and he would continue to fall prey to the demons of smoking and drinking long after I decided that it wasn't the thing to do. It was strange how differently life would be for all of us, but in those days, we were just kids and one big happy family.

My mother had another brother who was just a couple years older than my brothers and I. My Uncle Raymond was slightly retarded because of complications at birth. I would spend hours in his room playing with hundreds of little army figures and cowboys and Indians figures when I was growing up. Raymond was like a big kid; and as we all grew up, he stayed the same, watching television and staying in his room playing. Raymond would often have fits of rage when he would find something wrong in the world; he knew a lot more than we gave him credit for.

As I grew older and bigger, I would often be called over my grandparents' house to calm him down. I would sit and talk to him until he would tell me what was wrong. Often it would be something he saw on a television show consisting of violence toward little children or helpless women. He would punch holes in the walls, yelling at the television. He was too big and strong for my grandparents to handle.

I recall going over to my grandparents' house to calm Raymond down, and as I entered his room, he became very defensive. I was a teenager then, and I sat on his bed, asking him what the matter was. He began to tell me that he was mad at people for using drugs, and he wanted to be a normal person, and people were messing themselves up taking drugs. He said that he didn't understand why they would do drugs that made them more messed up than he was. I can't remember exactly how I explained it to him, but as I said before, Raymond knew a lot more than he was given credit for. He had a very good point, and it kind of makes you wonder who was really mentally challenged.

When I was a teenager, Raymond was put in a home for the mentally impaired when I was away from home for a long time. Later in the story, I will tell you what happened to Raymond with great sadness in my heart.

Raymond would venture out on his own, riding his bike to different parts of the city where older kids would pick on him and beat him until the police arrived or my grandpa would go and get him. As I grew older, I would see some of the cruel things done to him by older kids and adults. Most of the time, I would just take him home and deal with those people later. For that time period, I would spend a lot of time with Raymond when I found it too difficult to deal with fighting parents at my house. We would spend hours in his room playing with hundreds of little plastic army men or hot wheel cars. His world was all make-believe, and I would get lost in his world until the real world was livable again.

One evening things were getting rough at my house, and my parents were arguing. We took our usual hiding places—my sister in her room, and the boys ran downstairs to our room. I can't remember the exact issue my parents were in heated battle about, but their voices were getting louder; and from downstairs in our basement bedroom, with the door closed, we heard a loud crash—glass breaking.

My brothers and I ran upstairs and saw my mother lying on the front porch, bleeding mostly on her back. My father had pushed her out the front door, breaking the glass with her body, and she landed on her back. My sister stayed hidden in her room. We stood there in horror. "Mom, please get up. Mom, please stop bleeding!"

My mother lay there in silence. I was in fear of the worst; was she still alive? I saw my grandpa running across the yard. He was on the porch quicker than any world-class track star. Glaring into my father's eyes, chest to chest, my grandfather had a gun in his right hand, addressing my father, "If you weren't the father of these children, you would be going to hell tonight! Get your ass out of here before you make me a killer tonight!"

My grandparents helped my mother. My brothers and I were told to go back downstairs to our bedroom. We entered the room crying and still shaking in disbelief of what had just happened. My younger brother Danny was just four years old, and talking to him later, he recalled the incident as well as I can.

My older brother, Billy, and I were standing in the middle of the room when my father entered. He said, "Get in the bed and shut up and go to sleep!" Both my brothers were in their beds, and I stood in the middle of the room as if my father wasn't even there. "Timmy, did you hear what I just said?" I stood my ground looking at my father. He took this as an act of defiance, grabbing me, and shaking me about a half inch away from my face. "Do you understand what I just said?"

I never answered, which just sent him into a rage. I know what my mother felt like. I showed no signs of fear. He ran upstairs and came back to our bedroom, yelling and screaming at me, holding his whipping brush in his right hand. My father had a cherry wood brush that he'd whip us with. I will never forget the words "MADE IN JAPAN" on the neck of that hard long brush.

With his stern voice, he said, "So you think you're a man?"

Whack. I felt the sting of that whipping brush over and over until he got tired. I wanted to cry, but I kept thinking of my mother beaten and bloody, lying on that nasty cold ground on our front porch. I just stood there as the bite of that brush tore into me. Never once did I flinch or shed one tear, for hate cut deep into my heart and soul.

My father said, "Get in the bed. Do you have anything to say for yourself?"

I looked into his red bloodshot eyes, and glaring at the big blue veins in his neck and forehead, I still can't believe I told my father, "By the time I get big, you better be gone."

When my father finally left, I could not close my eyes, feeling the whelps and bruises from the whipping brush. I cried until I thought my eyes would fall out. I cried because I was hurting inside and out, but mostly I cried for my mother and my family. Most of all, I wondered about my mother, still seeing her on the porch bleeding. I still see that whole scene in my mind today.

That night I wondered why things were so bad and why did my mother have to suffer every minute of the day? Being raised in a Catholic school and going to church at least four times a week, that night I did not pray. I asked God why did this happen.

I often wondered if there was a God. We would go to church three and four times a week on schooldays and either Saturday or Sunday morning. We would pray for the poor, sick, and dying every day. I prayed for my mother and family. I also prayed my father would leave or something tragic would happen to him so that he could not come home.

Daddy

Life didn't seem to get much better. My father was a truck driver at Stroh's Brewery in Cleveland, near downtown. Sometimes we would pile into the station wagon to pick him up after work. Some of the guys my father worked with would often see us waiting and stopped to talk on their way home. I still remember a lot of those characters to this day, real stand-up guys. Everyone would say what a great guy Freddy Lowe was, except the people who were closest to him. We would never know what type of mood my father would be in, so we wouldn't talk until he started the conversation. The ride home would take thirty to forty-five minutes depending on traffic. Sometimes the ride home would seem longer than it really took, depending on what type of mood my father was in.

My father was a big man at about 6 foot 2 and about 275 pounds. One evening after work, he said he wasn't feeling well and went to the hospital. The doctor's diagnosis was an overactive thyroid gland. Maybe this would explain his bulging eyes and nasty disposition. Later on in life, I found out that the thyroid gland controls a lot of things that go on in the human body. Later on in life, my sister would suffer from the same thing. My father spent a lot of time in the hospital, and we spent a lot of time there too. My mother stayed right by his side until the problem was corrected.

He lost a lot of weight, and he came home a new man. Due to his illness, he came home weighing about 175 pounds, and he bought new superfly clothes. He was even worse than he was before—not only was he meaner, but he thought he was God's gift to women. The pretty boy he once was when he was growing up was reborn. With a ponytail hairstyle and nice clean clothes and lots of cologne, my father would take to the streets and sometimes wouldn't come home till late at night. My father was an avid bowler on a league; this would be his excuse for not coming home. We would see less and less of him. This meant fewer beatings for my mother and less yelling and less of the dreaded made-in-Japan whipping brush. Life was good, but my mother seemed to be sadder than before. My mother knew time was growing short for the newly found playboy.

One evening my father came home from work and got something to eat, took a shower, put on some of the superfly clothes, grabbed his bowling ball, and zoomed off in the family wagon. My mother also had a plan of action that night too. She went into the bedroom and started packing bags and boxes of superfly clothes, shoes, hair care products, and the rest of his belongings. Putting everything outside on the front porch seemed like poetic justice to me. Where she had lain on the front porch bloody and battered was where all his worldly belongings now lay. I can't recall what happened after that; when he came home, my brothers, sister, and I were taken to a safe place. Divorce entered our lives, and in the beginning, things got a lot worse before they got better.

Now we would let the courts decide the fate of four children and a mother who didn't complete high school. My mother had dropped out of Wickliffe High due to being pregnant with my older brother, Bill, something else I didn't know until I recently talked to my mother. She didn't have the money for a divorce, but a friend of hers paid the retainer to get the proceedings started. Beverly Warfield, who was the wife of Paul Warfield who played professional football for the Cleveland Browns, was and still is one of my mother's closest friends. The two young women met in the hospital and soon became the closest of friends.

I would often see the Warfields, and they did a lot more for my family than I ever knew about. I don't remember all the details, but I will never forget the bond my mother had with Paul's wife, Beverly. The Cleveland Browns gave Paul Warfield a forty-two-pound turkey as a signing bonus; the number forty-two was also Paul's jersey number. The Warfields came over our house and gave my family that forty-two-pound bird, and as well as I can remember, they also gave my mother an envelope that had a thousand dollars in it. I don't how the Warfields got my mother to accept the money. She would not depend on her friends to bail her out of trouble, and the Warfields were true friends and would have done anything for my mother and her children.

In my senior year of high school, Paul Warfield showed up at one of my football games. On parents' night, I quickly took a place at the back of the line. I didn't even know if my father knew I played football. As they would announce the players and their fathers, the closer they got to me, the more I dreaded walking out on the field alone. When they called my name, my stepfather in his Cleveland police uniform and Paul Warfield of the Cleveland Browns walked on the field with me. The good people of Wickliffe also announced that Paul Warfield was at the games in support of a local radio station. Paul quickly announced that he was there to see a local kid play football, "Tim Lowe." Later on in my story, I will tell you of such men of men bigger than life. My stepfather would be the biggest influence in my life and greatest person I could ever know. He made many great sacrifices in his life to make sure we lived a pretty much normal childhood after my father left us.

I believe I was twelve years old when all of this took place. My mother would work in the evening cleaning office buildings after she prepared our dinner. She also went to school preparing for her GED. We were left on our own to complete our schoolwork and clean house. Meanwhile my mother would fend off dirty old men after young, good-looking divorced women. We would get government cheese from our grandmother, who worked at a day care, and care packages from the church. The government wouldn't help us; my mother had three jobs, and they said she made too much money.

My mother would make ends meet the best way she could, and a lot of good people helped us along the way. My mother's oldest brother, Louis Massey the second, known to the entire family as Uncle Snooky, worked for a sausage company, making deliveries to stores all around Cleveland. Uncle Snooky would often come over our house and give my mother a case of sausage. He also had a family of his own who lived two streets away from ours. As children we would go over Uncle Snooky's house to play with our cousins Pam, Luigi, and Jerry. Uncle Snooky would take us to ball games, amusement parks, and the Cleveland Zoo. He was also an avid fisherman like all the rest of my uncles. He was a hustler and always knew how to get free tickets and money whenever he needed it.

Snooky was someone everyone loved, and he always took care of his children and my family the best way he knew how. Before my cousins reached double digits in age, Uncle Snooky and his wife were divorced, and they moved away to Mobile, Alabama. He would travel to see them every chance he could. Unlike my father, he always stayed in touch with his children. Snooky had more angles; he would always show up with food or something to help my mother when we were at the end of our rope. For a long period of time, Uncle Snooky lived with my grandparents next door and was always busy cutting the grass or fixing something on the house in his free time.

He had many girlfriends, and later in his life, he would marry again and have twin girls. Once again the marriage didn't last; and just like before, he kept in touch with the twins and his other children. To this day, Snooky is still around keeping up with his children and taking long trips to see all of them. He lives only a couple miles away from my home in a retirement community, still staying true to form hustling and living life to the fullest.

While all this was taking place, my mother had to deal with working, taking care of us, and dealing with many other things; and I would see her cry herself to sleep more times than I care to remember. One of her biggest disappointments was dealing with the Catholic Church.

God, Mama, and Family

The good Catholic Church decided my mother was no longer able to receive communion at church. The Catholic religion did not believe in divorce. As a woman, you were supposed to stay with the man that would beat you and cheat in the marriage. My mother was trying to make our lives whole by trying to be both man and woman for her children. My older brother, Bill, had a hard time without my father. He wanted him to be around to attend his basketball games like all the other kids did. My sister would never get over her daddy leaving. I believe my younger brother, Danny, and I were much different; we wouldn't miss a beat. We would go on beating up any one fool enough to cross us, and I believe he liked fighting more than I did. My mother told me I wasn't a mean kid. Other kids would bring out the fight in me when they called me a nigger or made fun of my weight problem. I would often get in to trouble defending the underdog kids that were small or would be bullied by the older bigger kids. My brother Danny also had the same type of fight in him.

My mother and grandfather attended classes and received their GED together. In the meantime, my mother also went to court for the divorce proceedings and cleaned office buildings. My brother Bill and I would attend Wickliffe Junior High together in the seventh grade. We were in the same grade; my brother was held back in the first grade. My sister and Danny would still attend Catholic school. My mother was told that the Catholic school system was considered a private school. We couldn't afford to pay. Later on my sister and Danny would also attend Wickliffe Junior High School.

Not long after my mother received her GED, she would seek better employment. My mother began to work in a local hospital. Not only were the paychecks a little better, she decided to give nursing school a try. My mother would work at the hospital on night shift, go to school, and raise four children. She would also maintain a house and make sure the bills were paid and our schoolwork was done.

We would go to school and help do the cooking and cleaning. My mother would make a list of chores and post them on the refrigerator. After school, my sister and I would work in the kitchen, making meals and cleaning after dinner. My brother Bill would vacuum and clean the living room, my brother Danny would have the bathroom detail. We would all clean our rooms and make our beds. In the summer, Bill and I would maintain the yard. After schoolwork and chores we completed, we would go outside and play with neighborhood friends or go next door to my grandparents' house.

Just like all the rest of the kids in our neighborhood, we would go to the park at the top of the street and play softball or go to the city pool, which was a couple miles away at another city park. The city of Wickliffe had a summer program in the community parks, where high school kids were given a job and kept the younger children out of trouble. I was about thirteen years old; many times we were alone but didn't really know it. We always had my grandparents to run to if something really went wrong. In today's world, I don't think the court system would allow us to be that independent as children.

We weren't just running around the neighborhood with reckless abandon. We were often told if we got into trouble, we would be sent away to live with our Grandma Rucker in Cleveland. She was like my father, with long hair. My aunt Tina lived with my grandma—what a team. Two people who talked a lot about God, but I don't think they really knew God. They were evangelists who would go to revivals with faith healers. They once tricked my older brother, Bill, into believing that they were taking him to a rock concert. I was really mad that they didn't take me with them until Bill came home and said they took him to a revival featuring a faith healer, Ernest Angsley. He would actually knock people down on television, telling the evil spirits to leave their bodies or pretending to heal their ailments.

We never had to stay with them, and after my father left us, we didn't have many dealings with them; although I would often overhear telephone conversations that my mother would have with them. Things never got that bad; we were well-disciplined children. Our struggles would make us strong and able to deal with life struggles. My siblings and I were never afraid to talk to Mom about anything, and Mom would always tell the truth whether we liked it or not.

We still do the same thing as adults today. We didn't have money and fancy things like most, but we had love and respect for each other. Looking back on those hard times, it taught me many life lessons, life lessons that a rich man couldn't buy. I think we were much happier with my father gone. Yes, my mother worked like a borrowed slave, but I think she was much happier also. We all learned a lot in the face of survival.

The Newspaper Route

My older brother, Bill, had a *News Herald* paper route. Sometimes I would help him deliver the papers in the morning. After learning the ropes from him, I got my own paper route. I would deliver the *Plain Dealer* at five o'clock in the morning and get ready for school when I finished. I liked delivering papers in the summer except when it rained. In the winter, it wasn't so bad either until we had monster snow. The neighborhood people would call my house screaming about where the paper was.

I learned how to keep track of money. In my day, the newspaper boy would also collect the money every Saturday. On Tuesday the collector from the company would come over to get the money and give me my cut. Many times my money would be cut short because some of my neighbors didn't pay, and there were about a dozen of those neighbors that never wanted to pay. Well, after about a week, I would stop delivering their paper, and it didn't take them long to call my house. Sunday would be the most trying day because I would get triple the amount of papers to deliver. Some people would get a paper on Sunday only, and I would get three or four sections that I would have to put together to make one big newspaper.

Delivering the newspaper wasn't a problem, just collecting the money was. A lot of customers would argue with you about their bill and would often argue about a nickel or dime. I kept my payment book up to date and carried it with me when collecting time would come. Some of my neighbors would absolutely lose their minds screaming and yelling at a twelve-year-old boy who was trying to make a decent living. They would often call the company and complain; usually the company would take the delivery boy's side.

Some of the same people would be the most difficult to deliver to because they had monster dogs that they would let out in the morning—two vicious German shepherds on one side of the street and a big black English sheepdog that resembled a bear on the other side of the same street. Every kid in the neighborhood would run from these dogs in fear of getting mauled or bitten by the gigantic beasts. When I was delivering my papers in the morning, I would come face to face with one or all three of the growling biting animals.

With my papers I would carry a small baseball bat; and when these nasty beasts would show up, I defended myself with my Louisville Slugger. Sometimes they would sneak up on you in the dark of morning, and I would swing the bat like I was hitting a home run. I was bitten more than once, but the dogs were hit many times. I would see some of the neighbors peeking out of their windows and laughing. None of them would come to my aid while I battled with the dogs that had teeth that would draw blood on contact.

When I delivered the papers for a few months, the dogs would leave me alone. I had gained their respect by beating the hell out of them. Just like some kids I knew, nothing like a good ass-kickin' to stop the madness. The two German shepherds would climb their fenced-in area and on top of a low-hung roof and wind up in the middle of the driveway, ready to attack at will. I would never run. A chubby kid had to be tough. I could only run fast enough to get bit. So I knew I would have to stand my ground with my baseball bat slung across my back. The owners of these dogs never confronted me about beating their dogs, and if they complained, they would probably have to go to court and pay huge fines. I actually thought they let the dogs out when they knew I was delivering the papers. The dogs were out almost every day I delivered the papers.

Many other things would happen. Sometimes I would have to get my mother to help me collect from an irate customer. I was taught to respect my elders, and I would never argue with an adult. One evening I was making collections, and I saw a group of neighborhood kids with a dozen eggs. They asked me if I wanted to join them in what they called fun. I just wanted to finish collecting, and before I could answer them, they were throwing the eggs at Coach Hughley's house. He was a man with a deep voice that coached football and baseball with his free time. Coach Hughley had two big boys and a nice-looking daughter that was one year older than me. He always had a half a cigar hanging out of the side of his mouth, and when he spoke, I listened. The deep voice and the smokey haze from the cigar would strike fear into any kid; we all knew he was all about business.

Well, when the eggs hit his house, he jumped out of the patio doors; and the chase was on. Coach Hughley had a hidden talent us neighborhood kids knew nothing about until that day. I watched him run out the door, and he was the fastest man I had ever seen. The kids that threw the eggs jumped his backyard fence, and I watched Coach hurdle the fence, never breaking stride. The perpetrators were all caught; five kids had to explain to their parents why they were throwing eggs at the Hughley home. Coach Hughley was a world-class hurdler in high school, and now every kid in the neighborhood knew. The coach's house never got egged, and he was respected and feared by every kid that knew him.

School, Sports, and Street Life

As Bill and I started the seventh grade in public school, I began a newly found passion, football. Being a big fat kid had its advantages when it came to playing football. I could be mean as a bear and knock down other kids and not get suspended from school. I considered this legal fighting, and everyone liked it when you trampled over your opponent. Now I had a purpose.

I was one of the Wickliffe Fighting Blue Devils, and every day we trained hard, and I got recognition from everyone. I also had to keep my grades up, to play. With my mother working so hard, I can't remember if she even saw a game. But my Uncle Tony went to most of my games, and I liked him being there. Football was a learning process. I was no superstar. I played second string. Most kids had been playing football on the Wickliffe Midget Football League for six years. I couldn't play because I was well over the weight limit. After football season was over, I joined the wrestling team; and after that, I ran track. Sports seemed to correct a lot of wrongs in my life plus it kept me out of trouble in school and home. Billy was also a sports fan. He played basketball. Uncle Tony also attended his basketball games.

Going to public school was just like Catholic school except more of the bad stuff. Wickliffe still had its Alabama feel. The public school went from seventh grade to the ninth grade. There were about 350 students, and about 15 of those students were black. We had our share of racial problems, and I was not even close to being the toughest kid. The city of Wickliffe had four streets of black families and is still pretty much the same way today. If a black family bought a house in Wickliffe, you lived on one of the four streets. We all knew each other very well.

The diversity was the same in school if you were black; at lunchtime we would sit at two tables in the corner of the cafeteria. No one ever went outside the imaginary lines that separated us from the white students. We all had friends, but no one dared date or seek males or females of a different race. That also carried over in sports and other school activities. If you were black, you had to be an overachiever. I was not exceptional in anything, so I had plenty of time taking up space on the bench, riding the pine.

We never broke that color barrier in Wickliffe, but some of my friends were exceptional athletes and scholars. One of my closest friends had both brains and natural athletic ability. Mervin Washington was one grade below my brother and me. This guy had all the tools, maintaining close to a 4.0 in school and one of the best athletes I ever seen. Mervin was carved of granite, a big dark-skinned brother with muscle and speed that no one in the school could match. Mervin was no fighter, so when I wanted to mix it up a bit, I would seek out another friend.

Greg lived up the street. He had three other brothers, and he was also the second oldest. First we fought each other and decided we liked fighting other kids better. By the time I reached the ninth grade, I was still a second stringer in sports, but Greg and I were in a class all our own when it came to fighting and getting into trouble. We had a little neighborhood bad boys' club, and when we couldn't find anyone else to fight with, we practiced on each other.

Greg and I would also go to Lincoln Elementary School where we could hone our fighting skill. We walked to the school where an old Italian man would teach us how to box. Kids from other neighborhoods in Wickliffe would show up, and we learned the true skills of boxing. At first we took a few good shots, but it didn't take us long to learn the game; and soon with some street skills and real fighting skills, we were unbeatable.

Later in the evening, we would go back to our own neighborhood group where we would put our new fighting skills to the test as we fought with kids from the neighborhood. There were about a good dozen of us and someone was always looking for a good fight. After that we still had enough energy to harass neighbors and going outside of our neighborhood to local playgrounds to play basketball or a good old-fashioned black against white football game. We were all so innocent. We would cuss and fight, but none of us were into the drinking and drug scene, yet!

Mom, Big John, and Us

While I was doing my own thing, my hardworking mother had earned her nursing degree and turned out to be valedictorian of her graduating nursing class. She now worked at a local hospital as a nurse. My father continued his wicked ways, and somehow the justice system was on his side. My mother received 125 dollars a month for four children; that's for food, clothing, and anything else we needed. Also if my mother didn't sell our house in three years, he would receive five thousand dollars for his half of the house—and we call it a justice system. Somehow my father proved to the courts he didn't make a lot of money. He also had some slick female lawyer who played with the justice system.

Many people would show their true colors, and sometimes that wasn't so pretty. My grandmother and Aunt Tina on my father's side of the family thought that my mother should give up the suburbs and take us to live in the projects in Cleveland. After all, that was where my father grew up, and there was nothing wrong with him. According to them, this was my mother's fault. They also thought my mother was seeing some rich doctor and that was where she got her money from.

The truth was my mom did have a man. My stepfather entered our lives when I was twelve years old. John Fryer was a Cleveland policeman, and I considered him the best man that I knew. I would never think of him as a stepfather, and he never consider me and my siblings stepchildren. Later on he would have two children with my mother, Little Jonn, and the baby of the family, Karla. We all blended very well together; at least that's the way I felt.

Cops and nurses always seemed to go together because they ran in the same circles, working swing shifts, and the police are always at the hospitals, getting people patched up who didn't quite agree with being arrested. John Fryer we called Big John because later on there would be a Little Jonn, my youngest brother. Big John proved to be more than anyone expected. My mother and Big John were married when I turned fifteen years old. No one every expected him to marry a woman with four children. Big John never raised his voice and had a way of showing disapproval by not saying a word, but we all knew when he wasn't happy with us. Big John was someone I could talk to, and there wasn't a thing I could beat him at, sports and wit. Instead of being jack of all trades and master of none, he was a master at everything. I would do things to try to gain his respect and approval. I don't think Big John, my mother, or even I knew what the future would hold for me and what kind of twisting-and-turning life I would create for everyone.

One sunny day in fall, I was sitting in algebra class taking a test. My mother was in the hospital, my family was preparing for a new family member. Looking out of the window, not really interested in taking a test, there was a knock at the classroom door. A cute little office aide gave the teacher a note. He called me up to the front of the class and announced to the class that I had a new baby brother and my mother was doing fine.

I watched the office aide as she walked away. She lived up the street from me, and at the time, I didn't know what a big part of my life Rhonda Hughley would be one day. I just liked the way she walked, and there was a mysterious feeling I got when Rhonda was around. Later on as I grew older, this girl would be special to me. For that moment, she was a very attractive girl who had just delivered a letter telling me of the birth of my youngest brother, Jonn.

Some say life is one big circle; I didn't know how right these people were. I was happy for my mom and Big John and my whole family. Everything in the world seemed right on that warm day in September.

Money Is the Root of All Evil

My brother Bill and I started the ninth grade, and my sister was in the eighth grade in public school with us. Danny was finishing up in the sixth grade, his last year of Catholic school. Big John was now part of the family. He was married to my mother, and we all loved little Jonn. Things began to change for us.

We still had some rough spots as my father would ask for his five thousand dollars, which was now seventy five hundred dollars through the court system. My mother was working to keep a roof over our heads, clothes on our backs, and our bellies full. To tell the truth, my mother didn't have a dime to spare, and she was too proud to ask anyone for it. She threw herself on the mercy of the court, and to no avail; she would have to pay my father.

Now comparing Big John to my father was like comparing apples to oranges. My father wanted his money and didn't care if it meant selling the house and putting us out on the street. Big John figured if he was living in the house then he would share the burden of debt to free us from my father Freddy. When my father received his money, my mother made a simple statement and said, "God will get ya for that." Little did he know, or anyone would know, Freddy would pay a heavy toll for collecting what he thought was rightfully his.

My father would come over to visit us. I don't think it was because he cared. I think he was shamed into it or because he thought it bothered my mother. I would beg my mother not to go with him or even see him. Well, as soon as he received his money from my mother, he came over our house driving a great big brand-new copper-colored Fleetwood Braham Cadillac. He was dressed in an all-leather suit that matched the car.

My mother made us go outside to meet him. There he was, big as life, and I thought to myself, "What a piece of shit." As I recall the whole scene, I still feel the same way today. Early in that same week, I would go out after school and cut grass to earn money to buy shoes to run track. I needed two dollars more. I called my father and asked him for two dollars, and he told me he didn't have any money. The track meet was on Wednesday, and as of Tuesday, I didn't have enough money. All members of the track team were told to get specific type of shoes, or they wouldn't be able to participate.

Well, Big John knew something was wrong; and when I explained my situation, we immediately went to the store, and he bought the shoes for me. Big John would also give me moral support, and he was also the voice of reason when I would come to a crossroad in my young life. Today as a man, I still need that blessing from him. He is and always will be the voice of reason for me.

I don't know exactly what happened, but to the best of my knowledge, that shiny new Cadillac my father was so proud of somehow burnt to the ground the very same day he bought it. A week later, he bought another shiny Cadillac. This was blue, and he liked this one even more. He drove the new Caddy over my Grandma Rucker's house to show his sister and mother how beautiful the car was. Freddy parked the car on the street, and someone driving by ran into it. The insurance company totaled out the car, which means it was a complete loss. My father vowed never to buy a big pretty car again, so he bought a big camper. I never saw the camper, but my brother Danny told me that on both sides in huge letters were the words, "KING FREDDY."

Out of all the people in the world to love, my father truly loved himself. He wanted to see the world and tour the countryside, and he had a young pretty girlfriend he lived with that he wanted to take with him. She didn't want to go anywhere; she said the camper was a piece of junk. So Freddy got a bunch of his buddies to take a trip with him, and they let him buy all the gas and all the food. When he came home, he sold the camper and bought a small older car. I do recall my mother telling him that "God will get ya for that." As the story goes, he also remembered that line. He called my mother and asked her to take the curse off him.

As I grew older, I do remember another part of that very story. Rumor has it that someone, or one of Freddy's coworkers, took a torch to that car or one of his girlfriends. As my mother had said, I actually believe that "God will get ya for that" is a true statement. Food taken from the mouth of babes, and so justice was served. The Lord gives it, let the Lord take it away. After that, my father's visits came few and far between; as a matter of fact, I believe that was the last time I saw my father. As for my siblings, they would have brief encounters with him from time to time when they went to Cleveland for business or pleasure.

Freddy lived in a big fancy apartment building in downtown Cleveland, in the Park Apartments. He had a young pretty girlfriend who lived with him. She also had a fifteen-year-old son who my father absolutely adored. The boy was taken better care of than his own flesh and blood children. My father would say how smart and good-looking he was, which tore a big hole in my older brother Bill's heart. My sister also felt a sting in heart. For Danny and me, we weren't impacted at all; with all the wonderful things Freddy had done for us, this was not out of character. Both of us expected it.

My father's girlfriend was around twenty years younger than he was. He was her sugar daddy, and he paid for everything she gave him. Later on in life, she would leave him, and he was able to see what everyone else was telling him. He felt like a fool because she used him, and the love of money was the only thing that kept the relationship alive.

Marvelous Mervin Washington

In the summer of 1977, I would head to the playground up the street and play basketball all day. Sometimes we would go swimming at other playgrounds; we didn't have a pool at our playground. Later on in the day, we would go to the high school and play basketball or lift weights. The football team would hold a training camp for those who were interested. A couple of friends and I decided to give it a try.

About half the kids who were interested in playing football showed up at the summer training camp. My friend Mervin Washington was one of best, and we walked on the practice field together. There were fifty to sixty young boys. This is where I had my first encounter with one of the football coaches, Mr. Robert Smith—one of the toughest coaches and teachers to ever walk the face of the earth.

It was a mid-June day, and we all lined up for a cross-country run through the woods next to the high school. I believe the course was about three miles of rough terrain. Mr. Smith put a whistle in his mouth, and his massive chest began to rise. Then he blew the whistle, and we were off and running up and down hills, through the creek, and over a couple of bridges. Well, I ran about a quarter mile before I started walking. There were about two dozen of us walking, some fat and some slim, just plain out of shape.

I wondered where Mervin was—he was nowhere to be seen. I believe it took me about an hour and fifteen other minutes to come crawling out of those woods. Mr. Smith, Mervin, and a couple of other guys were standing under a huge oak tree, waiting. I was the last one to come out of the woods. Mr. Smith put his arm around me and said, "Son, do you want to play football?"

As we went back to the locker room, he explained what I had to do to get into shape. Mervin and I walked home that day. He never told me he had the quickest times in school history, and he was about a mile ahead of everyone else—the first one to finish the course. He never once talked about himself. He told me to come to his house in the morning. Mervin had a plan of his own. I was totally defeated. I weighed about 225 pounds and ran like I was carrying a cement truck on my back, and Mervin was like black lightning. Mervin was only in the ninth grade, and he wouldn't even play or practice with me until he was in the tenth grade next year.

The next day I woke up, I felt like I had been run over by a truck. Every muscle in my body was sore; I took a hot shower and headed over to Mervin's house. He was sitting on his front porch drinking Gatorade. We walked to the high school, which was about three miles. As we walked, I began telling him how sore I was.

He had a funny type of grin on his face. He smiled and said in the next hour, I wouldn't feel a thing. We approached the practice field, and we lay down on the grass, which was still wet from the morning dew, stretching and feeling the warm morning sun. We headed over to the woods where the running course began, and we jogged into the woods.

We ran at my pace, and we crossed a creek and then jogged down the biggest hill on the course. We were about a mile into the three-mile course. We stopped at the bottom of the hill. Mervin said we needed to rest for a minute. Taking that short breather, he turned around and said, "This is as far as we go." I thought we were done.

Mervin faced the one-hundred-yard monster hill and sprinted all the way to the top and jogged back down to where I stood. He looked at me and said, "Next." I sprinted to the top and stopped.

He yelled, "Jog back down." I jogged back down, and we repeated this process about ten times. We rested and jogged a mile back out of the woods. Then we walked three miles back home. We did this every day that summer rain or shine, and soon I began to feel strong, and we were jogging the whole course and sprinting up the hill at least twenty times or more after we ran the course. Sometimes in the evening, I would ride my bike back to the course and run and sprint the hill on my own. I felt good, and I loved the me that I became; I weighed 175 pounds and felt like a champion. Mervin helped me, and no one would ever know the bond that we had. He was like a brother to me, and we did everything together.

In the later part of the summer, some of the hottest weather of the year known as the dog days of summer around the first of August, once again fifty to sixty young men headed for the practice field. Our football coach Mr. Smith lined us up and announced that he had so many uniforms and we had more men than uniforms and there would be a cut.

We warmed up and walked toward the woods where the course would begin. Mervin and I walked side by side, not saying a word. The coach's stopwatch and whistle hung in the middle of his chest. He raised the stopwatch to eye level and blew the whistle, and we were in full stride running into the woods. Mervin and I were in the middle of the pack.

Well, into the first mile all the guys that stopped there before stopped there again. I ran past them, and to their amazement, I kept on running. Also to my amazement, I kept on running, and I was running right next to Mervin, the fastest guy on the team. As we ran up hills and through streams and over bridges, I was now one of the leaders in the race. I wanted to play football so bad that I ran with fear of being cut, but I also ran with speed, and Mervin was pleased to see me trying with everything that I had.

As we approached the final mile, and I could see the edge of the woods where we started, I ran faster and now Mervin and I were the first two guys. Everyone else was behind us. We reached the final quarter mile in the grueling course. We were neck and neck, and I began to pass Mervin. To this day, I believe Mervin had a lot left in his fuel tank, but I reached the finish line first. As I passed the finish line, Coach Smith looked and could not stop grinning.

We walked over to the water, and I said to Mervin, "Thanks for letting me win." Mervin had been the front-runner for a long time, and coming in first was no big deal to him. He knew being first meant everything to me, and I still believe he let me win. To this day, I will never know, but what I do know is Mervin helped me and made me a real athlete.

After everyone came out of the woods panting, and some physically ill from the long grueling run in the hot, ninety-degree weather, Coach Smith gathered us in a big circle around him. He said some of us took him very serious when he told us he only had so many uniforms and there would be a cut. He raised his fist in the air and said, "Today I've seen who really wants to play football." He pointed in my direction and yelled, "Tim Lowe wants to play football. Son, you will get a uniform!"

I was so shocked, and I was proud of myself, I looked at Mervin. He gave me a half smile so that my fellow teammates couldn't see.

As we walked home, Mervin said, "Good run, man."

I learned a great lesson that day; the Lord blessed me with a good friend. The Lord also said the last would be first. I'm quite sure that phrase has another meaning, but it sure fit that day.

Mervin and I had a lot in common. He also had a father that he never saw, and he lived up the street at his grandparents' house. If Mervin had a purpose in life, he changed mine. I was no longer the fat kid that everyone ignored, thanks to him. I held my head a little higher that day. The bond would grow stronger as we worked and played together.

Mr. Woods and Hard Work, Molding Boys to Men

Mervin's grandfather, Mr. Eddy Woods, was one of the hardest working men I ever met. He didn't care too much about football. What he did care about was getting Mervin and me up in the morning to work with him, making driveways. At 5:00 a.m., Mr. Woods would knock on my back door, and my mother would wake me, and I would climb into his dump truck, sitting next to Mervin, who looked like he was still sleeping. We went over to Vic Salito's garage, where he would be waiting with another hardworking kid named Marty. We went to Mr. Donut and then to some unknown location, to break up an old driveway or set forms to prepare to make a new one.

These two old men worked us like borrowed mules, and I learned the value of a dollar and how to work from sunup till sundown. I learned many life lessons making concrete driveways. Vic Salito was pure Italian and about sixty years old, and Eddy Woods was about the same age. These two men would be the hardest working men that I would ever know. They were the finest teachers in hard work and role models for any young man willing to pick up a sledgehammer and shovel.

Eddy Woods not only taught us how to make driveways. He would sell vegetables in the neighborhood from his farm and distribute government cheese for the city. Sometimes we would cut beef at his house, and I would load up my wagon and take some of that beef home. My mother was very thankful. In the wintertime, Mr. Woods would plow snow from driveways in our neighborhood. He never asked for any money, but everyone in the neighborhood would give him a few dollars for his trouble. Even when I would stay up all night partying with my friends, Mr. Woods would be knocking at my door at the back door. Mervin would be in the truck, waiting.

Mr. Woods didn't have a regular job, but every day of his life, he worked from sunup to sundown. The work ethics he taught is something that no school could teach. He would pay us well for a hard day of work, and I learned a trade. I knew that I could use what I learned from him, if all else failed.

Education comes in many forms. I enjoyed making driveways and being with those two old men that had seen a lot and done a lot. This was one of the best jobs I ever had. I never had to work out because of the tough physical labor breaking out driveways and loading up wheelbarrows of concrete to the location they needed. When I see a cement truck with a group of guys making driveways, I say a prayer for Mr. Eddy Woods and Vic Salito, thanking the Lord for putting two old wise men in my path that taught me the ways of the world.

I also had a job at Ponderosa Steak House; and when I wasn't making driveways, I was a dishwasher, bus boy, and sometimes, cook. My younger sister also worked there. I rarely ate at home anymore and would often bring home lots of leftovers that my brothers and I would devour as soon as I walked through the door late at night after cleaning grease traps, washing dishes, and mopping the floors. It wasn't a bad job, and I would never go hungry, I was making very little money, but I ate my fill of steaks and baked potatoes.

Thursday night would be our peak time of the week because it would be family night, and every family in the world would show up. We had a full staff, and the families would keep coming till closing time. The grill would be loaded and every plate, fork, knife, and spoon would be used; and I would be the only dishwasher. It was hard work, and every night when I walked up the street to go home, the dogs in the neighborhood would follow me because I smelled like steak and potatoes. I would take a nice hot shower, wash my uniforms, and prepare for school the next day. I never had a problem sleeping, and the next day would come fast. After school, I would practice football and go to work. My schoolwork was lacking, but I would do just enough so I could play football.

From Boys to Men, Growing Up

In 1977 Bill and I were in the tenth grade, and we attended Wickliffe Senior High School. My sister was in the ninth grade, and Danny was in the seventh grade, both at Wickliffe Junior High. I still played a lot of sports, football being my favorite. Bill decided to go into auto body and would soon go to Mentor High School, which would end his basketball career in school. He would ride or walk to school with me and get on the bus to go to the other school.

I didn't really feel alone because I was playing football after school and had a new set of friends known as the jocks. Out of about 110 boys, there were 8 black guys, and 4 of us were exceptional athletes. I wish I could say I was one of those 4 gifted athletes. I was not, but it kept me out of trouble, and I also loved the game. I would also lift weights, and I loved this even more than football. I gained a lot of strength and had a sound relationship with coaches and other teachers that would lift weights in the bows of the high school. This was my newly found passion, and I would train and also diet.

Some of the guys from my neighborhood would often stay after school to lift weights. We would go to the locker room, get our lifting belts, and change into gym clothes, which consisted of shorts and a tank top, to watch our muscles develop in the huge mirrors in the weight room. One day after school, I went into the locker room to change when I heard voices over by the showers. I peeked around the corner to find a big blonde-haired guy riding one of my friends like a horse with a towel in his mouth, punching him in the back of the head, saying, "Getty up, nigger" as he rode him around the locker room. The skinny dark-skinned black kid was an upperclassman who lifted weights with me almost every day.

Seeing this, I became enraged. Like some wild animal, I charged the big blonde-haired kid, knocking him off my friend. I wrapped the towel around his neck and punched him in the face until my hands were bleeding. He lay on the ground in a bloody mess; I actually didn't care if he was dead or alive. My friend and I left him lying there on the cold locker room floor. After I cleaned the blood from my hands, we went to the weight room, not saying a word to anyone.

The next day, I saw the big blonde-haired boy with a couple of his friends. I looked him in the eyes as if to say, I dare you to say one word and I would continue where I left off yesterday. He knew better, and his friends wanted a piece of me, but no one dared come my way. The big blonde-haired boy looked like a train wreck and wore sunglasses to hide his battle scars, but it was easy to see he took a hell of an ass-beating the day before.

I heard rumors that they vowed to get even with me, so I learned to watch my back. I knew their only strength was in numbers, and I felt they might get me if there were more than two of them. They also knew that I would pick them off one by one, so they never bothered me or my skinny dark friend again. I had a reputation of being a fierce fighter, and I lived up to that reputation every day as I watched the big blonde and his friends stare at me as I walked down the hallway to my classes every day. I carried a roll of quarters rapped in duct tape in my right pants pocket for the rest of the year, hoping that they would be brave or foolish enough to tangle with me. That fight never happened, and they left me and my friends alone.

We continued to go to the weight room every day, and soon other kids that lifted weights on a daily basis found out what happened, and so did the rest of the kids at school. The decent kids praised me for what I did, and most of the troublemakers considered this a challenge as we would face many of them along the way. Sometimes it didn't always turn out this way, and sometimes I was the one that would get the short end of the stick, but I always managed to survive to fight another day. These incidents were far and few between as I began to get stronger and more fearless than ever, and most of the kids from the football team stuck together, forming and everlasting friendships. Soon I would pursue a whole new challenge, as the opposite sex seemed to take more of an interest in me as I shed the baby fat and gained more muscle from spending hours in the weight room.

I began to take on a whole new shape. I was no longer the fat kid with the huge afro. There were other people who noticed my new look too. Some of the girls began to talk to me a lot more, which made me feel better about myself. For the first time in my life, I would wake up and be happy to go to school. As my confidence level began to rise, so did my popularity, I enjoyed getting on the school bus.

I kept looking for Rhonda, a brown-skinned beauty in the eleventh grade. She lived on a side street connected to my street. I wouldn't see her on the bus because she had a car and would drive to school or walk up the grass hill at the top of our street. The school was about two and a half miles away, and most kids didn't like to walk because of nasty weather or mud from the hill. She liked to be alone and she enjoyed the walk.

I often wondered if she even knew I was alive. I would ask my aunt Linda, who was in the same grade as her. Linda was a very popular and good-looking girl in high school with lots of friends and boyfriends. She knew a lot about the girl I liked. I would see Rhonda in the halls at school, but I was too shy to say anything. I was just a kid who loved sports, and we wouldn't cross paths for a long time. She was also an upperclassman; guys in the eleventh grade would take her out. I didn't even drive; if I wanted to go somewhere with her, I would have to ask her to drive. I felt like such a loser, so I hung out with the boys and girls in the tenth grade just like me.

I wasn't that interested in driving. Back in my day, most kids would take the written test and then actually drive. If you passed, you got a driver's license. Some kids took the driver's education course; it wasn't a requirement like it is now. I would ride my ten-speed bike and walk to anywhere I wanted to go. I was too busy playing football, wrestling, or running track to drive. Sometimes I would ride with some of my friends. Most teenagers would get into accidents and get injured or even killed. Teenagers were drinking or doing drugs while driving, and I didn't do either at the time. Also girls came with a host of problems; I didn't have time for driving or dating girls. I was busy working or playing sports, and I stayed out of cars and trouble. The drug scene was not part of my life at this time. I am sorry to say that later on I would be involved in all of it. I would be known as my mother's worst child.

From Sports to the Streets

In 1978 my brother Bill and I were in the eleventh grade. He still went to another school for auto body, and I still played football and other sports. I had a few friends in the tenth grade and my first steady girlfriend. She lived one street over from mine. Her friends were my friends, and we were together all the time. We took some classes together and rode the bus to school together. I would go over her house after practice. She was very pretty, and I thought we would be together for life.

Things changed, and I started dating other girls from other cities. I still didn't drive, but love conquers all. Mervin and I would double-date; he would drive his parents' Cadillac or his grandfather's Ford LTD. We started drinking and smoking a little grass. This was the start of many things for both of us; we were experimenting with all types of things. We thought this was what adults did, and we would stay out later and later. The world was going too fast for two young naive boys who thought they knew everything. This is where my troubles began. I still played sports and so did Mervin, but little by little, we were in way over our heads; but no one could tell us we were headed for a long line of trouble. Right now we were just having fun. We were starting out when some kids had been doing drugs and drinking as early as the fourth grade.

At the top of my street between the playground and the church, two picnic tables were set up, and these was where all the smoking and drinking would take place. Neighborhood people would drive by and see a couple of new faces with the regulars stationed at this area. The good kids never ventured over to the party area, and when I started hanging out there, my mother was getting bad reports.

She would say, "If you are with them, you must be doing the same things they are doing." I would lie and tell her I wasn't, but my mother knew I was. None of my siblings ever sat at the drug-infested area, I was the only one. Big John used to ride the bus home from work, and he would see me with my new group of friends. He wasn't very pleased. He would talk to me about the company I was keeping, but just like every teenager, I wouldn't listen. This was just the beginning, so I still respected my parents' wishes, and I would make rare visits to the area. For now I was still influenced by good people, and I kept away from the area.

The party place was occupied all day and night with every smoker and drinker in the neighborhood. The police would drive by and just look and keep on going. The community tried to shut the area down; and the more they tried, more people would show up, and the partying would continue.

This strong black community was embarrassed with all the drug activity and drinking that took place there, right next to a church and playground where children would come to play. Sometimes young mothers and fathers would sit there smoking a joint and drinking with their young children sitting at the picnic tables. I didn't see the damage these people were doing, and I slowly began to be one of them. The five streets of black people in Wickliffe had an area for all to see when they went through our area. People attending church functions ever day of the week would pass by and see all the things they were against happening fifty feet away from one of the church entrances.

On Sunday the parking lot would be filled with people from everywhere going to church. This was a Presbyterian church, a predominately white church with very few people from the black community attending. The pastor would stop by the party spot and try to talk to some of the people sitting there. As soon as he would walk away, it was back to the same old business. This was the black eye of the community, and no one could stop it. It looked like some ghetto scene from some big city. I am ashamed to say I spent a lot of time there as I grew older.

How could I have been so blind, now as an adult with children? I hope the good God-fearing people in that community will forgive me for all the damage I did and also the influence of the youth that community. We were our own worst enemy; this was black-on-black crime in its worst form. We helped our friends and family members become drug addicts and alcoholics. Lord help the children.

Still a Good Kid

I was in the eleventh grade, and I was just experimenting with the party spot at the top of my street. I still was not a full-blown member. I was still into all sports in school, and I still loved to work out. I was at the halfway point, and I could go either way at this point. I would like to say I chose the right path, but I would be lying.

In the eleventh grade, I sang in the choir, still had my cement job, and worked at the Ponderosa Steak House. My grandmother worked at a day care by Wickliffe City Hall in a church. They needed help with mopping the floors and helping watch the children. After meeting with the lady that was in charge, I was hired, and I began working there five days a week after the football season ended.

My older brother, Bill, had worked there for about three years; one of the young girls fell in love with him, and that ended his career there. She was a young white Jewish girl a little older than Bill, and soon black people and white people began to see the relationship and decided to break up the two. In 1978 Wickliffe was not ready for black and white to come together. There was a big playground and pool at Wickliffe City Hall's Colby Park. Often Bill and his girlfriend would take the kids to the park and were seen walking hand and hand. People from the day care and police department would see them together. That's when it was decide Bill needed a new place to work.

When I took over, my duties were to mop and wax the floors and be a big brother to small children aged four to about twelve years old. I would mop the floors, help my grandmother in the kitchen, and play with the kids. On warm spring and summer days, we would play outside near the parking lot or go to the playground until the parents of the children would come from work to take them home.

One spring day, the five girls that worked there and I took the kids behind the day care to play. We would play games in the church parking lot and the big field. A small boy and girl were picking dandelions and other flowers in the field. They would give me flowers and plants from the field. I looked closely at some of the plants they handed me. One plant had leaves that looked very familiar. Taking a closer look, it turned out to be marijuana leaves. I asked the kids to show me where they got them from. We walked fifty feet into the field and found a whole field covered with marijuana plants. It was about as big as a football field.

We took all the kids inside and called the police. It didn't take long for the police to show up; the police station was only one hundred yards away. Soon there were about five police cars and detectives going over the area with a fine-tooth comb. They came inside and asked me over a million questions. Because I was a teenager, they believed I knew about the field; the truth was, I didn't know who planted it or how it got there.

The area was roped off for the entire summer, and when we took the children outside, we went straight to the city hall playground. Nothing else was said about the field, and no newspaper articles were written. I never did find out if the police got anywhere in their investigation. I continued working and playing with the kids at the day care. No one ever blamed me, and the police believed I was totally innocent. This time I was totally innocent.

The girls and I were only allowed to take the children to the city hall playground. We thought Colby Park was a pretty safe place; the police station was in the north corner of the park. How wrong we were. Things were normal for a long time. We would go to the park and push kids in the swings and watch them go down the slide or play on the monkey bars. The park had a couple of auxiliary police officers stationed at the entrance and exit areas and one officer riding around in a golf cart.

We would go to Colby Park every chance we got. The summers were long and hot with very little rain. In the beginning of July, we would see lots of people. Around July first, the girls and I were at the park as usual, and all the kids were playing. The kids were running around, and we were watching them when I noticed a few kids gathered around in a circle. I walked over to them, and in their tiny little hands were little Mickey Mouse tattoos.

I asked them were they got them from, and they pointed to a big old oak tree right next to a long line of police cars and the police station. I took every tattoo from the kids, wrapped them up in a piece of plastic from one of the trash cans, and put it in my pants pocket. I started walking toward the oak tree, when I saw a tall teenage boy with long shoulder-length blond hair, bell-bottom jeans, and no shirt on. He didn't see me walking toward him; the boy was busy giving more tattoos to other kids in the park.

When he finally looked up, I was staring at him eye to eye. It was too late to run. I asked him why he was giving tattoos to my kids. He said, "I don't see no nigger kids around here."

I said, "Give me those tattoos," as I snatched a sandwich bag from his hand that had over three hundred tattoos in it. I said, "Are you giving acid to these kids?"

He grabbed my shirt with both hands, and I immediately punched him in the face. We rolled on the ground, and I hit him about fifteen to twenty times in the face and stomach. The girls and the kids from the day care were screaming and crying, and a police officer was getting into his car when he looked up and saw the fight. The police office grabbed us and picked us up from the ground.

The boy could barely stand; I was still ready to fight, with my fists clenched tight. My shirt was torn and bloody but not with my blood. The officer said, "What the hell is going on?"

I showed him the tattoos, and the officer reached into the boy's pocket and found a couple of joints and a small glass bottle with an eye-dropper top and a sandwich bag with more tattoos. He handcuffed both of us, and we walked to the police station. I told the girls to take the kids back to the day care and make sure they didn't have any more tattoos. The girls did as I said, and they also told the lady in charge and my grandmother.

The boy and I were both handcuffed and sitting on a bench at the police station. A few officers walked by and were surprised to see me there. I was a good kid, and they knew me from being at the football games and the day care. One officer went and got the major. The major came out and had a talk with me. I knew him because I was friend with his son at school.

I explained to him what happened, and the slimeball sitting across the room on the other bench never said a word. Soon I was released, and I walked back to the day care. Everyone was asking me if I was all right; my grandmother laughed. I didn't have a scratch on me, just a bloody torn-up T-shirt. One of the girls gave me a T-shirt, and I went back to play with the kids. The lady in charge sent me home because she thought I was in trouble with the law.

After a long detailed explanation, I returned to work, but things weren't the same for a long time. The children feared me, and so did the girls I worked with. After a while, one of the girls I was closest to said she and the other girls didn't know I had a temper that could go from zero to sixty in less than two seconds. I explained that I was fighting for the children—that junk could have killed them. Slowly I began to gain their trust, and they knew what happened wasn't my fault; and if it happened again, I would react in the same way. A few of the children told their parents about the fight and talked to the lady in charge. She defended me well, but I almost lost my job and a lot of good friends.

As for the greaseball that I turned up for trying to poison the kids with acid-laced tattoos, some of my cop buddies told me they found over a thousand acid tattoos and a couple of joints, and the bottle with the eye—dropper lid was liquid acid, to make more tattoos. I didn't have to go to court, but I was told that teenage boy wouldn't be getting out of jail for a long time. He was tried as an adult because he was eighteen years old. The judge gave him a maximum sentence of fifteen years in prison; maybe with good behavior he would be out in ten years.

I don't believe my mother or siblings ever heard this story. My grandmother was busy, and other things were happening in her life she had to deal with; she had teenage children too. At the time I was still consider a real good kid, and the police and my neighbors didn't have any problems with me. Who knows what the future would hold? Hopefully I would not become a product of my surroundings. Would I give into peer pressure or remain good and pure?

The Prom

School started. I played football, wrestled, and ran track. I still did enough schoolwork to remain eligible to play. I also sang in the school choir and the all-boys choir. I learned how to talk to the girls a little more. I became friendlier with Coach Hughley's daughter Rhonda. She was in her senior year of high school. It seemed like she would get prettier ever year, she had a dynamite shape, and I could look at her all day. She was gorgeous, and I still didn't have the nerve to ask her to meet me after school or go out with her. Other guys would hit on her, and I was always in the background watching.

In the spring of 1978, the seniors had a prom, and all the buzz in school was who was going. I didn't drive, and a lot of my friends in the eleventh grade that did drive went to the prom with some of the senior girls. I didn't feel left out, but I knew Miss Rhonda Hughley had a date, and she would be going to the prom. All the guys were going to the tuxedo shop and renting big fancy cars. The girls were buying gowns and shoes. I would go to the gym and lift weights. I didn't concern myself with things I had no control over. I didn't drive, and there was nothing I could do about it. So the girl I liked was going to the prom with a guy I didn't like. There was nothing I could do about that either, so I continued to lift weights.

The prom went off without a hitch; it was a great success. Many of my friends went. The prom was Friday night. One of my closest friends went with a senior girl, and he called me after the prom was over. He told me that Rhonda's prom night didn't go so well. He wanted to know if I would double with him and his girl to the after prom at Cedar Point Amusement Park in Sandusky, Ohio. The park was about seventy miles away, and my friend said he would drive.

I never spoke to Rhonda, her girlfriend set up the date. When I hung up the phone, I just lay in my bed staring at the ceiling. I couldn't believe what just happened. I was on cloud nine. I just couldn't stop thinking about her. I visualized the two of us walking hand and hand through the park. We would ride all the rides; I would spend the whole day with her. Now I was really nervous! The after-prom was on Sunday, and we would pick the girls up at their houses early in the morning.

Sunday morning we picked up the girls and drove to the amusement park. We were all good friends, and we talked about the prom as we drove to the park. Rhonda told all of us about her prom date driving into some type of wire attached to a telephone pole. She said she tried to help him and give some moral support.

He was extremely mad at her and said it was all her fault. To me I thought this was one of the greatest things that ever happened. I felt bad that her prom night didn't go well, but I figured it was the best thing for me. He was too mad to go to after-prom, and with any luck, hopefully he wouldn't ask her out again.

We had a great time at the park, and we enjoyed talking to each other. I told her I didn't drive; she knew that, and that's why she didn't ask me to go to the prom. As we talked, I asked her if she would like to go out again. She told me anytime. We rode a lot of rides and went outside the park to eat. We ate in the car and went back to the park. We rode some more.

I really felt very comfortable with her. It wasn't like being on a date. We talked and laughed with each other. As it grew late in the day, we all decided to leave and head for home. The last thing we did before we left the park was squeeze into one of those tiny little picture booths and take a couple of pictures. It was a great excuse for getting close to her; the booth had only one seat. She sat on my lap and put her arms around me. I had never been this close to her, and I felt very calm as we embraced to take the picture. We drove home and talked the whole way home.

When we finally got home, I walked her to the door, and we kissed each other. The night was a complete success for me. That night I didn't have a care in the world except when would I be able to go out with her again. I would see her in school the very next day.

Rhonda and I dated a little here and there but nothing serious for the time being. We would see each other in school, but we didn't run with the same crowd. She was a good student with good grades, college material. I was more blue collar, had grades nothing to be proud of, my circle of friends were a bunch of rowdy partying jocks and burnouts. We liked to fight, play sports, and dabble in a little alcohol and grass ever now and then. Even though we didn't view the world the same way, we always had time for each other. I had other girlfriends, and I'm sure she had other boyfriends, but when I would see her, I would ask her out. She never turned me down, and I would jump in front of a train if she asked me too. Opposites do attract.

Driveways and the
School of Hard Knocks

In the summer of 1978, I was still making driveways with Mr. Woods and Mr. Salito. Mervin and I would get up at five in the morning. It was the same old routine: Mr. Woods took us to the donut shop where we would meet up with Mr. Salito; then we would head to the jobsite and prepare for the cement truck to arrive. Sometimes it was just getting forms in place and getting the wheelbarrows and tools ready. Other times we would get the sledgehammers out and start breaking out the old cement and preparing for the new cement. No matter what, it was never a short day, five in the morning until late in the evening.

After work we would always find time to go to the top of our street to play basketball or hang out at the picnic tables and drink or smoke with the rest of the neighborhood kids. We began to hang out there more and more. We were beginning to be regulars at the top of the street, which was not good. We continued to idolize and follow the people that were bringing down the community. We were slowly changing into part of the problem and not the solution. Our reputation as good kids was fading fast, and all the good people in the black community were seeing more and more of us at the local party spot. We still weren't considered fully fledged members of the party people, who did nothing but meet at all hours of the day and night at the picnic tables.

I still worked with my grandmother at the day care center. In my spare time, I would go to the high school to lift weights and run. All the kids in Wickliffe would go to the high school and play basketball, run, or lift weights. This was a mini-training camp for all the kids that would play sports while attending the school. No one was ever excluded, and sometimes kids from other cities and schools would show up and use the gym. The football coaches would supervise the activities. We never had any problems; no one wanted to be banned from the high school.

I didn't know that some kids involved in sports smoked and drank like the party people at the top of my street. Some of them were even worse than the local drinkers and smokers I knew. I tried to be like them, and now I was being taught how to smoke and drink with kids who were considered good kids and great athletes. These weren't just the black kids; these were mostly white kids with well-to-do families. I found out that no matter who you are or where you're from, people good or bad are all the same.

Superstar high school athletes that were in the paper one day would be smoking grass, drinking, or doing drugs with us the next day. I was still in the beginning stages, and I wouldn't do all the things that I saw. Some guys were taking enhancement drugs like steroids, but there wasn't a lot of that. The drugs of the sixties still had a tight grip on the youth of America at the time. Kids smoked marijuana, sniffed cocaine, and drank alcohol, and lots of it. I drank a little and puffed on a joint to be in with the crowd.

Pride, Prejudice, and Crossing the Line

My brother Bill and I were entering our senior year of high school in 1979, and we were growing further apart. Bill was in a different high school, and he would drive to see his friends. I still didn't drive and had no desire to drive. I would go out with my buddies on dates or just to party. We would often go to other cities that had more of a black population and more black teenage girls. I would go over girls' houses in my neighborhood, and we would walk to the park or make out when their parents weren't home. None of the black kids in Wickliffe ever dated white kids in our own city.

In school I had many friends because I was considered a jock, one who would play sports. Some of the girls in my classes would talk to me all the time. This little Italian girl and I became close friends, and I would walk her home, and sometimes I would talk to her mother. Then I would walk to my house by myself. We were in a couple of classes together.

One day she asked me to study with her at her house. She told me her mother wouldn't mind. We did study a couple of times at her house, but that changed when her father found out. Her father was a Wickliffe police officer, and his cop buddies would tell him that they saw his little girl walking home with a black kid. I'm quite sure they didn't say black kid. The Wickliffe police department didn't have one black policeman, so you could imagine what his buddies were saying about me and his daughter.

One day I was over my Italian female friend's house studying, and her mother stepped into the room and found us with a pile of books researching history and math. Her mother told me to stay for dinner. I tried to say no, but her mother insisted, so I stayed. We prepared for dinner. Both mother and daughter treated me like a king. In the middle of the meal, we heard a car in the driveway. Soon her father was entering the room. He didn't look to happy.

He took one look at me and said, "What is that sitting at my dinner table?" Before I could stand up, he grabbed the table cloth and everything on it and threw everything out the door. He was still in his police uniform; he grabbed me and took me outside. His wife and daughter just stood there in total silence. He looked me in the eye and said, "Do you know all the trouble you've been causing me? I go to the police department, and guys are razzing me about having nigger grandchildren. I want you to never walk my daughter home, and I don't ever want you in my house again, or I will throw you under the jail after I kick your ass!"

After that day, I had little to do with the girl, and she apologized for the way her father acted; but I learned a good lesson. I would never get close again to any girl outside of my race. Hispanic or Puerto Rican girls were okay, and most of their folks thought that I was one of them. I am a light-skinned black man, and I could pass for some type of Hispanic person. Actually I am a mixture of many races, so people didn't know what I was. I never dated a white girl, and I knew there would always be trouble if I did. Personally I preferred black women, thank God for the sisters.

My Italian friend's father would see me on the street, and I would never look his way. One day he decided to get out of his police car and talk to me, but I ignored him and kept on walking. My mother taught me to respect elders, so I figured if I didn't have anything nice to say I just wouldn't say anything at all. Besides that, he had showed his true colors when I was at his home. This whole incident shook my faith in good people of different races, but I came to understand when I saw a black girl try to bring a white boy to her house. I never told my mother about this because I didn't want to cause her any more trouble. I can't remember if my siblings ever found out, I know I was too embarrassed to talk to anyone about it.

Soon the Italian girl was a thing of the past. I respected her father's wishes and stayed away. I saw her in school hanging out with some of the long-haired dopers. This group was known as the burnouts. Soon she had one of the worse guys in school as her boyfriend. He was often seen hitting her, and he taught her how to smoke dope and drink. This fantastic person spent more time at the juvenile detention center then he did at home or school. I believe he spent a lot of time with her father because he was always sitting in the backseat of a police car. He was also allowed to go in and out of the girl's house freely. I wonder how her father's fellow police officer felt about this fine citizen.

I don't think her father was pleased, but this guy wasn't black, and his first grandchild would be born before his daughter could complete high school. She didn't graduate at all. Her father didn't have any nigger grandchildren either. I would see her father driving up and down my street in his police car. We never spoke, and he would give me a long stare. The truth was I had no love interest in his daughter. We were just friends. She was a very pretty girl, but I knew the boundaries of the territory, and I had a strong love for pretty black women. I wanted a girl just like mom.

As an adult, I would run into the Italian girl and her father when I would go to Wickliffe for football, basketball, or baseball games. Her father would sit in a lawn chair. He's about seventy years old, and he would throw up his hand and wave. I would do the same. I still don't speak to him, but I can see great sadness in his eyes. I felt an old leopard couldn't change his spots either, so I didn't care to talk to him at all.

His daughter and I stepped around the corner, where we wouldn't be in her father's line of sight. We talked as friends. She has three children, and her husband is in jail. The cute little Italian girl is now a mother and weighs about 250 pounds and barely five foot tall. She lives with her parents and works at a local gas station. Her children act and think just like her husband did when he was growing up, 100 percent pure trouble. Apples don't fall far from the tree. I feel sorry for her and her family, even for her father. When I think of them, I often say a prayer for her and her family.

Living in Wickliffe was pretty much like the girl and her father. Black children knew how the good people of Wickliffe felt when one of us would venture out and play on their streets with their children. Anyone with ideas about changing or bringing diversity to the community was taught a quick lesson on the differences between races and religion or any other thing that separated human beings. Sometimes I didn't blame them; some black people were just as mean and hateful when it came to the mixing of races.

We didn't help the situation. I would like to say that we were all good, God-fearing people. That wouldn't be true, when we spent most of our time up the street at the picnic tables smoking and drinking our lives away. White communities in Wickliffe had the same things going on in their neighborhoods too. I would often go to other playgrounds in Wickliffe to do the same thing we did at ours. So people are all the same; for every bad black kid, I can show you a bad white kid or Chinese kid or any other type of kid. Lord help the children.

The Jocks and Dope

In the winter of my senior year in high school 1979, I was on the wrestling team. We would run up the stairs, do wall pushups, and learn takedowns and other wrestling moves. I was a heavyweight at 190 pounds, which was five pounds over the last weight division. I would wrestle kids weighing as much as 250 pounds or more. Needless to say, I didn't have much of a winning record, but I still had plenty of fun. The workouts were absolutely insane, and one of the hardest things I've done in my life. The wrestling team had two black kids, and one was real good; once again I would like to say I was this gifted athlete. Guess again.

Wrestling had its share of partiers too; I fell in with this crowd. I wasn't concerned with being a great wrestler, but I showed up for practice because I liked the training. After school we would change in the locker room and go upstairs in the gym and warm up. By the end of practice, we were all one great big nasty, smelly pool of sweat. We would take showers and get our winter clothes on, preparing ourselves for the long cold walk home.

Occasionally one of the guys from the wrestling team would pull out a joint or two. This junk was everywhere, poisoning the minds and bodies of good kids and adults who were willing to take a drag of the demon weed. I soon learned that better than half of the kids on the wrestling team smoked weed. I began to feel nothing was wrong with it, and soon I thought only the nerds or weird kids didn't smoke dope. Kind of makes you wonder who was the real dope?

One day before wrestling practice, the team was in the locker room dressing, and one of the superstars of the team pulled out a sandwich bag half full of pot and a pipe out of his gym bag. He showed it to me and a couple of other guys. Before we changed into our wrestling gear, we decided we would go for a smoke before practice. There were five of us heading upstairs to find a remote, out-of-the-way location where we could smoke a little wild wood flower before we went to practice.

We found a bathroom at the southern tip of the school where no one would go after school. We had a small radio. We tuned into WMMS 100.7, the Thundering Buzzard, our favorite rock station. Some of you old-time Cleveland boys know what I'm talking about. Well, we got the party started, and what was supposed to be a little turned out to be a lot. We soon forgot about wrestling practice and everything else; we were smoking bowl after bowl in the pipe. The whole bathroom reeked of pot, and smoke filled the air. A janitor opened up the door and found us inside. He told us to get the hell out of there; we laughed and laughed while exiting the building. We were so high there was no way we could show up for practice.

All of us snuck into the locker room, gathered up our things, and went home. My eyes were as red as the sun, so when I finally got home, I crept threw the back door; and lucky for me, nobody was at home. I raided the kitchen and found some cold pizza my family ate the night before. I ate the entire twelve cuts and a big bag of potato chips, and drank six cans of pop. This was known as the munchies, a by-product from smoking pot. I went downstairs to my bedroom and fell asleep before anyone came home.

I slept through the entire night. The next day I got up and went to school. My wrestling buddies and I were in a world of trouble for missing practice. We didn't get in trouble for smoking weed; the janitor never told on us. When we showed up for wrestling practice, everyone knew we were in the doghouse.

The coach lined up the wrestling team; I could see the fire in his eyes. It was so quiet, you could hear a single ant piss on cotton. The coach asked all six of us why we missed practice. No one said a single word. The coach sent the whole wrestling team home except the six partiers.

First we started out with wall pushups; and then we did up-downs followed by more wall pushups and more up-downs with about thirty hundred-yard wind sprints. The coach continued this routine for three hours. The pizza and chips along with everything else in my stomach came up all at once. My buddies all threw up too, but the coach continued his crime-and-punishment routine. Three of my buddies quit the team before we could finish half of the coach's punishing practice.

I had never worked so hard in my life. The three of us that didn't quit were considered men among men to the rest of the wrestling team, but the next day we had to join the others and practice just like we never had the day of workouts that could beat all workouts. They continued to smoke and drink, but we never skipped another practice. I decided to give it a rest and didn't do any of it until the wrestling season ended. As I look back on things, I should have quit smoking and drinking forever, but I still had a lot of lessons to learn and a lot of growing up to do.

Graduation, California, and Uncle Walter

When spring had finally sprung, my brother Bill and I were ready to graduate. We had two or three months left of school. Bill was still a great kid and didn't fall into the same trap as I did. Drinking and smoking just seemed to me a normal way of life. Others that loved and cared for me would continuously try to talk some sense into me. I wouldn't listen, and I even did more of the things that hurt my parents and family. The damage was so deep, I don't know how they could ever forgive me.

After school was over and I graduated, I was invited to spend the summer at my Uncle Walter's house in Englewood, California. I had never really been anywhere in my life, and this was the opportunity of a lifetime. I couldn't believe it, and this would be the first time I would get on a plane. I don't know why my mother let me go, the only thing I could figure out was that I would be away from my buddies at the top of the street smoking dope and drinking. My Uncle Walter and his wife were two of the most decent people on God's green earth, and maybe being around them, I would learn a few things. I couldn't wait to get on the plane and leave all my troubles behind; it was as if I was starting a new life.

The plane ride took a little over four hours, and when I arrived at LAX airport, it was about ten o'clock at night. With the four-hour time difference and the jet lag, I felt like I had been awake for a week. I was exhausted. My Uncle Walter met me at the airport, and I was glad to see his smiling face when I got off the plane. As always he made me feel good when he said, "Looks like you been hitting the weights pretty hard." In all actuality, I was still pretty fit from all the high school sports I participated in, but the truth was, I was partying my brains out every chance I got. I think my mother gave him all the ugly details before I left. They talked on the phone every other day.

Englewood was about forty-five minutes away from the airport, and Walter made me feel comfortable asking me about home and family. He never asked me about smoking and drinking. I knew he, a Vietnam vet, was around guys that did those things. It was totally dark, and I didn't see much of Los Angeles that night. We drove to his house, and my Aunt Averill was waiting for us as we walked through the door. She looked well, and she had always been a pretty lady. We talked for a while about home and California, and soon everyone went to bed.

The next morning, Walter took me to a small apartment-type home that was in the back of his house. It was a guesthouse. For the first time in my life, I was living alone, and I loved it. I didn't have to report to anyone, with the freedom of coming and going as I pleased. Walter never let me get wild. He would always check on me to see how things were going. As the people in California used to say, I was a small-town boy in a big city.

My Aunt Linda took me to see all her friends. The California girls were very forward, and soon I was on my own with them. Linda was a free bird, and she made sure I was comfortable with her girlfriends before she left. These girls weren't that much different than the girls back home in Ohio. They asked many questions and liked to party just as much as I did. They were also interested in me because I was something new; they invited me to go to an amusement park with them the next day.

The next day, the girls picked me up, and we went to Magic Mountain amusement park for the whole day. They smoked and drank more than I did, and I was falling into the same old crowd back home. After the day was over, one of the girls drove me home, and she decided to stay with me until the late hours of the night. We listened to music and smoked and drank until we fell asleep. She stayed the night and got up the next morning, telling me she would be back after work. This would continue for weeks, and she was picking me up on a routine basis.

After a while, my uncle started to see a pattern and decided to step in. He could see trouble before it got started. Walter took me to work one day. I toured his place of work and headed outside to walk along the beach, people watching. I walked on a huge pier where people were fishing, and I rented an ocean reel and bought some bait. Ocean fishing was different than lake and stream fishing, and I looked like a fish out of water. People stared at me as I tried to bait the big hook. They could tell a rookie when they saw one.

I befriended a Mexican boy who was about my age. He showed me how to bait the hook and cast out into the deep blue sea. I caught some small ocean fish and shared a six-pack of beer with my new friend. He pulled a joint out of his pocket, and I kindly declined his offer, I knew after a while I would have to go back to the police station where my uncle worked. Soon the day was over, and I went back home with Walter.

Walter took me all over California; I went to the La Brea Tar Pits in the heart of the city of Los Angeles, where I went to the museum and viewed dinosaur bones and many other things that were pulled from the black tar pit. We also went to Tijuana, Mexico; San Diego; and the Mojave Desert, where we spent a couple of days. All this time, Walter went to work and also spent time with his family. I enjoyed all the time I spent with him as I explored a completely different world than what I was used to.

We stayed a couple of days in the Mojave Desert, and at this time, Walter and I had a couple of heart-to-heart discussions. He asked me about things back home, and somehow I told him the truth about all the things I was doing back home. Walter never passed judgment on me and was able to give me a little advice, and I figured that he was such a wise man that I would listen. Later on in life, I would understand all the things he was telling me, and he was 100 percent correct. If only I had taken his advice; I would be a lot further today.

With all the time we had together, I asked him about his time in Vietnam, and he didn't spend too much time on the subject, and I'm sure he would have liked to have forgotten everything. Walter told me about fighting at the foot of a mountain and how he would have to take off his helmet putting one dog tag in it from each man, to pick a guy to go on point. I could see the hurt in his eyes and feel the pain as he told me of screams in the night and the point man never returning to the squad. I would have liked to ask him more, but I knew that it really bothered him to talk about it. He didn't say much on the war, and we quickly found more pleasant things to talk about. We were on our way to Tijuana, Mexico, and that's what he talked about as we drove through the hot desert in his Volkswagen van.

I enjoyed my time in California with my uncle and his family. I will never forget the time spent with them, and little did I know how much it would mean to me later on in life. Walter would leave this world in an untimely manner, which I will discuss later on in my story. He would be missed by all. He was one of those men I talked about as being a man among men bigger than life itself. To Walter's wife and children, I can surely say he's gone but not forgotten; and as I live my life, I often think of him and say a prayer thanking the Lord for the time I spent with him. He also showed me a way of life that I use today with my own family. He taught me how to be a good family man as I watched him with his own family.

Home Again,
the Underground Fighting Scene

When I came home from California, things were a little different, and the first tragedy that I would face was my Uncle Raymond being gone and put into a home. I was very sad when I found out he was gone, and I knew it was better for him, but somehow I blamed myself for being gone for so long. When I went over my grandparent's house and entered his empty room, I sat on the edge of his bed and cried. I still feel like if I was home, he would have been able to stay in his room, watching television and playing with his action figures.

Raymond stayed at the home for about two years until one day we got a call telling us he was in the hospital. He had been given his medication and left unattended, and he choked on his own vomit. He also choked on a bottle of mouthwash, and the fluid entered his lungs, causing him an infection. Raymond didn't survive; only a week after the incident, he died in the hospital.

My mother was deeply saddened, and I remember her telling me she took care of Raymond like he was her own kid when they were growing up. He was the first one in my mother's family to pass away; we all knew he was in a better place. Raymond would suffer no more, and if anybody entered the gates of heaven, I know that Raymond would be there watching over the rest of the family.

Only a few days later after I came home from California, I was back at the top of the street partying with a few of the same guys that were there when I left. As we smoked and drank, I told them about all the things I did when I was gone. We had run out of party favors and money, so we had to find a way to make some money and continue the party. We learned of a dangerous game and decided it was an easy way to make some quick cash. A couple of brave white boys that hung out in my neighborhood told us of a place where we could make a quick hundred bucks. We all listened intently; the plan was to go to this warehouse in downtown Cleveland and fight for money. We piled into a car and went to the warehouse.

There were six of us, and only three of us that knew how to fight and not get the hell beat out of us. We entered the building and watched a couple of fights. I volunteered to fight, but we had to come up with one hundred dollars to start. We scanned the crowd and found a guy that we knew, and he spotted us the money as long as we would pay him back plus fifty dollars. I approached the desk where the contestants would sign up and pay the fee. I gave them the money, and they told me if I lost, I would go home with nothing but a good ass-beating. This didn't scare me. I told my buddies to make a couple of side bets. I wasn't planning on losing. My good buddies bet up to five hundred dollars. I couldn't lose; we didn't have any money to pay anybody.

I watched a couple of guys get dragged out. They couldn't walk out on their own—they were knocked out cold. I wasn't scared. The announcer called my number first; then he called out my opponent. A big heavy kid stepped out of the crowd. He was the same height that I was; I weighed about two hundred pounds even. This guy looked like a biker with a couple tattoos and plenty of battle scars, long, shoulder-length greasy hair and outweighed me by about sixty pounds. This would be a fight until one of us could fight no more. This wasn't your standard ring, just a concrete warehouse floor, no gloves and no referee. This was a good old knock-down drag-out street fight that I couldn't lose.

We faced each other, and the announcer yelled, "Fight!" And so we did. I moved around this guy until I saw an opening. He raised his thick arm and punched me square in the jaw. I heard the crowd yelling and screaming. I also heard a ringing in my right ear close to where I was punched. After that, I realized I might take an ass-kickin'.

I never got hit again. I punched the guy right in the throat on the Adam's apple; and he winced in pain, dropping to his knees, trying to find some air. My buddies went nuts, yelling, "Hit him again, go 'head, take him out!"

I waited for him to get up. I guess the crowd wasn't too used to that because they yelled, "Kick his ass, stomp him in the ground, and other fun things like that."

I wasn't taught how to fight dirty, but there were no rules to this game. I waited for him to get to his feet; he was holding his throat like he'd swallowed a piece of food that wouldn't come up. The look on his face said, "I had enough."

His eyes were watering, and he came toward me as if he had a job to do and wouldn't rest until he got it done. I waited for the attack, but as he came closer, I hit him in the gut. And as he doubled over, I hit him three hard shots straight to the temple. He fell down like someone put a building on his back. He never got back up.

My friends and I collected our money and paid back the guy for the loan plus fifty. We took home about four hundred dollars that night. This was too easy, and we thought it would be like this all the time. We thought this was the answer to all our money problems. Every time we would run out of cash, just go fight and get some more, right?

My smoking and drinking partying buddies and I had a plan we would be rich. We were unbeatable, we thought. We decided to go down town to the warehouse every Friday night and make some big money. The plan was to make side bets and collect double, maybe even triple the cash, after we won every fight.

Somehow our plan backfired. The first time we went back, we tried to work our plan. I told the guys I fought the first fight, and someone else needs to step up. Jerry said he wasn't afraid of anything and claimed to be the toughest out of all of us. Well, we paid the entry fee and had two hundred dollars for side bets. That meant if Jerry won we would have eight hundred dollars and build more cash out of that. Jerry said, "Don't worry, dudes, it's like money in the bank." Somehow Jerry didn't seem to me to have a certain set of skills that would make him a contender. He also didn't show any signs of a killer instinct.

So Jerry got his number, sat down, and watched a couple of fights until they called his number. The fighters that night looked different than the night I fought, as I looked out at the guys holding the numbers. They all looked like well-conditioned athletes. Not one fat boy in the bunch, a couple of long, lean fighters, but no one looked like a pushover. This wasn't their first rodeo, and it was only our second. I knew we were outclassed, but Jerry was pumped and primed. He started pounding his fists together and screaming about kickin' some ass!

Jerry's number was called, and he stepped into the center of the place. He took off his shirt, and he looked like a plucked chicken with pale lily-white skin. He wore his bell-bottom jeans and cowboy boots. Actually I never saw him wear anything else, minus the plain yellow-tinted, white-pocket T-shirt that he threw on the ground as he walked to the center of the floor. Now Jerry was nothing special—a regular type of guy about five foot nine and 170 pounds. Jerry had never worked out a day in his life and smoked a hell of a lot of weed and drank every day that I had known him. Jerry start bouncing on his toes and jumping up and down. He threw a couple of punches in the air as he shuffled around the ring. Not because he knew what he was doing; he saw the fighters that had fought before him doing it.

They called another number and out walks this dark-skinned black fighter about six foot four and thin, without an ounce of fat, weighing about two hundred pounds. This guy looked like the fighters you see on television on *Friday Night Fights*. He was also dressed for the part: he had a pair of red boxing shorts on, his boxing shoes matched, and no shirt. With the lights on his body, he had a shiny wet look. He had this fierce look on his face and danced around the floor, throwing a series of punches in the air. This guy meant all business.

I tried to talk Jerry out of it, but he said, "If you can do it, so can I. You're no better than I am. Besides that, I'm tougher than you ever been in your life. Do you think I'm some candy-ass pussy who can't fight?" All the things he said to me I thought were exactly right. I knew he was no fighter, just a street punk with a big mouth added to what he said. I just walked away. I knew there was no turning back.

The announcer yelled, "Fight," and here we go. The black beanpole stepped around Jerry with his hand held high, took one step toward him, and hit Jerry about fifteen times before he knew what was going on; and that was the first ten seconds of the fight. Jerry was swinging wildly and never connecting with one single punch. Jerry's nose was bleeding, and both his eyes were closed from the awful beating he was taking. Well, all of us just stood there in complete shock. No one said a word.

Jerry lasted about thirty seconds, and his face looked like a piece of raw hamburger. Jerry was on the ground, and the way things looked, he wouldn't be getting up. The fighter stood over him like a hawk looking at an injured field mouse. He looked over at his boys and said, "This white boy didn't bring nothing. Maybe I should have fought his sister!"

I walked over to the center of the floor where Jerry was and picked him up, swinging him over my shoulder like a big sack of potatoes. All our money was gone; we patched Jerry up as best as we could. He had a large cut over both his closed eyes, and his nose was broken, along with a couple of teeth missing.

Before we left, one of the guys in charge asked if Jerry was going to be all right. He said, "Your friend took one hell of a beating. Did you know this was semipro night?" We had no idea what he was talking about; he pulled a card out of his pocket. I started reading the card out loud, "Semipro night at the end of every month of Underground Street Fighting." I was very lucky, and Jerry was the result of six idiots not knowing what we were getting into.

We piled into the car and laid Jerry across the back seat. I wondered if we should take him to the hospital. We all knew that if we took him to the hospital, we would have some explaining to do. Instead we took him over an old fighter's house, and he helped us with Jerry that night. He asked us what kind of fools would step into the street-fighting scene, and all we did to prepare for the fight was smoke and drink before we would fight. He told us, "Don't ever do that again because one of you could get killed." We knew he was right, but we tried it a couple of more times. But we stayed away from the semipro nights.

Eventually I got my ass beat too, but I played a smart game. When I knew I was beaten, I continued to put on a good show; and when the crowd would roar after I took a good shot, I would lie down and not get back up before I took a severe ass-whippin'. I also knew how to cover up and block some of the blows with my arms, and I held my hands high so my face didn't take a beating. That was the end of our get-rich idea.

Jerry's battle wounds begin to heal; he was a different person after that. He would stare into space, and we never heard a word from him about being some real bad ass. We stayed close to home and went back to the top of the street and sat on the two picnic tables smoking and drinking. We had to find another way to make money; we definitely weren't fighters. God looks out for his children and fools.

Taking a Deadly Ride

No more school. As soon as I graduated, I began to seek employment. I still didn't drive. I continued to work with Mervin and his grandfather Mr. Woods, along with Mr. Salito, making driveways all summer long. We went to the top of the street even more, and now with a couple of freshly graduated high school students, we were regulars at the two picnic tables. My parents hounded me to go get a real job. My brother Bill got a job at a small-time auto body shop. I didn't have any skills. So I went to local small-time factories, and pretty soon, I landed a job.

I worked on the night crew at a small steel factory; I was what they called a chipper. I would clean the steel chips out of the machines that milled the steel parts, making them ready for shipping. I worked seven days a week with no time off, for twelve hours a day, six in the evening to six in the morning. A couple of 1978 Wickliffe graduates I played football with worked there too.

I would wrap a harness around my shoulder and chest to drag a regular-size steel trash bin around the factory. It weighed about three hundred pounds empty; when it was full, I'm sure it weighed over a thousand pounds. I was equipped with a couple of steel washtubs, large paintbrushes, and a pair of rawhide working gloves. I would take a washtub with my paintbrushes over to one of the milling machines and clean all of the steel chips out of the machine. I would fill the tub up till it couldn't hold anymore, pick up the two-hundred-pound tub, and walk it over to the trash bin about twenty yards away, dump it and put my harness back on and drag it to the next machine. Even though I wore gloves, I would get small, microscopic steel splinters in my hands. My hands became very sore, and soon they got infected. I still went to work, ignoring the pain.

The guys I made friends with smoke and drank on breaks and lunchtime. Once again I was hanging out with the wrong crowd. Every Friday after work, we would pile into a car and go to one of the guys' apartments to eat, drink, and smoke while watching television. This was their enjoyment in life, and now it was my only enjoyment. We all worked every day of the week on night shift, twelve hours a day. I never saw any of my friends, and I was too tired to do anything. I was always asleep when normal people were awake. The only good thing about all of this was I didn't hang out at the top of the street anymore.

I did this job for about three or four months in the summer. One Friday, when we got off work at six in the morning, we did our normal routine and headed for the apartment for our usual dinner and a movie. There were eight of us; we quickly piled into the car. We went to the store and bought a case of beer. We started drinking and smoking before we left the parking lot.

The apartment was about six miles away we argued about who was going to sit in the middle; we called this riding bitch. I was forced to take the middle seat, and each guy grabbed my leg and tried to put their arm around me. After loads of playing grab-ass, we were drinking and smoking all the way, and not a cop in sight. The driver was drinking and smoking too, but he carefully watched his speed. No one wanted to go to jail. We were traveling at a speed of about forty-five miles per hour; the guys on each side of me decided to stick their heads out the window and see who could yell the loudest.

As the yelling kept getting louder, I told them to knock it off, but they laughed and kept sticking their heads out of the windows. The guys that weren't doing it were telling them to stop. One guy was almost completely out of the window, and I grabbed his belt, trying to pull him back in the car.

Just then I heard a loud thump, and his body went limp. I pulled him back in the car, and his face was crushed. He had hit a telephone pole with the side of his face; the guy on the other side of me took one look at him and started screaming to stop the car. We pulled over on the side of the road.

I said, "He needs to go to the hospital now!"

The driver said, "How are we going to explain this?" We turned around and headed for the hospital. We pulled in the parking lot, and the driver grabbed his buddy and said, "All you guys need to get the hell out of here." They all took off, and I stayed, helping the driver take his buddy through the emergency room door. The interns came through the doors and put him on a stretcher. The front desk nurses were asking the driver questions as I just stood there. He asked me why I stayed. I told him, "I guess it was the right thing to do."

After about waiting an hour, with the driver I decided to go get a cup of coffee. I asked my friend if he wanted one. He just sat there with his head in his hands. I think this guy was one of the saddest people I ever seen in my life. I really didn't know these guys that well. I was new to the group. The guy in the emergency room I didn't know at all; this had been the first time we met. I left the room and went down the hall to find a coffee machine.

When I got back with my coffee, the place was loaded with police. The driver never moved from the spot that I left him in. There were two police officers sitting on each side of him, and a detective sitting in a chair in front of him. The police didn't even look at me; they didn't connect me with him. He was a long-haired, blue-eyed white kid. I was the only black guy in the car that night. Now I was the only black guy in the room and the only black guy in the hospital. The driver raised his head, and when he saw me, he gave me the high sign; in other words, get out of here. I walked out of the hospital, and not one police officer even looked my way.

I walked home and thought about people I was hanging around with. I also thought about the crappy job I had. My hands ached from all the steel splinters I collected in them from cleaning those grimy machines. It was noon before I got home; I crept down the basement steps. I sat on the edge of my bed and cried. I was physically and mentally exhausted. I took a shower and slept the rest of the day.

I woke up to my mother yelling down the steps, telling me it was time to go to work. I never moved. I slept for two more days and thought about my life and my job. I talked to my parents, and I never told them what happen. I decided to quit. Later in the evening, I went back to the factory and talked to the foreman. I walked through the factory and found the driver. He told me his buddy was in a coma, on life support and a ventilator; he couldn't even breathe on his own. He was considered a vegetable, and they didn't know how long he would live.

A day later, I went to the hospital, looked in the room; the guy didn't even look the same. His face was swollen and scratched up from hitting the pole. I walked back down the hall to the emergency room and took a seat. I walked up to the front desk and showed the nurse my hands. They were swollen and painful to the touch.

I went to see the doctor. He examined my hand; then he took an X-ray. When the results came back, he showed them to me. I had what looked like thousands of tiny microscopic steel splinters in my hands. I told the doctor about my job, and he said if they got infected, I could possibly lose my hands. I told him I already quit the job. He instructed me to use Lava soap and Comet Cleanser and wash my hands as much as possible in order to work the splinters loose. He also prescribed a cream to use. My hands healed in about two weeks.

Once again, I had no job and walked up the street to complicate my life even more. Back to the picnic tables, I was getting a real fine education from the school of hard knocks. But that was my choice. There were other ways out; I just didn't have the drive, or as some people would say, I didn't have the balls to make the change. Giving up was easy, smoking and drinking were easy too. When I was high, I was a legion in my own mind. I could talk the talk, but I couldn't walk the walk.

The Plaster Factory

My brother Bill started working in a small plaster mold factory, and I followed him there. It was a day shift, eight hours, five days a week, Monday thru Friday, weekends and holidays off. There were about twenty-five employees, and the owners treated them like they were slaves. It was all the same at small factories. They would work you like a borrowed mule, and if something happened to you, they would hire another person to replace you.

I had a set pattern. I fell in with the same old type of people, young dopers and drinkers. For lunch we would smoke and drink in our cars, and then go back inside to work. This factory had about six party boys, and once again I was the only black one.

My brother Bill did not participate in the extra activities in the parking lot. Bill never had anything to do with the people who liked to smoke and drink. He would always do the right thing and was never in trouble. For lunch he would eat with the girls and old people who worked there.

The only reason they hired me was because they thought they we getting another hardworking kid like my brother. I worked harder than three men all the time, but I was a drinking and smoking bad boy. Bill and I were like night and day, and we always respected each other. If we ran into problems, we were always there for each other, but Bill stayed clear of me and my friends in the parking lot.

The people that owned the company and the foreman would give the party boys the most demeaning jobs and threaten to fire us if it was done in an untimely manner or by the end of the day. We would dig ditches, sweep the warehouse, clean, and do everything that no one else would do.

One day another guy and I were given the assignment to paint every door in the factory, which consisted of about forty doors. This guy was doing something I had never seen and would never try ever! We opened up a gallon of green paint and started painting. Every time I would open a can of paint, this genius would stick his nose as close to the paint as possible as and suck in a gigantic deep breath as much as possible.

By the time we got to the third door, this guy was higher than the sky. He could barely stand or hold a paintbrush. He had green paint on his nose and all over his face. I looked at him, and he had more paint on him than the three doors we painted. He looked like one of those crazy football fans that painted themselves the team colors before a big game. I took him outside under a big shady tree. It was about ninety-two degrees that day. He took off his shirt and passed out on the lawn.

I painted the rest of the doors all by myself; it took me all day. Before it was quitting time, I went back outside where I left the little green man. He was the greenest blonde-haired blue-eyed white boy I ever saw. He wasn't under the tree where I had left him; I looked around and didn't see him anywhere. I went to the back of the factory by the trash bins. I found him stretched out on a picnic table where the guys took smoke breaks. He was still covered in green paint; his skin was fire-engine red from being exposed to direct sunlight for about six to eight hours. The spots on his face that were painted green looked like it was baked into his skin.

I rushed back in the factory and called 911, and then I told the foreman. Everybody ran outside as the emergency squad arrived. The foreman started yelling at me, telling me I should have been watching him. I knew somehow this would be all my fault. I yelled right back, "You should have told me that guy was my responsibility. I didn't know I was supposed to do my job and babysit too." The squad picked him up and quickly zoomed up the street to the hospital. I was sent to the office.

The factory owners and the foreman started the interrogation, asking me one questions after another. They were firing questions so fast I didn't have time to think. I told them that the guy said he felt sick and went outside. I thought he would come back in on his own. Then they asked me why did he have green paint all over his face and on the inside of his nose?

"He was on one side of the door, and I was one the other. I looked up and he was gone." I should have said, "Look, this idiot was sniffing paint like it was going out of style and blacked out."

After all, I didn't owe this guy a thing; if it wasn't for me, the little green man would have been dead. This time I actually had nothing to do with this guy sniffing paint. I had told him to stop. As usual I was in trouble, and Bill as usual wasn't; he was with his group of people that just came to work and did their job. I was with individuals that would have trouble all their lives; was I one of these people? My mother always told all of us, "Be careful of the company you keep. Misery loves company."

The next day I was in the office with the foreman and the owners of the company, explaining the whole thing over and over again. Police detectives were also in the room, asking me questions. I thought this was the end of another job. After the detectives left, the owners and my foreman decided I would be given another chance, but I was on thin ice. I was told one more just being the victim of my surroundings, and I would be looking for another job.

After about a week later, the paint sniffer came back to work, and he got into less trouble than I did. He had permanent marks on his face, arms and chest, where the sun had baked the paint on his body. He wore permanent scars that would remind him of his foolishness. He told me he had been burned by the sun so badly that he stayed three days in the hospital. The doctors told him the scars would fade in time, but he would never be completely healed. Once again by the grace of God, I didn't participate in the deadly game that he played.

I was put on a real working crew; I would clean the warehouse and every hard job that they could find. Every Monday I would go to the shipping yard where the freight trains would come in. There were six of us. We had the pleasure of unloading box cars with one-hundred-pound bags of plaster and stacked them on skids, so the tow motor could pick them up and load them on a box truck to take to the factory. Each boxcar contained fifty-two tons of one-hundred-pound bags of plaster. Each of us had our own boxcar to unload in nine hours; we had an hour for lunch.

The crew was comprised of all the young misfits of the factory, and one fifty-six-year-old frail man. We were in the hot sun all day; we bought beer and other drinks on the way to the shipping yard. This was a type of punishment for the screw-offs; if we didn't finish by the end of the day, we would be fired.

I worked like a mad man, and so did the other boys; we were all young and strong. I don't know why the old man was there or what he did to deserve such treatment. He had been a faithful employee that did his job and never missed a day of work in his fifteen years of being with the company. He began to fall way behind, and by noon he sat on the edge of his boxcar, crying and telling us this was the end for him.

I was finished with my box car by noon, and the others would soon finish. The old man was working through lunch. Sweat poured from his body, and so did the tears of the depleted old salt. I watched for a while, and so did the others. I drank half a forty-ounce of beer and decided I couldn't take it anymore. The old guy looked like he was going to fall out at any minute. I walked over to his boxcar and started grabbing two one-hundred-pound bags at a time and loading them on the skids below.

The old guy said, "I don't need any help from a smart-ass punk like you." I ignored him and continued to unload the boxcar. I had heard him talking to people at the factory, telling them he had two children in college to pay for and a wife that also worked at the same factory. The truth was, I admired the old boy for telling me to get lost; he had a lot of balls. He was willing to accept the worst but wouldn't put up with the likes of me and the other smart-ass punks working in the yard.

One of the other guys asked me why I was bustin' my ass to help the old guy. I told all of them, "They are expecting to fire this guy by the end of the day. I would do anything just to look at their faces when they drive up here and see his boxcar unloaded and his work completed." Well, that was all those dudes wanted to hear. All of them started grabbing bags of plaster and unloading the boxcar.

As usual we were drinking and smoking while we worked. Why not make it a party? No foreman and no supervision. The old man didn't have a drop of beer and didn't smoke with us either; he just kept working, not saying a word. We got into a groove and formed a chain. We unloaded the entire boxcar in two and a half hours.

All the work was completed, with an hour and a half left to spare. We migrated over to a shady spot and drank the rest of the beer. The old man came over and sat down beside me. Putting his hand on my shoulder and looking into my eyes, he said, "Why did you and your buddies help me?" I looked him square in the eyes and said, "You are a good old soul, and you don't deserve to be treated like a piece of crap by some rich fat cats that have all the money they ever needed. All you want to do is send your kids to school. Maybe when I need a hand, someone will have the decency to help me. Plus I can't wait till they come back and see all the work completed!"

The owners and the foreman drove up with three eighteen-wheelers and found us sitting in a shady area, waiting for them to arrive. They would walk up to a boxcar and look inside, making sure we did all our work. The old man's boxcar was the last one to be checked, and before they checked it, they were giving him this speech about his work not being done and how he couldn't keep up anymore.

They looked inside and didn't see one bag of plaster in the boxcar. They were dumbfounded and asked how he completed the job. I looked over at him, put one finger to my lips, giving him the sign to be silent and not tell them. He just looked and smiled. "I just put in a routine hard day's work."

As the six of us drove back to the factory, the old guy was very humble with tears coming from his eyes. He said, "I owe you boys a lot, and I thought you were all a bunch of smart-ass punks." We were a bunch of smart-ass punks, but we hated to see a good, hardworking family man that worked every day to send his children to school get treated like a broken toy that the rich could throw away after they used it all up.

We would get paid every Friday after work and have the weekend off. Everybody got paid and would go their separate ways. When Monday morning came, and everybody was in the break room getting ready for work, the old man and his wife came over to the table in the corner where the five outcasts of the factory sat. His wife had coffee from McDonalds for all of us and two dozen donuts from the best place in town. Everybody that worked there, including the owners and our foreman, were sitting in the room.

The old man reached into his pocket and pulled out five envelopes with our names on it. I immediately opened the envelope, expecting to find a thank-you card. Each envelope had money in it; he had divided his check into five equal shares and given it to the boxcar crew. I saw the money and gave it back to him as I looked at the other guys. Every guy tossed their envelope in the center of the table.

The old lady started crying and said, "Thank you and praise the Lord." The old man had tears in his eyes and said, "I terribly misjudged you boys. God bless you. The only thing I can offer you is my prayers, and my family will pray for all of you." He walked away holding his wife's hand, and he gave a stern look at the owners and the foreman as he walked by. Everyone else just looked at us, and it was totally silent. We drank our coffee and ate the donuts. I was proud to be with those dope-smoking idiots that day. The meek shall inherit the earth. Thanks be to God.

The Good Job
and Driver's License

My brother and I worked that job until something better would come along. My Uncle Tony told us of a job at his place. Uncle Tony worked at a place called Lubrizol where they worked on engines and oil products. He had started out as a security guard and worked his way up to foreman. The job was for a mailroom helper, and Bill and I both put in an application.

About two weeks later, I received a call from Lubrizol and was set up for an interview. Bill was still waiting for a call. The following Monday, I cleaned myself up and went in to be interviewed by one of the managers.

The interview went well, and they wanted to hire me. The manager had one last question. "Do you have a driver's license?"

I was twenty years old with no driver's license; the manager told me he couldn't hire me without one. I was completely outdone. I asked him, "Could I go get my driver's license and come back?" The answer was no, so I told him about my brother, and he said he would consider it.

I didn't get the job, but a few months later, Bill started working at Lubrizol. I was happy for him; after all, he was better suited for the job. I still had a lot of growing up to do, and I was still trying to find myself. I was still playing bad boy. Lubrizol was the type of place where people retired from with good pensions, and I was not ready to have a serious job. Bill was the right guy for the job.

I borrowed my brother's Chevy Nova the day after the interview and drove down to the License and Title Bureau. I took the test and drove the course with an evaluator. I finally got my Ohio driver's license that day. Now all I had to do was buy a car; I didn't have a dime. All my money was invested in smoking and drinking with the party people at the top of my street.

The Black Crows

I worked a little longer at the plaster factory, and soon it came to an end. I don't remember what exactly happened, but I'm sure with the way I was thinking and behaving, it was my fault.

I partied a little more, and soon I found another job with another group of bad boys. I worked as stockroom help in a huge factory that made expensive sweaters for woman. The factory employed over one thousand women. There were only eight guys that worked in the stockroom. With those odds, a guy that played his cards right would soon score.

The boss was an old Jewish guy who smoked big black cigars every minute of the day. We would meet in the warehouse, which was about one hundred yards away from the main factory. Our crew would load trucks and put stock in order at the warehouse in the main factory. Six of the eight guys would actually do the work. My boss and his foreman were the only two other males in the entire plant. There was one more male, the security guard, who was about seventy years old. His job was to check people going out of the plant for stolen merchandise.

I soon became friends with a young white kid who had a left arm that wasn't fully functional from a car accident. There were two black ex-convicts that were on a work program through the state. I called them Heckle and Jeckle, like the cartoon of the two black crows on television. They were really different; these two characters liked to beat up the white kid in their spare time when they weren't smoking weed or screwing off somewhere. One of them had a hairdo just like Don King, and the other one had a wild look in his eyes. He would pour sugar in his coffee until it had the consistency of maple syrup and drink it down in one big gulp. Their hygiene was terrible. I don't think they ever brushed their teeth or bathed from the time of conception. They were two hood rats that had trouble written all over them. I stayed as far away from them as I could, and so did everybody else.

I always started out by trying to do the right thing, so my new friend and I would do exactly what we were told. As I got to know him, he told me he had a little girl and a new wife to support. He lived in a small house with his in-laws. He was just what I needed to keep me in line, but things began to change.

One morning we were working in the warehouse, taking inventory and stocking some shelves. He told me he was going to get some more boxes and disappeared for a long time. I went looking for him, and as I turned the corner, I saw Heckle and Jeckle tuning this kid up; one held him, and the other one just beating the crap out of him. As soon as they saw me, they turned around and told me it wasn't my fight and to mind my own business. Well, the two black crows learned a valuable lesson that day.

I told them they were pretty tough beating on a one-armed man. That's when the real fight broke out. I grabbed one of them, and they tried to double-team me. Little did any of us know the boss man was standing in a corner, watching the whole thing. I threw up my hands like a prizefighter, and they laughed, until I started throwing punches. I landed a series of blows that stunned both of them; I have to give them credit, they didn't stop until they were both battered and bloody. I let my one-armed partner get in a few great shots.

Heckle and Jeckle were on the ground and begging me for mercy. I let them up and said, "Let's go for a couple more rounds." They decided that wouldn't be a good idea. I told them there was a new game, and I was the new warden. "Every time you look at my pal wrong, I'm going to beat the hell out of you two jokers."

Later that day, the boss was leaning back in his chair and decided he needed to have a talk with me. He was chewing on the end of a big black cigar and looking at me for what seemed like a decade.

I said, "Is there a problem?"

He said, "I'd like to know where you learned how to fight. You didn't take one punch from those two ex-cons pounding the crap out of your pal." I didn't know what to say, I thought he was going to fire me.

He started laughing and telling me that before I showed up, they would pound on the kid every chance they got. He told me to be careful; those two guys had a bad track record. I said I had a bad track record too. I've been around the block a few times, but I never got thrown in jail.

For the next couple of days, I didn't let the kid out of my sight, and the black crows watched him like a hawk. They tried to take me out with knives, box cutters, and anything else they could find. I didn't consider them a threat. Every time they tried something, they found themselves looking up from the ground. It got so crazy that every time I saw them, I would just punch one of them in the side of the head or give them a gut shot to keep them on their toes.

One morning we were all having a meeting, and the boss was giving us our daily schedule. Heckle and Jeckle were feeling their oats; and when the boss wasn't looking, they knocked a cup of coffee from my buddy's hand, and it fell into his lap. I looked over at them, and they were both laughing. My boss turned around to get something off the shelf. I was sitting next to one of them, and in on swift quick motion, I balled up my fist and punched one of those assholes right out of his chair.

The boss turned around and saw the guy laid out cold on the floor. I looked down and said, "He shouldn't lean back in the chair so hard, he could get hurt." The other one just looked at me but didn't say a word. My one-armed friend had to get up and leave the room, he was laughing so hard. The foreman saw everything and left out of the room, with tears rolling down his cheeks and holding his stomach as he broke out in uncontrollable laughter.

Soon the young girls working in the factory began to treat me like a king. Whenever I picked up stock in their area, they would flirt with me. I didn't understand what was going on until one of the older ladies told me that the girls found out about my little war with the black crows. My boss told me Heckle and Jeckle would harass the young girls, and they loved me for kickin' their ass.

One long, lean, beautiful Puerto Rican girl would go out of her way every day to make me a cup of coffee. I would always make her the last stop on my route to pick up stock, so I could talk to her and smell her perfume. She had one killer body and a face to match. She would speak Spanish to me and call me *pape*. I asked her out a couple of times, but she refused. She had a big boyfriend that would pick her up every day.

We were getting off work, and Miss Puerto Rico was waiting for her ride. She saw me and raised her hand to wave at me. Her boyfriend just pulled up and saw the whole thing; he got out of his car and slapped her in the face, knocking her down. I was getting ready to run over there and knock him down, when my boss grabbed me by the arm and said, "Let it go. That guy is the leader of one of the biggest Puerto Rican gangs in Cleveland."

The next day I was waiting for her to show up at our morning meeting, and she never did. I was making my rounds, and I went to her station. She was sitting in her chair, and when she turned around, she had sunglasses on and a busted lip. She looked up at me, and I could see the tears rolling down her cheeks from under the sunglasses. She told me I must never be outside when she was waiting for him to pick her up. He was insanely jealous and always had a gun with him. She kissed me on the cheek and said, "I would like to go out with you, but he would kill both of us." I never saw her again after that day.

I worked in that factory for about three months, and they laid me off. Heckle and Jeckle didn't get laid off; they were protected by the state. My boss told me he would have liked to keep me, but I was the lowest in seniority. My one-armed friend cried and told me the black crows were going to whip his ass when I left. The black crows found out about me leaving and decided to tease me about it. I told them I had eight more hours to go, and I was going to give them a nice going-away present.

About four hours into the shift, Heckle and Jeckle came in the warehouse looking for me. As they turned the corner, we saw them. I told my one-armed friend this would be my gift to him. The black crows jumped on me, and I grabbed one of them by the left arm and twisted it as hard as I could until I heard a snap. He was rolling on the ground screaming in pain, and I saw my boss out of the corner of my eye. I quickly grabbed the other one and beat him until he couldn't stand up. Both of them were on the ground, one screaming in pain and the other one out cold.

I looked over at my boss and said, "I'm ready to go now." My boss put his arm around me and said, "Let's go."

As I was passing my friend, I said, "I hope this well keep them off you for a while"—one with a broken arm and the other one banged up pretty good. Maybe because one of them had a broken arm, they would finally leave the kid alone. They always fought as a team. I hugged him and told him to take care of his family. Keep your friends close, but keep your enemies closer.

The Grinding Wheel Factory

Once again I was looking for a job; I collected unemployment for a couple of months and did odd jobs in the neighborhood. Back to Mervin and his grandfather Mr. Woods once again, I would be making and breaking driveways. It wasn't a bad job, and I liked being outside all day. A good hard day's work for a good honest dollar also kept me out of trouble. I enjoyed working for them, and I never felt more at home with them. I was beginning to think this would be my life profession. Soon I joined the same old crowd at the top of the street, sitting on the picnic tables, smoking and drinking. Once again my parents began to wonder if I was a lifer at the top of the street.

After a couple of months, I found another job in a small factory in the fall of 1980. This time I worked in a grinding wheel factory on second shift, three in the afternoon till eleven at night, five days a week with weekends and holidays off. This place was three miles away from my house, and I would walk to work every day.

Mervin and a couple of guys from my neighborhood soon worked there also. Later my younger brother, Danny, would join us there. The second shift consisted of seven guys, and the work was very physical: mashing down grinding-wheel mix with our fists into great big steel molds and put in an oven for six to eight hours, then pulled out and left to be cooled and taken out of the molds and finished, then packed for shipping and loaded in an eighteen-wheeler.

The second-shift guys helped each other and learned every trick in the book to cut corners and complete the work in half the shift. There were four black guys all from the same neighborhood in Wickliffe, and three white guys—two Wickliffe boys and one originally from Euclid, which was the city next to Wickliffe.

Our foreman was a roughneck that went to Wickliffe High in the early '70s. He was superstrong and knew how to work like a mad man. John was not only our foreman, he was our best friend. He didn't just put us to work; he worked with us side by side. He worked like ten men, and we all did the same. John told us stories and laughed and joked with us as worked. John loved policemen and the Wickliffe police would come down to the factory and jaw with him when they weren't on a call. The second shift put out three times the product the day shift did. Day shift consisted of about fifteen guys and couldn't hold a candle to seven strong, young, rough-cut boys and a couple of young men.

We would do our work and smoke and drink at the same time. My brother Danny and John never participated in our bad habits. The rest of them were just like me, always smoking and drinking with not a care in the world. John would talk to us and tell us exactly how he felt about drugs and excessive drinking. We were too stupid to listen or thought we knew better and didn't care. I was a main offender, and John would always give me a good sermon on the evils of drug abuse.

John walked up to me one day and said, "Let me get this straight. Your father is a Cleveland cop, and you use drugs and drink. So while he's out cleaning up the streets of Cleveland, you're out polluting the streets of Wickliffe?"

I looked him in the eye and asked, "What gave you the right to say all those things to me? I'm sure you did some things you aren't too proud of." I was on a tow motor, looking down at him; I had anger in my eyes.

John must have sensed it because he said, "I am not afraid of you or your dope-smoking buddies. The reason I'm talking to you is because I think you're the ringleader." I drove away, and yes, I was mad; but I knew he was right. I continued to be a bad influence to everyone I worked with. That night I disregarded everything he said, and soon we were all smoking and drinking again.

John was no pushover; he looked like he worked out and always wore a dark blue sweatshirt with the sleeves cut off to show his big arms and a pair of Levi's jeans. I don't think I ever saw him in any other clothes. John looked like the singer John Cougar with darker hair, weighing about a solid two hundred pounds and around six feet even and only twenty-four years old. All the guys on were the ages of eighteen and twenty-four years and in tiptop shape.

Bob, the white guy from Euclid, might have been the oldest of all of us and definitely one of the strongest. He had a pretty blonde-haired wife and two kids; she was a 1978 Wickliffe graduate who I knew from high school. Her younger brother, Roger, was part of our crew. Together we were a well-oiled machine. We worked as a team, and sometimes we would get together on our off days. I worked there for about four years. John and Bob became close friends to all of us.

This wasn't the safest place to work; dust filled the air with fine grit from grinding-wheel mixtures. We also worked with some harsh chemicals. The walls were literally brown from grinding-wheel dust, the windows were also coated with the dust, and they were also brown. The clothes we wore were thick with grinding-wheel mixture. Water would not penetrate them; when I washed my clothes, they would never come clean. The dryer would only harden the stuff, and my work shirt and pants were like wearing a suit of stone. Our work boots had about a two-inch sole of hardened grinding-wheel mixture that would never come off. The air in the factory was thick with grinding-wheel dust, and we were breathing in this dust every day. When I would wake up in the morning, I would cough up black mucus. I believe we were as close to coal miners with black lung disease. All this unhealthy employment and smoking and drinking added to it.

I never worked out anymore and started picking up massive amounts of weight from eating fast food, smoking dope, and staying up late at night partying and eating. My weight peaked out at 275 pounds; I continued all my bad habits. I was out of control and didn't have a clue I was literally destroying myself. I really didn't care about myself, and hurting the people who loved and cared about me didn't seem to affect me either.

I never missed a day of work despite staying up all night partying and eating. I wouldn't go out and have a good time anymore I only associated with the guys at work. They contributed to my bad habits; and we smoked and drank before, during, and after work.

The Intruder

In the hot summer heat of July, I decided to go home and get a bite to eat after sweating off about ten pounds in the extremely hot dirty factory. I drove my beat-up car to the house. It was a quiet evening at around 8:00 p.m. I was in the kitchen making a tuna sandwich; Big John was taking a shower after a hard day working at the police department. My mother was cleaning up after dinner, and my little brother, Jonn, was playing with our little sister, Karla. All was calm for the moment, and little did we know what was happening with our next-door neighbors. Soon trouble would rear its ugly head, and the things that were about to happen would be something that I thought only happened on television.

One of the teenaged kids from next door came running across the yard, telling Big John to call the police. There was a man in their house with a gun threatening to kill everyone. The man was looking for his wife and kids; the couple were in the process of getting a divorce. Our neighbor, just recently divorced herself, was helping out one of her friends, which was the wife of the man with the gun next door. Soon all four of our neighbor's children were in our house, fleeing from the enraged man at their house. Our back door kept flinging open, with more of the people next door running from the man that had somehow lost his mind and family.

Big John told everyone to go in the bedrooms and not come out until things cooled down. My mother stayed closely behind Big John, trying to find out exactly what was going on; she made the call to the police. I continued making myself something to eat as if nothing was going on. Big John sat on the couch watching television after his shower. He also acted as if nothing was going on; he looked as if he had a hard day at work and just wanted to relax. Sometimes he was hard to read; he is a quiet man and really didn't talk about work at all.

Soon I heard the front screen door forcefully opening, and there stood a big man with a gun in his left hand. Big John stood up as the man yelled, "Where are my wife and kids?"

Big John told him to put the gun down, telling him that there was a better way to deal with the situation. The big man seemed to get angrier by the second as he said, "I'm going to ask you one more time before I start shooting." All of a sudden, he began to raise the gun in his left hand; and before I knew what was happening, I heard a loud series of gun fire as the smoke filled the room. My ears were ringing, and I could hear screaming coming from the bedrooms down the hall.

I looked in the living room where Big John and the man were standing. The big man was down on the floor near the coffee table, with blood flowing on his dingy white T-shirt. Big John stood above him and reached down, taking the gun from his hand. I watched in horror, thinking that Big John was shot; I looked at him and realized he wasn't shot at all. The man on the floor was bleeding all over our brand-new shag carpet; he had six holes in his body from the 9mm hollow-point bullets, one bullet in the left shoulder and another in his wrist closer to the gun; he had two bullet wounds in the center of his chest along with two holes in the center of his pants, near the groin area. I could hear the police sirens in the distance getting closer by the minute.

There were about six Wickliffe police cars in the front of our house with every officer not knowing what they were getting into, ready and armed for battle. They approached the scene with extreme caution, definitely not wanting to be the next casualty. As they found out that the danger was over, they entered our home immediately, seeing the wounded man on the floor with two guns on the coffee table and Big John wisely away from the guns and the man. My mother standing right next to Big John and me was standing in the kitchen, looking at everything going on just twelve feet away. I listened as Big John explained what happened. He showed the officers his badge as they handcuffed him. My mother told the policemen that they were treating Big John like a criminal. He told her to be calm down and go check on the children and everyone in the bedrooms.

The wounded man that was on the living room floor in a huge pool of his blood was just like a piece of furniture to the police officers as they walked around him as if he wasn't there. The ambulance was outside, and the EMTs were waiting to treat the victim. There was also a massive crowd forming outside, with everyone from our neighborhood and news people arriving, waiting for a story. Our front yard looked like a movie scene: more than fifty people, and the crowd getting bigger by the second; six cop cars, an ambulance, and news reporters. Red-and-blue flashing lights from the ambulance and all the police cars lit up the entire area; I scanned the crowd, not believing all the people and drama outside and inside my house. Police radios and scanners were all blaring in the mass confusion as more reporters arrived, asking people in the crowd what happened.

After about thirty minutes, Big John was escorted outside in handcuffs by the police and put in the back of the police car. I looked outside through our bloody picture window as the police drove away with Big John in the back seat. The EMTs were finally entering the house after about forty-five minutes. It seemed to me as if the police wanted the injured man lying on our freshly installed new carpet in a massive pool of his own blood, with six gunshot wounds continuously bleeding from his body, to leave this world.

My mother was in the bedroom with all the children. We opened up a bedroom window that faced the backyard. Each child, along with my little brother and sister, were handed out the window to me and my brothers. We didn't want them to see the man and all the blood that covered the entire room, along with all the police still in the house. We cut across the backyard over to my grandparents' house, away from the crowd and all the police and news crews.

It was about an hour after the man was carted away by the EMTs that an undercover police car brought Big John home. Late in the evening around 11:30 p.m., the crowd had dissipated, every policeman and reporter were all gone. My family stood in the kitchen, preparing for a messy cleanup job. The living room was covered in blood, with a huge deep crimson stain on the new carpet, which my parents had worked and saved for. The walls looked like someone had splattered blood over the entire room. The lampshade in the corner was covered in blood, the picture window was covered in blood, and even the ceiling had blood on it.

The room that we had worked on only one week ago was totally ruined, and that evening we stayed up late into the night, trying to at least make the room livable. After we cleaned the whole room, I looked at the television. Reaching down into the pinkish-colored water and ammonia, I pulled my cleaning rag out of the water, wringing it to clean the television. It was the last thing to be cleaned, and it was covered in blood with a full handprint of blood in the center of the screen.

The next morning, there was a small article in the newspaper, not mentioning any names or location, saying that an off-duty Cleveland police officer shot an intruder in his own home. Big John often did undercover work, and his superiors at the police station didn't want the incident to link back to him. The Wickliffe police department tried to say it was domestic violence due to a lovers' triangle. Their small-town mentality and racial profiling always tried to make it as if all black people were bad. The Wickliffe police knew who my stepfather was and what he did for a living, long before this incident occurred.

After a couple of days, things seemed to get back to normal, but not too many neighborhood kids cared to come near our home. Not even some of my closest friends wanted to come around. It would take a long time for all the gossip to stop. Everyone in Wickliffe knew the story, and even the guys at my job wanted to hear the story.

Big John was no rookie officer and spent many years fighting crime in some of the toughest parts of the city of Cleveland, always being able to solve most problems without drawing his duty weapon. He would often go to shooting matches and lined our basement with many first place trophies for shooting. He was on the combat pistol team at work, and I was always proud to see him come home with another trophy or first place—loving cup.

Soon things would change, and he no longer enjoyed shooting matches. What was once a great hobby and means for survival on his job became something that he only did for his job. The man that entered our house on that memorable night took something that was good and pure and turned it into something else. In the comfort of our home where Big John came for his peace of mind, with all the people who loved him, he had to deal with shooting a man in his own home. I often wondered how he felt and all the things that went through his mind after that. To me he was and still is the greatest man I would ever know, and he could do no wrong. I learned another great lesson that night: survival of the fittest protects the family.

That summer I would stay up late after work when Big John was on night shift, wondering if the intruder would come back. For a long time, I watched cars go up the street and listened to every creak in the house. The intruder survived the shooting and stated that he was too drunk to remember what actually happen. I'm not sure if he ever did any jail time, but he never came to our house again.

Accident on the Job

I was back to the same old thing only days later, partying with the boys and living like there was no tomorrow, partying at work every chance I got and working on the loading dock, when a truck would come for a pickup. On this particular hot summer day, I was loading up a truck with the tow motor, zooming back and forth like a mad man. Sweat was rolling down my entire body, but I never stopped even when the sweat was stinging my eyes. I considered myself the best tow motor driver this plant ever had.

While loading the truck as quickly as possible, I decide to pull up next to an I beam where the water fountain was; I never got off the tow motor. Instead I leaned over to get a drink, and my foot slipped off the brake, and I hit the gas pedal hard. The back wheels were spinning as the tow motor cage dug into my back, and the I beam crushed my chest.

I looked up and yelled, "John!" He ran over to me quickly and jumped on the tow motor, putting it in reverse. I crawled off of the tow motor and fell to the ground in tremendous pain. The tow motor cage had left a big bruise from the top of my shoulder blade, leading across my spine to the lowest part of my back. I didn't know if I had any internal bleeding. I was very light-headed as the pain began to increase.

John rushed over to me. I could barely breathe, and I looked up at him and said, "John, we have to go!"

He looked at me as if he didn't know what I was talking about, and I repeated the same thing over. He finally said, "Go where?"

Before I blacked out, I said, "To the hospital."

John and a couple of other guys I worked with lifted me up and loaded me in the backseat of his used-to-be-St. Regis police car. As big as I was, this was no easy task. I was face down across the backseat, and I winced and moaned in pain as he drove. I felt every bump in the road. The hospital was about five miles away, and that was one of the longest rides in my life.

We finally arrived at the hospital; John pulled in front of the emergency room doors and helped me out of the car. I decided to walk in. I was hunched over like a ninety-year-old man without his cane. I was trying to breathe when the receptionist came to my aid. She asked me what happened, and I was in too much pain to tell her. So I looked up and told her to ask John. He explained as they put me on a stretcher face down and carted me off to the emergency room.

The doctors cut my shirt off and examined the large bruise on my back. They gave me a shot of morphine and took me to get X-rays. The drug took effect immediately, and my world was in slow motion for a couple of hours. I had slurred speech and blurred vision as I explained the accident to the nurses and doctors. John sat in the waiting room for a couple of hours until I finally returned.

The doctors told me I would be very sore for a couple of days, and I didn't have any internal injuries. This little Chinese doctor said, "You so fat, that why you not get hurt so bad." My massive body had cushioned the impact; for once being so fat was a blessing.

John drove me to my house. I hunched over in the seat; my back was too tender to sit in the right way. He talked to me all the way home, telling me how he tried not to laugh at the little Chinese doctor when he told him I was too fat to get hurt. I thought it was funny too, but for some reason, humor seemed to escape me for the moment.

John walked me to the front door and explained the accident to my mother. I was still in slow motion from the drugs in my system as my mother walked me downstairs to my room. She turned on the television; I couldn't see it because I had to lie face down in the bed. As the drugs wore off, my back throbbed with pain and began to get very stiff. The doctors gave me a prescription for some painkillers; I took two of them every time the pain returned.

I stayed in the bed doped up for two days. Mervin and a couple of the guys I worked with stopped by. They all knew the story John told them about the little Chinese doctor calling me fat. When I finally got out of the bed, I called John, and he was still laughing as he repeated what the doctor told him.

He told me to take a couple more days off from work; and then he laughed and said, "Let's see if we can knock a little weight off you, so the doctors won't call you fat anymore."

After a complete week off work, I was ready to get back and face the crew with their new form of entertainment, making fun of me by repeating in full Chinese accent what the doctor had told John. I took it well, and I was glad to be with the crew again. They never let me live it down, repeating it over and over again. I couldn't wait until someone else screwed up so I could join in the fun.

Soon the next accident happened, but nobody was laughing. It was a fatal accident, and I was crushed, better than any tow motor or I beam could do. I would never be the same. The next accident changed my life forever.

Things went on in the factory without any problems. We got a couple of new guys, and it was fun watching the rookies on our shift try to match our hard work and great strength. Every now and then, guys would tell the new guys my story. We continued to smoke and drink before work, lunch, and after work. All the new guys fit in very well; they were just as bad, if not worse than we were. John and my little brother also remained the same, never taking one drink, and smoking pot never entered their minds. John would continually ride my ass every day to quit smoking and drinking. I never once considered quitting. I was a party boy in full stride, that's all I lived for.

Losing a True Friend

Every now and then, John's cute little Italian girlfriend would show up. She was superpretty and always wore a tight-fitting pair of Levi's jeans on her perfectly shaped body. John was truly in love and dated her for a long time. We teased him about marrying her; he never denied it. I knew her whole family. They owned two gas stations on each end of Wickliffe, and they treated everyone well.

John had a twin brother named Nelson, and he dated John's girlfriend's sister. They were one big happy family. John's girlfriend, Silvia, had a couple of tough brothers and a couple of even tougher sisters. I knew her brothers well and always respected them; I don't think anybody ever gave them trouble. They liked to party and had lots of Harley-riding friends. I would see these guys every time I bought gas at one of the family-owned stations. John or his brothers Nelson were always around. Silvia's dad was a good man that always did more than his share of community service, helping people get their cars fixed that had very little money to pay him. He was also a rough costumer that told it straight. He was a well-liked business man.

John had a snowplowing business he operated with a couple of trucks. He also owned a couple of old police cars and a royal blue 1968 Dodge Cornet, which was his baby. John also owned a German shepherd that went everywhere he went. John would bring the dog to the factory when we were done with all of our work.

Even though John and I argued about many things, we often had heart-to-heart talks. He told me that he had an older brother that died in a motorcycle accident. He also said if he had to die early, he would like to race his car and beat a much faster street car, and he would be happy. I never thought about death, and I thought I would live forever. John was still trying to convert me into a decent human being, and I fought him all the way.

One Saturday evening, I was up the street with the party crew at the picnic tables when a friend of ours said John was in a car accident. I asked him if John was all right, and he said he saw the emergency squad pull a sheet over John's head as they put him on a stretcher. I started yelling at the guy and told him he was lying. He looked me in the eye and said, "Go check it out for yourself."

I started walking down the street, and before I got too far, I started running. If you can imagine a 275-pound man running, I ran as fast as I could, which was probably a slow crawl for anyone else. I was out of breath as I opened the back door and ran down the back steps of my house. My mother was calling me from upstairs. I never answered.

I just ran for the phone and called his house and called his girlfriend's house. I just kept calling and calling, and no one answered. My hands were shaking; I was beginning to panic more and more. Finally the phone rang. It was John's girlfriend's sister. She said, "Tim, John died in a car accident."

My mother told me I let out a scream so horrifying, she knew something terrible happened. I ran out the back door, and I never saw my mother. I just kept running; it was like someone had taken a knife and cut out my heart. I ran to the top of my street and kept running until I was on a big hill at the top of my street, where I sat down on the cool grass. I looked out where I could see the city of Cleveland. I cried until I had nothing left. I just sat there trying to find a reason why such a tragic thing had to happen.

I talked to God over and over, still not believing this happened. I blamed God; then I blamed myself. When John died, he took a huge chunk of me with him. I thought God was punishing me for all the wrong I was doing. I pleaded with God for one more chance. I promised to change, anything just bring John back.

Life's Change

I sat on that hill for a long time, all alone thinking about all the wrong things happening in my life. Had I brought these things on myself? If I was a good person, would all these bad things that were happening be different? As I sat there all alone, one of my friends came and talked to me. He told me he was sorry about my friend; and as he walked away, he reached into his pocket and pulled out half a bag of pot, rolling papers, and a lighter.

I sat there staring at the items my friend had left behind. I finally stood up, and I grabbed that bag and threw all the pot into the wind, with the rolling papers and lighter. Was this the end of all the partying and hanging around the picnic tables at the top of my street? I had a lot of sorrow and grief in my heart. Did I finally learn my lesson? On this day, was I born again?

I didn't ask God for forgiveness. I was angry at the world. Angry that in the prime of my life, something was taken from the world that was good and pure, and all the evil was left behind. Was I different when I came down from that hill?

I was very tired. I went home and slept. For days I didn't want to come out of my room and face the world. This seemed so surreal; I wondered if this was all a bad dream.

I took a shower, hoping that the hot steamy water would wash away all the pain. I sat on the edge of my bed, staring into space; my brothers went in and out of the room. I never even acknowledged their presence. I sat in silence and stared into space. Life wasn't the same, and I was at the lowest point in my life. When some people hit the low points in their lives, they drink or smoke to mask the pain. I did all that before I reached my low point. I didn't know what to do to mask the pain. I was in limbo with nowhere to go. I didn't even pray or go to church; I was lost like Moses in the dessert. How long was Moses in exile? How long would I wander in my own desert?

John's car was barely damaged in the accident, a slight bend in the bumper of the 1968 Dodge Cornet. This wasn't enough to kill him; to this day I don't know what killed him. I have my own theory, but I don't want to say it; it really doesn't matter as it won't bring him back. John lives on in my heart and in my soul and will never be forgotten. I was told you only have so many true friends in your life; John was one of my true friends. How many more true friends will leave this world and join God's army?

John's funeral was one of the biggest I've ever been to, with people from all walks of life, from the biker types to businessmen in suits, and about six black guys that John worked with. It seemed like a day where everybody left their differences elsewhere. We were all there to wish a last good-bye to a truly decent person that left this world unexpectedly. The world was at a great loss, and little did anyone know I among others felt the sharp swift pain of never seeing him again. If things were different, or I was different, would I have ever met John? The Lord makes you humble.

Work at the grinding-wheel factory went on as normal; the second shift crew felt the loss of our friend in many ways. We all told different stories about John and enjoyed the memories that we shared. I continued to work; the owners gave me one of John's old duties. I would come back to the factory to unload the grinding wheels in the big oven with the tow motor at two o'clock in the morning.

My mother and Big John noticed how I was suddenly a loner. I wasn't hanging around my usual crowd, and I didn't feel like being around the party people, or anyone else for that matter. My mother made an appointment for me to get a routine checkup at the doctor's office. To please her, I decided to go and get checked out. I knew I was feeling fine, just depressed with my life. How did I let it get this bad, and what was I going to do to change it? The decisions I made at this point in my life came back to haunt me. I didn't know where to turn. I was spiraling deeper and deeper into a depressed state, but I created this hell. I was my own worst enemy. Could I be saved? I didn't pray. I was mad at God and the world; I just wanted to dwell in my own misery.

I went to the doctor's office and sat in the waiting room until I was called. A little Indian doctor walked in the room and asked me to take off my shirt. My weight was around 275 pounds. On a good day, I knew I was extremely out of shape. He examined me and never said a word. He left the room and returned with the results after about forty-five minutes.

With his strange Indian accent, he said to me, "You have high blood pressure due to being grossly overweight. It you continue in this direction, you won't be long for this world. I will prescribe blood pressure medication. Try to get some exercise and modify your eating habits. Good day, Mr. Lowe."

Reality, Facing Life, and Finding Myself

After that great news the doctor gave me, I went to the drugstore to get the prescription filled. It was a nice sunny day, and as I drove to the drugstore, my mind began to wander. I thought about what the doctor said, and I was in a more depressed state than ever before. I felt all alone weighing 275 pounds and not knowing what was going to happen next. I decided the doctor was right: exercise.

I walked to work every day and came back late at night to unload the oven, for a total of four trips to and from work five days a week. I was walking three miles there and three miles back home and walking the whole route again late at night, for a total of twelve miles five days a week. This was no easy task walking all that way weighing 275 pounds, and currently the exercise I had was the physical labor at work. Other than that, my exercise routine was walk to the television to change the channel—back in the day when a remote control was unheard of—and lie back on the couch and eat everything known to man while watching television.

I did take the blood pressure medication the doctor prescribed, and of all things, it made me hungry. After taking it twice, I decided the last thing I needed was something that made me hungry. I dumped every pill in the toilet and contemplated on eating right. Every vice that I had was something that could kill me—smoking, drinking, and now eating.

I walked in the rain, snow, or extreme heat in the peak of summer. The walking was very refreshing. I would often think of John and all the time I wasted at the top of my street with the party people. I never ventured back to the picnic tables, and I was ashamed of ever being seen at such a useless part of the black community. From the time I was sixteen to around twenty-two years old, I was a regular face at the top of the street, smoking and drinking. Eight years of precious life literally wasted; some would do a longer penance wasting their life away. How could I have been so blind not to see there was no future in living life on the edge?

I was twenty-three years old, wondering what was I going to do with my life. I had no idea, walking to work every day. John had passed away a couple of months ago, and I still felt the pain and suffering of losing a more-than-close friend.

Instead of walking to work, I bought a couple of large sweat suits and jogged from one street pole to the next. I lost a lot of weight, but I was still a very big boy. Physically I was better, but mentally I was much worse, caught in a world of indecision and loneliness. It wasn't for the sake of friends not wanting to be around me, but all the friends and associates I spent time with were smoking and drinking continuously. I chose not to be a part of that world anymore, so I jogged and walked to work and came home, never deviating from my day-to-day routine and trying to find some direction in my life.

One hot summer day, I decided to go to the high school and hang out with some fresh out-of-high-school jocks. I walked over to the football field and saw some well-conditioned athletes running lap after lap around the quarter-mile track. After they ran for many miles on the track, a few of the guys that knew me walked over and talked to me. They all had dark blue running suits and warm-up sweats with bright yellow script lettering, "Wickliffe Cross Country Running Team" written on the front and back.

After talking to a few of the team members, they welcomed me with opened arms and invited me to be a part of their fine running team. I talked to the coach and asked him, "Could I be a part of the team, not as a runner but a water boy or team helper?"

He said, "You're so fat that all you can do is eat. All you can do is walk to find your next meal. I wouldn't want you hanging around my team. You're a physical disaster. Stay away from my team."

That warm summer day, I walked home in tears and feeling like lesser of a human being than before. The coach's words cut deep in to my already damaged self-esteem. I sank deeper and deeper into my depression. How much more could I take? Was the Lord making me pay for all of my wrongdoings? I was as close to the bottom as I can get, but I still hadn't reached the deepest level of the ocean floor as far as depression went. I would endure more heartache and pain before I would actually rise above it all. My suffering would continue for a long time, and I felt like I deserved it. I had turned my back on everything that was good, and now everything that was good was turning its back on me.

The Party

On the fourth of July, I was invited over a high school friend's house for a party. In my present state of mind, I didn't want to go, but they came and got me. There were lots of cars in his driveway and parked on the street. Loud music blared from his house, and people were scattered throughout the house and backyard. The smell of dope in the air overpowered the smell of ribs and chicken cooking on the grill, beer and wine in every corner of the house and in big washtubs in the yard. Dancing and laughter as people ate tons of food, and smoke and drank even more. I was one of very few people at the party not smoking and drinking. I ate very little food and sat on the patio watching all people. There must have been fifty to sixty friends and relatives there.

People are very amusing when they are drunk and high. I watched all the middle-aged ladies known as cougars dressing sexy to compete with the younger, more attractive females for male companionship. The young men showed off their prefect bodies dressed in shorts and tank tops, and all the young teenage girls were in tiny shorts and halter tops that barely covered their almost fully developed bodies. The older crowd was much less revealing but still tried to show off their best assets. I sat in the lawn chair people-watching as I tried to cover all my flaws with and oversized shirt and shorts.

The younger crowd picked up teams to play volleyball; each side had ten people. I watched the intense game, and one of the older ladies decided to sit down. They looked for another player and coaxed me into playing. I entered the field of play, wishing I could go back to my comfortable spot on the patio.

I took a spot in the back and prayed the ball never came my way. The other team served the ball in my direction. I reached up to hit the ball, and my shirt flew up over my head, revealing my huge stomach and man boobs as I fell to the ground. The ball bounced off my belly, and the entire crowd roared with laughter. Some fell to the ground holding their stomachs as tears rolled down their cheeks from laughter. I was so embarrassed, but I continued to play until the game was over.

After that I took my seat in the lawn chair on the patio, hoping I would blend in with the woodwork. My buddy and a group of young, pretty, barely clothed girls came and sat next to me. They enjoyed making fun of me, and each one of them told their own version of the fat boy trying to hit the volleyball. I pretended not to let it bother me, but I sank deeper into my chair as they entertained themselves at my expense.

A pretty girl sat next to me and asked me if I needed a drink. I thought she was nice, and as the partying continued, I asked her if she would like to go out with me. She said, "If we go to the movies, I would need two seats just to sit down. This would be like a triple date." She had a bunch of fat jokes and battered me until even her friends told her to stop.

I walked home before the party ended. I cried on the way home feeling rejected, and a deeper depression set in. The party only confirmed that I wanted to be alone, away from everybody and everything. I do believe this was the bottom, and I was at the lowest point in my life. The ocean floor was cold, dark, and deep. I was an outcast, and the only time people wanted me around was to provide entertainment by pointing out my flaws. I became more of a loner, and the only people that felt any compassion for me were my immediate family members. I became my only best friend.

Running from the Past

I walked and ran to work five days a week, three miles one way on a heavily travelled road. Everyone that lived in Wickliffe traveled on Euclid Avenue, and it was the major street to get to the freeways. People from everywhere used this road; it was the only way to get to work. I walked and ran on Euclid Avenue four times in the day and two times in the dark of night.

People were cruel, and some would throw trash and beer bottles at me as they yelled, "Fat ass" or "Nigger" out of their cars. I even got hit by a car as I crossed a four-way intersection. The guy stopped and got out of his car, not to see if I was hurt but to yell at me and look at the damage to his pearl-white Cadillac. I got up and ran the rest of the way home; when I got there, I took a hot shower and looked at the giant bruise on my side and hip. The next day I woke up with my whole left side aching. Battered and bruised, I put my sweat suit on and ran to work.

I ran the entire summer with a Sony Walkman in my hand, with music playing so I could be in my own world, not letting people in my head or heart. I listened to Bruce Springsteen, Marine Corps cadence songs, and old Motown as I freed my mind of pain, guilt, and people. Running became easier and easier; so I ran longer, quicker, and faster. My body was changing, and I never realized it. I ran every day for a long time, I would have made Forrest Gump look bad. I ran through all the seasons: summer, fall, winter, and spring, every day no matter what type of weather. I passed other runners along the way, waving and keeping my pace. The loneliness and pain never went away. I couldn't run away from the past, but I tried to do it anyway.

The Shape of Things to Come

The summer of 1983 was approaching fast, and I was still running every day. I ran for two years straight, and I never took a day off. I was 23 years old, and in the best shape of my life. I weighed about 135 pounds with a 28-inch waist, but in my mind I saw the 275-pound man that I was. As the summer was drawing nearer, I ran more and more. Every weekend I would up the mileage until I was running 18 miles every Saturday or Sunday. My mother and family members were very concerned with my state of mind and well-being. My mother asked me to go to the doctor's office for another routine checkup. To ease her mind, I told her to make the appointment.

I went to the same doctor as before, sitting in the waiting room to be called. The receptionist called my name and took me down the hallway into a room. She looked at a clipboard containing my medical records. She told me to take off my shirt. As she scanned the records, she made idle conversation, and she looked at the charts over and over again.

Finally she asked me my name and social security number. She said, "You are Mr. Lowe?" She continued scanning the charts, not believing what she saw. She said, "The records show you as a 275-pound man. Am I looking at the right records?" She looked at my well-defined body and six-pack abs; there wasn't an ounce of fat on my body.

I told her the records were right and explained to her a blow-by-blow running routine. She was amazed, not believing me or the records; I had lost all that weight in less than a year. She asked me what was my drive or motivation. I looked up at her and said, "Pain and suffering can do a lot for a man."

She walked out of the room, shaking her head and holding my records in disbelief. I sat in the cold room with my shirt off, waiting for the doctor to arrive.

The same little Indian doctor entered the room with my medical records in his hand. He looked at me over and over again with a more puzzled look on his face than the nurse. He took the stethoscope and put the two ends in his ears and then listened to my heartbeat with the cold stainless steel end. He cleared his throat and said, "Mr. Lowe, you have the heartbeat of a well-conditioned athlete—many, many changes from the last time I saw you. Are you eating right?"

I told the doctor I was feeling fine and eating well. The doctor told me I was deceiving myself, and the truth would free my tormented soul. He could read the pain in my eyes and the heaviness in my heart. The doctor knew modern medicine but also knew people very well.

The truth was I was in the best shape of my life, but I was hurting so bad on the inside that running was the only thing that put me in a euphoric state of mind; it was my new drug of choice. It was my world, and no one could enter. The more I thought about the real world, the world I created was perfect for me. I would drift in and out of reality. If something was bothering me, I would run longer or faster or both. My world—it was perfect. I had no one to answer to and was a perfect hiding place.

People began to take notice, and curiosity would get the better of them. Soon I would be questioned as neighborhood people would see me running miles and miles away from my home. Once again people ruined the perfect world I created for my own sanity. I was so confused about life. What was I going to do to earn a living? I kept running and trying to figure out what I was going to do with my life. People would often say God has a plan, and I didn't have a clue what it was.

Trying to Find God

While running for miles at a time, I would often ask God, "What do you want me to do? Help me find a way." God didn't actually speak to me, but he began to mold me like a piece of clay that would be made into something useful. As I took on the hardships in life that I created for myself, I felt stronger and better, but I still didn't have peace of mind. So I continued running and searching for a way to heal old wounds, at the same time basically starting life over in a new direction.

While running, often I would see a car with a bunch of guys I used to smoke and drink with. They would hang out of the windows, yelling at me to get in the car; I would wave at them and keep on running. I didn't want to travel down the same bad road I was trying to get away from. The path was clear for me, and any deviation would send me back into the world of drugs and alcohol. I stayed on the straight and narrow path and prepared myself for the long hard road ahead.

One evening while running home from work, a group of old-time party boys decided to force me into their van to join in the smoking and drinking festivities. While I was waiting for a traffic light to change, two neighborhood guys pulled me into the van and tried to make me smoke and drink with them. I asked them to let me out, and they passed me a bottle and a lit joint. They told me to start drinking and smoking or take an ass-whipping.

I didn't fear anybody in the van, and I said, "Well, I guess you fellas are going to have to hurt me." I took the bottle and lit joint and tossed them out the window; then pushing the sliding side door open, I jumped out of the moving van. I rolled on the hard pavement, scraping my knee and face. The van was traveling at about thirty-five miles an hour.

I ran along the road as we had a yelling match. They yelled, "Wait until we get back in the neighborhood. We will see how bad you are."

Actually I couldn't wait to get back in the neighborhood on equal fighting ground. I knew that my cousins would be at the top of the street, and it would be a fair fight; and if it turned out to be anything else, I wouldn't be the one getting hurt.

I ran about twelve miles and turned the corner at the top of my street. The van was parked at the picnic tables by the park. I could see the six guys from the van waiting for me as I approached the fence by the park. The smell of pot filled the air, and each guy had a beer in their hand, a case of beer sitting on the table.

I walked by the tables, and there were twelve partiers sitting there. The driver of the van threw his beer at me and pushed me as he raised his hands ready for a fight. I was already mad and scraped up from jumping out of the van. I grabbed him, and we fell to the ground throwing punches at each other, and a couple of other guys joined in. It was a four-on-one fight, and I was holding my own but taking a pretty good beating when a couple of my cousins showed up. Everybody scattered, and I got up battered and bloody. It looked like I'd been in a fight with a couple of Wolverines. My shirt was ripped to shreds on the ground along with a lot of skin from my body. My cousins said they were going on a hunt; they wanted to even up the score.

I picked up my shirt and held it up to my nose to stop the crimson stream of blood from flowing out of it. I started walking toward home as my cousins waited by the van for them to return. I thanked my cousins for the help and told them to forget it, but they sat next to the van drinking and smoking the stuff that was left behind. They looked like a bunch of campers; they would wait deep into the night. I walked home battered and bruised. I felt like hell and looked worse than that. While walking home, I was deep in thought about the way things were going, I really didn't feel the pain from my wounds; that would change as the night grew older—making a decision that if I wanted to change, I would have to leave Wickliffe. The place where I grew up was full of bad memories and getting worse as I tried to right all the wrongs I created.

That sleepless hot, summer night, I stared at the ceiling in my room deep in thought about the things that happened that day. Maybe I deserved the awful beating that I took from a couple of guys I used to call friends. I crawled out of bed and put my running clothes on to go shut down the ovens at work. My body ached and my face looked like I went a couple of rounds with Mike Tyson. Physically and mentally beaten, I walked up the back stairs in my house and prepared myself for the three-mile run to work, which seemed like thirty miles that night.

As I ran down the street, I felt every footfall hit the pavement as I listened to Bruce Springsteen on my headset of the Sony Walkman. I ran hard and fast, feeling the heaviness in my chest as I increased my speed and ran with reckless abandon. I ran so hard that night, sweat poured out of my body as tears ran down my cheeks. I cried out in anger, "God, what do you want from me?" The night was silent as I looked to the heavens on a crystal-clear night; it was a hot night, and the air was still. I was so confused, and every fiber of my being ached as my mind ran a thousand miles an hour with turmoil. Was this hell on earth?

As I unloaded the oven, I thought of all the things that were happening to me; and for the first time in a long time, I prayed with my heart and soul, not for me but for my parents and siblings and for my brother and friend John because I finally got it. I knew they were the ones that prayed for me, and I finally felt their pain dealing with me. I finished my work and ran home as the world around me didn't exist. I was in a world of my own filled with sorrow, remorse, and confusion. How could I have let it get this bad? What was the solution? How could I live a good and fruitful life? That night I fell into a deep sleep until it was time to go to work the next day. I put on my running clothes and ran to work.

The battle between good and evil was getting very old. I remember what my mother kept telling me, "The Lord only gives you what you can handle."

Things began to change. Life was slowly getting better; I tried a different approach toward life. I stayed away from the top of the street where I thought hell and heaven met on earth. I also kept to myself and stayed away from all people that didn't have a positive outlook on life. I began to pray every day, not just in the morning but all the time. God put good people in my path; the battle of good and evil wasn't that difficult anymore. I stayed close to my loved ones, and they guided me out of my own fire pit from hell.

I was twenty-three years old, and I experienced a lot of things that people didn't experience in a lifetime. I had been running for about two years straight. I can say I literally ran with the good and bad. My good old partying buddies from high school and many others were still at the top of the street at the picnic tables, doing what came naturally to them, smoking dope and drinking. The Lord gave me a second chance, and I prayed for all of them, hoping they would see the light; but the world remained very dark for those individuals. After many encounters with them, they finally gave up, knowing I would never enter their cold dark place in the world again.

I was finally free. My mind and body became one; I was strong mentally and physically. Little did I know that my pain and suffering was far from over. I would look death in the face and stare into the eyes of the devil over and over again. What does not kill you can only make you stronger.

Running with the Real Runners

I no longer ran in pain but ran with the hopes of finding myself. I would run to work as usual, but other local runners joined me along the way. I ran with old men and women with a much slower pace than mine. Other times I would run with seasoned young guys and girls that actually ran, like some of those Africans that you would see on television. I couldn't believe how well I could keep a steady pace with them. Sometimes I would find myself leading them and turn around to find them trying to keep up with me. I ran every day, but something was still missing. I didn't know what it was, but I was willing to spend a lifetime finding it.

The Saint Patrick's Day Brawl

Just when you think everything is going well and your life is almost perfect, the world throws in a monkey wrench, and reality sets in: it's never over. On Saint Patrick's Day, I was running my usual route on the way home from the factory when I saw a crowd of people standing across the street in front of a bar. On my route, I would pass about eight local bars; I never had a problem until this night. The bar was called The Country Inn, and from the looks of the crowd outside, its name fit. About twenty-five good old boys were outside with lots of pickup trucks with rebel flags in their back windows, and country music blared from inside the bar. As I approached the bar, I decided to cross the street to avoid the cowboy hat-wearing crowd.

I began to pick up my pace to move past the crowd quickly to avoid any trouble. Rocks and beer cans were being thrown from across the street, with people yelling, "Hey, nigger, come on over and drink some green beer with us. Come on, boy!" Some of the angry mob stepped in the middle of the street to get a better aim with the rocks and beer cans.

All of a sudden, half of a red-alley brick struck me directly in the temple; and I staggered, losing my balance, dizzy from being struck in the head with the rock. Blood began to flow from the side of my head, covering my white T-shirt. The crowd cheered, "Ten points for the guy who hit the nigger!"

Feeling dazed, I rose quickly as I could see some of the more aggressive rock-throwing good old boys crossing the street in my direction. I grabbed a handful of gravel, throwing it at them when I looked down at my feet and saw a whole rock garden filled with baseball-sized stones. I threw stone after stone, hitting everything in sight. I watched some guys falling to the ground as the stones hit their targets. I threw stones at the crowd and some of those nicely dressed pickup trucks. I remember smashing the windshield of a shiny big blue F-350 Ford truck. I immediately found out who the owner was as he yelled, "Nigger, I'll kill you!"

That started the mad dash for home. I started running as fast as I could, and half the crowd followed me down the street. I could hear the roar of the big truck's engine as I ran, picking up rocks and throwing them at the drunken mob following me. I was about two miles away from my street, running through backyards and jumping fences as I heard screeching tires and voices getting nearer. I was running for my life, and I knew if I made it to my neighborhood, the partiers would be at the top of my street at the two picnic tables. This place in my neighborhood was occupied all day and all night.

I rounded the corner to my street and ran as hard as I could for about a quarter mile to the top of my street. There were about twelve people at the picnic tables, and four of them were my cousins. I was covered with mud and sweat, and my white T-shirt was covered with blood. My cousins stood silently waiting for my explanation as we could hear the tires screeching and roar of a big truck barreling up the street.

Before I could say anything, the truck skidded sideways in front of us. About eight guys jumped out of the bed of the truck and two guys from the cab. I stood my ground, and my cousins lined up next to me as the angry men approached us with tire irons and other weapons in their hands, the driver of the truck screaming about how I busted his windshield and he wanted a piece of me.

My oldest cousin said, "Fair fight, one on one, and throw down your tire iron. If anybody joins in, we'll all fight until there's no one left standing." The rules were set; little did anyone know my cousins were well-versed in martial arts, boxing, and other styles of fighting. They were a bunch of army brats that had fought all over the world; they didn't lose any fights they were in.

The driver balled up his fists and lunged toward me; he could barely stand due to all the drinking he and his buddies did before all this happened. I danced in and out, waiting for the opportunity to land one good one. He was swinging wildly, and as soon as I saw an opening, I landed a big shot with all my might; and before he hit the ground, I landed four more power shots.

All the fight was knocked out of him before he landed one single blow. I stepped back and asked if there were any more takers. His buddies loaded him in the back of his pickup truck as we heard the police sirens in the distance. All his buddies piled into the truck and drove off.

When the police finally showed up, all the good old boys were long gone. They never stopped; the usual groups of partiers were sitting at the picnic tables as if nothing ever happened. I was sitting down with my bloody T-shirt on the ground, drinking a bottle of water. I explained what happened to everyone sitting there, and they laughed as they drank from their bottles and took long drags from their joints and cigarettes. I believe my cousins were upset because the drunken good old boys didn't put up much of a fight. They tried to coax me into joining the party, but I quickly refused and thanked them for helping me out. I threw my T-shirt into the garbage can and walked home.

The next day I had a cut on the left side of my head near my hairline, leaving a permanent scar, and a closed left eye from the red-alley brick that had found its home on the side of my head. I put on my running clothes and a pair of sunglasses to hide my battle scars. I ran out the back door and down the street before anybody at home could see me. Later on in the day, I would have to come up with a good explanation for the folks at home.

When I got to work, I put on my work clothes and headed for the break room for a cup of coffee. I never took off my sunglasses as I sat down in front of my coffee. The room was silent until one of my coworkers said, "Well, we're waiting. Did you get your ass kicked?"

I laughed as I stood up and walked out to the main floor to go to work. I never took off my sunglasses, and at lunch I gave them a blow-by-blow of yesterday evening.

I never changed my route, and I ran past The Country Inn bar two times in the day and two times at night. All the trouble on Saint Patrick's Day was the only time I ever encountered any problems. I still tiptoe around the area as I ran to and from work, never seeing any of the faces I saw that memorable night.

The Marathon Man

As the spring of 1984 vastly approached, I was still running to and from work four times a day. I was in my fourth year at the same job, making seven dollars an hour. I was one of the highest-paid employees at the factory. It was beginning to look like this would be my lifetime career; I continued to beat the pavement looking for a good paying job that would take me to the next stage in my life. Depression was starting to settle in again. I prayed every day in hopes of making my parents proud and becoming a useful part of society.

I began to run great distances, trying to free my mind; I also decided to pump a little iron after my long runs. In the hot summer of 1984, I would run distance races every weekend, piling up the mileage more and more. I ran six marathons in the summer of '84 along with other smaller races all over northeastern Ohio. I went to before-the-race-day parties with lots of pasta, pizza, and beer; the runners would call this carbing up before the race. I would ride to races with local guys who would pick me up in the morning and head off to the races.

My first marathon was in downtown Cleveland with over a thousand runners from all over the world. There were wheelchair racers, fat guys, young kids, pretty girls, and the long lean runners from Kenya and Africa who were actually in it to win. No one I ran with had ever won a race, except an older lady from Wickliffe who would win her age division in every race she ever ran.

Before the race began, I saw a group of runners with matching dark blue shorts and tops that had "Wickliffe Running Team" on the front and back of their shirts. With them was the coach who had told me I was too fat to do anything. My blood boiled, and I made a pact with myself that none of these guys would even come close to me at the finish line. I would die before I let that coach have the satisfaction of one of his runners beating me.

It was a cold spring day as all the runners were taking warm-up laps around Cleveland State College. The wheelchair people started one hour before everyone else. All the rest of the runners began to line up as they announced the start of the race; I fell in with a couple of local buddies in the middle of the pack. The gun went off, and the huge crowd filled up both sides of the street for twenty-six miles of the Revco Cleveland Marathon. After the crowd thinned out, my pace would quicken as I navigated through the pack of runners, who were at about an eight-mile-an-hour pace.

As we reached the thirteen-mile maker, I could see the pack of Wickliffe runners ahead of me. I decided to gain a little ground on them. As we were running across a big iron bridge, I watched the six leaders of the race on the other side of the street on their way back, running at a pace of five minutes per mile or less. All of these runners were the long lean runners from Kenya and Africa. The women from Kenya and Africa were trailing the men. My quest in the race was to beat every Wickliffe runner including their antisocial coach.

As all the runners that started in the middle of the pack at the start of the race were crossing the finish line, I had passed every Wickliffe runner a couple of miles back in the race. I crossed the finish line thirty to forty minutes faster than any Wickliffe runner, and their coach was about an hour and a half behind me. As he crossed the finish line, I looked him square in the eyes, as he showed many signs of pain as he stumbled across the finish line. This was the guy who had crushed a little fat kid's dreams of becoming a runner with insults that made me think I was nothing. I had cried on the way home that day.

Looking at him now, I realized how small he was and he was actually nothing. I felt good, and my race quest had been fulfilled. I was top dog in the city of Wickliffe. No special awards or piece of paper with this statement written on it, just pure self-satisfaction.

The Car

A few weeks later, while taking a long run after work, I passed a car dealer and saw a shiny black 1977 Trans Am parked on the lot. I walked over to the car and looked at the price; it was in my budget. I had saved all my money from the factory and decided that this would be a nice ride for me. I finished my run quickly that day and ran home to get Big John to go down to the dealership with me.

The salesman met us in the car lot in front of the car; he wore a cheap suit and talked a good game. I didn't say a word as Big John worked all the angles. We walked in the dealership after Big John and the salesman came to an agreement. Big John asked me how much money I had in the bank, and to his surprise, I had more than enough money to pay cash for the car. We put down a hundred-dollar deposit and went home.

That night I was so excited I could hardly sleep. I thought it was too good to be true—the shiny black Trans Am that looked exactly like the one in the movie *Smoky and the Bandit* that Burt Reynolds drove. I didn't sleep at all as I pictured the car in my mind. I remembered every detail starting with every chrome piece in the engine compartment down to the special Keystone Classic Rims and the Radial GT Dunlop Tires. The next day couldn't come quick enough as I watched the clock on the wall tick away every second.

I finally fell asleep in the early morning hours, and when I woke, I put on my running clothes and took my short route for the first time in a long time. I ran three miles and took a shower, hoping Big John was awake and ready to go. That wasn't the case. Big John had worked all night long, and while everybody was sleeping, he was at work. I wasn't very understanding at the time, as I kept asking my mother if he was up yet. Later on in life, I would completely understand because I would work the same way he did, long hours and rotating shifts.

At about four o'clock in the afternoon, Big John woke up; and about an hour later, we were at the dealer. I had a money order from the bank, and we sat down with the dealer to complete the paperwork. I never realized there was so much paperwork involved in purchasing a car. By about 6:30 p.m., the dealer handed me the keys, and we walked out to my car. My heart began to beat so fast as I sat down behind the wheel of my car. Big John followed me home as I drove the two-mile stretch home; I decided to drive around the block to show off my new hot rod. I drove past the partiers in the park and waved that day. I was never happier, and I felt like the car was a reward for staying away from all the dope and booze.

I parked the car by the garage in the backyard, and my brothers looked at the car in amazement, going over it from bumper to bumper. They were both motor heads, and my car met their approval. I couldn't stop smiling. As soon as they asked for a ride, my mother reminded me about buying some insurance and told me not to move that car from the spot it was in until I had some insurance. I gave her the keys and went into the house; it hurt, but I knew she was right. The car would sit in that very spot for a full week before I got some insurance. It really didn't bother me. I knew the car was mine, and it was in my driveway.

The car didn't take the place of my running routine; it enhanced it because now I could drive myself to races and different places where I could run. I enjoyed the change of scenery. I would run at different metro parks and on the beaches of Lake Erie. Life was good again, and it was true love for a man and his machine. My car was never dirty, and before the summer was over, I had spent lots of money on car washes and car wax. For the first time, I would be able to ask a girl out and drive her to our destination. I thought about Coach Hughley's daughter, Rhonda. Within a couple of weeks, I would ask her out, and we would go to the movies. I finally felt like a man instead of a boy. I had a beautiful girl in my shiny beautiful car.

The car was great, but I never fell out of my daily ritual of waking up and running to and from work. The car was basically a toy and couldn't take the place of running because the long grueling workouts helped me clear my head. With the car, I could venture further away from my home to put in job applications. The results were always the same, and I would I remained at the grinding-wheel factory.

After parking my car in the driveway, I ran in the house put on my running clothes and bolted out the back door. I completed my long run on that hot sunny evening in the later part of June. My friend saw me walking down the street and asked me to go to his family reunion party. Again, he wouldn't take no for an answer, so I told him I would be there. This was the party where I had been embarrassed when my shirt had gone over my head while playing volleyball and exposed my less-than-perfect meaty body. All the same people would be there, including the young girls that had laughed at the fat guy trying to play volleyball. The party was on the fourth of July as usual, and I planned to be somewhere else. I didn't care to face the gauntlet of people who had been less than kind to me a couple of years ago, laughing and telling me how fat I was.

The Second Party
and the New Me

On the fourth of July, I woke up at five in the morning to go running with a guy who lived up the street and ran every single day. We decided to get our workout in and enjoy the rest of the day. That day we ran about fifteen miles, talking about what we were going to do the rest of the day. Carl was old enough to be my father. He was an ex-military man that had traveled all over the world. Carl was very inspirational and always pointed me in the right direction.

As we ran, I told him about my dilemma with the party, hoping for some great words of wisdom. His advice was actually something I didn't want to hear. He told me to go to the party and have a good time. I wasn't the same guy that people had made fun of a couple of years ago. He said, "Enjoy the fruits of your labor. Show them the new Tim. Be proud of all that you have achieved in the last couple of years."

He was right, but I didn't want to go. I would be around people smoking dope and drinking, which I didn't consider fun anymore. These were the very things I was trying to get away from.

After the long run, I took a shower and headed upstairs for breakfast. Just as I turned on the television, the doorbell rang. I looked up and saw my buddy asking me if I would help set up for the party. I knew there was no getting out of the party now. I gathered my things, and we walked to his house up the street. He was very clever, knowing I didn't want to go to the party and showing up at my doorstep early enough to catch me.

We finished setting up for the party as friends and relatives started showing up, all the same people that were there every year including the group of young girls I had met from the volleyball game. The girls were now young women; some had babies but dressed in the same small shorts and tops just as before. Seemed to me that the shoe was on the other foot—I was this lean muscular guy, and they were a little bit beefier since the last time I saw them. They were still beautiful young women, but I ignored all of them as they walked through the door. I was also dressed in a skimpy little outfit, my running shorts and matching tank top. My friend told me that they were all asking him about me; they didn't even know who I was.

I sat in a lawn chair on the patio as they all stared at me, whispering to each other and giggling with each other. Each one of them paraded in front of me, and I totally ignored their passes. I believed that I was still the same person inside, and so were they. All of the ugliness that I had encountered with them years ago was still fresh in my mind; they were still the same catty little girls that I remembered. Their bodies had matured, but it seemed like their minds didn't; as a lot of guys would say, "Body by Fisher and mind by Mattel."

By noon the party was in full swing, and the dope was cooking quicker than the ribs and chicken on the grill. The beer and alcohol was being consumed quicker than the pop and water. I sat in my quiet little corner on the patio, people-watching as usual. I got something to eat and talked to a couple of the older middle-aged women sitting next to me. These women were on the prowl too; they dressed very sexy and tried to dance with me and take me home. These groups of ladies were known as the cougars, and I knew not to get involved with them. I could overhear them talking, and they called me a boy toy. The cougars were very cunning when stalking young prey to take home. The cat fight was on, and I felt like a bright yellow canary in a cage full of wild cats.

The annual volleyball game was about to begin, and as usual, I tried to stay away from the game. My friend came over to where I was sitting, rescuing me from the cougars and dragging to the volleyball net. I didn't know which one was worse, the same group of people that played years before plus a few young studs flexing their muscles for the catty girls that were just a waste of time for me. I took my usual spot on the back line, wishing I was somewhere else, anywhere but here.

The game was on, and at first I watched everyone else hitting the ball. All positions were rotated, and I moved from the back row to the center of the net. The ball was served in my direction, and I jumped up and spiked it right down the center. For some reason, I was hitting everything that came in my direction, and the catty girls and young studs on the other side of the net began to bicker more and more as I spiked the ball each time it came my way. Without realizing it, I took my shirt off as sweat poured down my body. There was a silence as the young girls and the old cougars gazed at my well-toned body; even the people just watching seemed to take an interest in the game. I was no longer the fat guy with rolls of fat but a well-toned athlete with six-pack abs and muscles similar to models on the front cover of fitness magazines. All the running and weight lifting had paid off, and I enjoyed being the center of attention.

After a couple of games were played, I picked up my shirt and quietly went back to my little corner on the patio and sat in the lawn chair that seemed like it was made for me. The catty young girls and the old cougars followed me to the once lonely corner of the patio. As I sat there, every young girl and middle-aged lady tried to win my affection by offering me drinks and sitting as close to me as possible. I was in total shock, not realizing what all the fuss was about. To me I was the same guy as before; but to them they acted as if I was God's gift to women.

The still very attractive young lady that I had asked for a date before pulled up a chair right next to me and began talking as if we were Romeo and Juliet. I remembered her exact words when I had asked her to go out with me. I remembered the laughter of all her friends as she totally embarrassed me with all the fat jokes. This time I didn't have to ask her; she did all the talking and asked me for a date. I tried not to be as cruel as she had been, but I felt she needed to be taken down a peg or two. I told her I wouldn't take her to a dogfight if she was the star attraction. She quickly rose from her chair as the laughter began to grow from all who were there. In a way I felt bad, but I also felt he who laughs last laughs best.

Before the party was ended, I was asked out by every single female and a couple of married women there. To me I was still the fat guy that just wanted the whole thing to be over with. As the partiers started leaving, I saw a very lively young girl in a cowboy hat that I hadn't seen before. She was my buddy's cousin, and I decided to see if I could get to know her. We hit it off right away, and little did I know it at the time, but she would be my steady girlfriend for the next couple of years. She turned out to be everything the doctor ordered. The only thing that separated us was her family, and that would be a devastating blow for the both of us. She was my first love, and I was her first love.

Carl the Runner,
Man of Great Wisdom

The next morning, I woke up at five o'clock, put on my running clothes, and ran up the street to meet Carl. He was stretching in the middle of the street as he waited for me. He asked me how the party was, and I gave him a blow-by-blow of the whole thing as we ran down the street and out of the neighborhood for our long journey. Carl offered a little fatherly advice as usual, and I listened intently, soaking up everything he had to say like a giant sponge. I loved to hear him talk with his deep voice and intensity, eager to help a young man trying to find himself in his very confusing world.

He laughed as I told him about the young catty girls and the old cougars as if they were looking in the window of a butcher shop with freshly cut meat. I could see the gleam in his eye as he listened intently, picturing all the colorful charters of the evening in his mind. I don't know who enjoy the story more, me telling it or him listening to it. I believe I covered the whole story, and before we knew it, we had run an effortless fifteen miles. We walked up the quiet street of our neighborhood, not a soul in sight as the sound of chirping birds filled the motionless air as we watched the early morning sun rise in the east. It was going to be a hot sunny day, and at the moment, the world felt right for both of us as we enjoyed the morning and each other's company.

The Family Reunion

The hot days of summer dragged on, and each day I went to work and ran every day. As the dog days of summer came in August, my family decided to have a family reunion at the park at the top of my street in Wickliffe. Relatives from all over the country would show up; for the most part, we were all located in or near Cleveland. The date was set in the middle of August when we would have our family reunion. Friends, relatives, and neighbors were notified.

The day of the reunion finally arrived, and I woke up at five o'clock in the morning, put on my running clothes, and ran upstairs out the back door and down the street. I was prepared for a long hard run; the sun was rising, and the warmth of the day was starting. I felt good as I ran through neighborhoods in Wickliffe, looking at all the burned-out lawns from the hot August sun. It was already seventy-five degrees and rising. It was going to be a hot day, and I was looking forward to seeing family members and friends that I hadn't seen in years. While I picked up my pace, I thought about what a great day it was going to be with family, food, and fun. All my troubles seemed to be light-years away that day. It didn't even seem like I was running as my mind drifted, thinking about all the activities of the day.

I was home by eight o'clock, with a three-hour run under my belt. I took a nice hot shower, put on some cool summer shorts and a tank top, and went upstairs to cook myself a good breakfast. I sat down with my big breakfast and turned on the daily news just in time to hear about the Cleveland Browns trying to create a winning season after a decade of losses. Just then, I heard a knock at the front door, looked up, and saw a couple of my cousins standing at the door. I had just finished breakfast and was about to take a midmorning nap when they decided I needed to help them prepare for the party. We left the house and walked up the street. I was tired, but I was happy to be with them as we laughed and joked about all the things we did as children.

By noon there were more than fifty people at the small park and more people arriving every minute. I believe you could smell all the food cooking for about a six-mile radius, which seemed to attract all the people in my neighborhood. The family reunion turned into a huge block party; the music was loud, and everyone was having a good time dancing and playing games. The beer was flowing freely as the party spot at the two picnic tables seemed to be a popular spot. There were more than two dozen people there talking, smoking, and drinking to the extreme; and better than half of them were my relatives. I was invited to the area many times by old friends, aunts, uncles, and cousins who wanted the old me to make a comeback. I never went close to the area. I stayed with the older wiser people and the children. I didn't miss being over there and had no intention of ever going there again, no matter who invited me; even Bob Marley himself couldn't take me down that road again.

Everyone was having a good time, and as the day progressed, the sun was high in the sky, and the temperature was in the midnineties. No one seemed to care, and we headed for the baseball diamond to choose sides for a softball game or two. My Uncle Robert pitched for one side. He had a cooler on the pitcher's mound that was full of his favorite drink, Rolling Rock Beer, and nothing else but ice. His six children who were all older than me would play in the games. Their mother, my Aunt Stella, sat in a lawn chair in the shade, with the older crowd and children too young to play. My Grandpa Lou was the oldest player on the field but could run, hit, and catch better than most of the people playing.

We played about three to four very competitive games, but after all was said and done, we had a load of laughs and plenty of sweat as we ended the day. The park was clearing out, and the sun began to fall low in the sky. The music was softer as people gathered their things and go home. I sat on a park bench away from everybody, drinking ice water. As I watched people leave, my Aunt Stella came and sat beside me. She was a very caring person with good intentions but was not always perceived that way.

Aunt Stella could read me pretty well as she asked me how things were going in my life. She said she had noticed a drastic change in me and felt I was searching for something. She asked me questions about many things but most of all about God. I never really gave her a good answer, and she gave me a piece of advice that would last me a life time. As I am writing this, tears are rolling down my cheeks as I think about her and the significance of our brief encounter that day. She looked me in the eye and said that she could see I was missing something. She told me to go to the Our Lady of Lourdes Shrine in Euclid; this was holy ground where some claimed to have seen the Virgin Mother Mary. I will never question this because a miracle happened to me as I took my aunt's advice.

I believe God sent me one of his angels that day. If my Aunt Stella's job here on earth was to save a few souls in her life's journey, she did her job well because she played an intricate part in my life and many others. I am quite sure God opened the gates of heaven for her, God rest her soul. As long as I live, I will never forget her; and every time I think of her, I say a prayer. It is true that the Lord does work in mysterious ways.

I Want to Be a Marine

I didn't take my aunt's advice right away to go to the shrine. I was still very confused about the things happening in my life. I did my job and ran every day as I began to think about all the events of the summer including what Aunt Stella had told me. September was less than two weeks away, and I was still trying to find a good job. I began to feel depressed again, so I ran harder and longer each day along with lifting weights in the basement of the house. In the next few weeks, my life would take many drastic changes that I had no control over. I would be challenged mentally and physically. I decided to go in the service to become a United States Marine.

The next morning, I put on my running clothes and ran to work, not telling anyone my plans. I thought about my decision all day and felt this was the right thing to do. I would drive to the recruiter's office as soon as I woke up the next morning before work. The recruiter's office was in Painesville, which was about twenty-five miles away from my home.

It was around the first of September, and the leaves began to slowly fall from the trees. I was twenty-four years old and about to make one of the biggest decisions in my life. I woke up that morning, and instead of putting on my running clothes, I put on nice clean, freshly pressed jeans and a form-fitting polo shirt. I went up the backstairs and avoided my siblings and parents as I opened the back door and jumped into my car and took off. I put in my favorite Bruce Springsteen cassette tape as it seemed just right for the mood I was in.

I reached the recruiter's office in Painesville in about twenty-five minutes pulled up in the parking lot and killed the engine. It was about ten in the morning, and my mind was already at 100 percent power as I turned the doorknob and entered the building. I walked in the office and faced every branch of the service recruiters possible: army, navy, air force, marine, and even the coast guard. Each recruiter looked sharp with a fresh haircut and perfectly pressed uniforms. I walked up to the marine recruiter and looked him right in the eyes as he said, "Is there something I can do for you?"

I cleared my throat and said, "Yes, I want to take the test to become a marine." The recruiter stood up and told me to step outside; being the professional that he was, he didn't want to discuss business in front of the others.

This young, slightly built, well-polished black recruiter asked me, "So what makes you think you have what it takes to become part of one of the finest group of fighting men in the United States? Let's see what type of brain power you have." I could tell he had been through this many times before, and he clearly had what it took to talk to people and make it sound so glorious, making you feel like this was the best thing in the world.

He sat me down at a desk and told me to study the six pieces of paper he laid in front of me. I quickly scanned over the papers, looking at spelling words and what looked like grade school math. Within five minutes, I handed the papers back to him, telling him that I didn't need to study the grammar school literature.

He looked surprised and asked me where I went to school at. I told him Wickliffe High and some college at Lakeland in Mentor. He went in a room and came out with the real test; he also told me that the local boys from Painesville failed the test on a routine basis. From what I saw on the study guides, I was surprised that anybody that attended high school could possibly fail the simple test. He wasn't impressed with me until I completed the test, telling me I scored very high compared to most of the local guys. He also said that I was a genius, but I was far from being the village idiot. In an off kind of way, I felt he gave me a compliment.

The next phase of the test would be my physical capabilities, which would prove even easier than the written test. The recruiter asked me a series of questions about my physical capabilities: how many pushups can I do, how far can you run, and what do you do to stay in shape? Without batting an eye, I told him I worked out every day, and I don't think they invented an exercise that I can't do. There was a moment of silence in the room; I could see a look of doubt on his face. He cleared his throat and said, "We'll see about that."

Before I knew it, I was on the ground in front of him doing push-up after push-up. In a matter of minutes, I did over two hundred perfect push-ups before he said, "Enough." We moved over to a small corner of the room with a pull-up bar mounted to the cinder block wall. I did thirty front-grip pull-ups, and he decided that was enough. I could tell he was impressed as he told me most guys that were a couple years younger than me could barely do twenty-five pushups and the pull-up bar was out of the question.

We went to the front lobby and bought a couple cans of Coke. He looked at me for a while before he spoke, then asked me to come back at 0800 hours in the morning. He said, "Tomorrow we'll go to the high school track and do a three-mile run. I hope you can run. Most of the young recruits puke their guts out after the run test." Little did he know that I had been running every day for the last two to three years; this was my thing, and I was looking forward to the test. I wouldn't be the one puking my guts out; he said he would run with me.

The next morning I was up bright and early. I was at the recruiter's office at 0730 hours, waiting for him to arrive. Just like a serviceman, he was prompt and drove up in his little car with recruiter signs about the Marine Corps plastered on the doors and rear bumpers. Of course, in big yellow and red letters in the back window were the words "*Semper fi.*" I was stretching next to my car as I watched him park his car under a big oak tree shading the north end of the parking lot.

He walked toward me as if he had a purpose, dressed in shorts and a tank top with the Marine Corps symbol on the shorts and tank top. This guy was a class act. He looked very fit, and everything about him was just like the all the stuff you'd see on television and recruiter signs. He greeted me and marveled at my shiny black Trans Am. He played with the stopwatch that hung from his neck and opened the passenger door of my car; without any hesitation, I knew which car we were going to drive to the high school track.

As I drove, he told me the test was to run three miles in under eighteen minutes. He also said he would be running beside me; and with a sly little grin on his face, he said, "If you can run faster than me, go right ahead." I considered this a challenge because he said no one had ever beaten him before.

For the remainder of the short ride, we were silent as the radio played an Elton John song. It was my friend John's favorite song. I thought it was a sign; and if John was here, he'd say, "Run like the wind, Timmy." And that's exactly what I did.

There was no one at the high school running track. The recruiter told me to try to be under eighteen minutes as he put the stopwatch in his hand and wrapped the string around his wrist. We walked up to the starting line, and he held the stopwatch in front of his face, yelling "go" as he pressed the big button, which started the time.

We ran the first four laps around the track side by side. For that first mile, he proved to be a pretty good runner. As we stayed side by side for about six laps, I began to pull a little in front of him as I heard labored breathing and heavier footfalls. With only six laps left, I ran harder and faster. My training over the long hot summer with nothing better to do than run made me a serious runner. I ran past one of the corps' finest twice before we were finished.

I waited by the finish line as I watched the recruiter complete his last lap of the three-mile run. As he crossed the finish line, I tossed him a water bottle. He walked back and forth drinking the water and recovering from the fast, hot run. He walked past me a couple of times before he looked at the stopwatch. He held the watch in front of my face so I could look at the time; I had run three miles in fifteen minutes and forty-two seconds. The recruiter was just under eighteen minutes, which was still something to be proud of. He told me that I was the first guy in a long time that he had seen run like that. I believe he was impressed as he kept looking at the stopwatch.

On the way back to his office, he asked me how much running did I actually do. I decided to have a little fun with him and told him I had never run a day in my life. He was silent for what seemed like a long time and all at once blurted out the words, "Bullshit!"

As we laughed uncontrollably, I told him the truth, and his eyes widened with amazement. He repeated what I told him, saying, "What on earth would make a man run for two or three years every day and for long distances for hours at a time?"

He waited for an answer. And I said, "Pain can do a lot for a man," as I explained the last three years of my life.

We were back in his office, and I watched him shuffle through my paperwork. All of a sudden, he looked up and said, "What do you want to do in the corps?"

I said without hesitation, "I want to be a drill instructor."

He stopped everything he was doing and sat down, looking me up and down, inside and out, when he said, "You could be anything you want. Why do you want to be that guy?"

I told him that physical fitness was my life, and this way I could get paid by the government to work out. He was even more shocked when I told him I wanted to be a D.I. for the next twenty years, a lifer. He stood up and shook his head as he continued going over my paperwork. Finally he looked at me and said, "Be careful what you wish for."

God's Second Chance for Me

I went home, and later on in the evening at dinner, I told my parents and siblings of my plans. Big John gave me his blessing and said the service would make a man out of me. My mother wasn't too keen on the idea but knew I had to make my own way in life. They asked me if they could talk to the recruiter to make sure I wasn't getting a raw deal.

Big John also said a couple of officers he worked with had talked about Cleveland Electric Illuminating Company hiring security guards to work at the Power Plant. He had a connection and knew the guy doing the hiring; also a Cleveland police officer that lived in our neighborhood said he would pull a few strings for me. Joe McTier was a lifelong friend who knew almost everybody in Cleveland and did everything possible to help me. I grew up with his children, and his wife Marge was like a second mother to me.

I decided to put in an application, and if they hired me, I wouldn't have to go to the Marine Corp. It seemed like all the cards were on the table. It was up to me to follow through on my end. I went from nothing to two solid job opportunities. If one failed, then it would be clear which path I was to take. Well, nothing in my life was ever easy, and the only thing that was clear about this was that it would clearly cause me much pain and confusion. I put on my running clothes and hit the streets for some serious running and more serious decision making.

The following Monday, I woke up and took a nice hot shower, put on some of my best dress clothes, and went upstairs to get my mother's approval on my attire. She said I looked nice and neat and to be positive in the interview. After all the practice I had putting in applications and taking interviews, I thought I couldn't fail. I drove down the street and got on the freeway, heading thirty miles east to a place I had never even heard of until two days ago. It was a nice sunny day, and my Trans Am was cleaner than I was as it caught the eye of everyone traveling on that freeway.

I really didn't notice anything, and I didn't really hear the music on the radio. I was so nervous. There was a great big world that disappeared that day as I traveled down the freeway to what could be my life's work. I prayed for the entire trip, asking the Lord for one more chance. I wonder how many times the Lord heard that from me. No matter how many times I asked the Lord for one more chance, I know my mother asked that very same question not for herself but for me more times than I care to think about. Thanks, Mom.

The freeway finally ended, and I traveled about six more miles and took the only turn in the whole trip as I looked in the sky at the cooling towers of the Power Plant. I was headed north, and as I entered the parking lot, I was amazed at how high the cooling towers were in the sky. I was in a strange land that I knew nothing about. I looked at all the pickup trucks in the parking lot and contractors walking around with hard hats on. There seemed to be a shortage on black contractors too. That didn't bother me because I was used to being the only black guy all my life. As I entered the building, all that seemed to disappear as the receptionist asked, "Can I help you?" She gave me directions to the room where the applications were taken.

I entered the room and filled out an application and took a four-hour psychological test with weird questions the made no sense to me. There were about a dozen people in the room and they seemed to know each other. I didn't know anyone. A few of the guys were laughing as they went over some of the questions on the test. I thought the questions were pretty ridiculous myself and laughed to myself also. After I turned in the test, I got in my car and headed for home, wondering what they could find out about me from the bizarre questions on the test.

A couple of weeks later, while I was on a tow motor at work, my younger brother, Danny, gave me a letter from the Nuclear Power Plant. I sat on the tow motor and opened the letter. The news was just devastating, and I felt a deep sadness. As the tears rolled down my cheeks reading the letter, telling me I failed the psychological test, my brother asked me if I was all right. I nodded my head as I sat on the tow motor in the middle of the factory, wondering what happened. How could the questions on that test determine anything?

After work, I took a long hard run for many miles, wondering what went wrong. I decided to go to the Marine Corps. I ran until I couldn't run anymore, and I sat on top of the hill, looking out over the city of Cleveland feeling very depressed and confused. Why was God punishing me so badly? If it wasn't meant to be, I would just have to accept my fate and sign up for the Marine Corps.

Aunt Stella's Soul-saving Advice

The next day I put on my running clothes and stepped outside in the early morning and started running down the street, searching my soul for answers. Not really thinking, I ran to Our Lady of Lourdes Shrine which was about fifteen miles away from my house. The early morning was crisp and cool, but the run heated up my body. There were a few cars on the road, but I barely even noticed them. I finally reached the shrine, which was tucked in on the side of a hill. I entered the woods where the shrine was. I didn't see one single person.

I sat on one of the pews by the shrine. I saw a few nuns lighting candles and praying. It was a very quiet place. I could hear birds in the distance as I sat there resting, not tired from the run but resting my mind; and I felt at peace. I got up from the pew, lit a candle, dropped to my knees, and prayed for my great-grandmother Margret Massey. After I said a couple prayers for her, I said out loud, "God, don't let me spend the rest of my life at the top of the street smoking dope and not being more than anything but a drunk and a dope addict. God, don't let me be an asshole the rest of my life! Please God, give me a good job and a family with a nice house. That's all I want, nothing more. God, don't let me live a living hell on earth. I am sorry for all the wrong things I did!"

After that I ran home, thinking about my next move. I just wanted to leave town so I wouldn't go back up the street with the things that were haunting me for what seemed like a lifetime. That day I stayed in my room thinking about how I was going to change things and try to make my life worth living. I wanted what everybody else had: a good job and family. I was determined to make change even if I had to go make a life in the service.

The Lord Works
in Mysterious Ways

A few weeks passed, and I was working in the factory when my brother Danny gave me another letter from the Nuclear Power Plant. I sat on the tow motor in the middle of the factory with my hands shaking, not wanting to open the letter. My brother Danny said, "What are you waiting for? Read it!"

He was right. What would it hurt? I had already been rejected; what else did I have to lose? I opened it and started reading. They wanted to see me on Friday for a reassessment. I wasn't happy or sad; I didn't know what to think.

That Friday I woke up and put on some of my best clothes, a suit coat and tie. Looking in the mirror, I felt confident but still unsure what I was being given a second chance for. I went upstairs to hear some reassuring words from my mother. She liked the clothes I picked out and told me to stay positive. I went out the door, started my car, and pulled out the driveway for the twenty-five-mile trip.

I reached the plant, and the receptionist greeted me and directed me to a room. I sat in the room and a well-dressed older black man entered the room. He had salt-and-pepper hair and real dark skin that made him look like somebody from Hollywood. He sat down in front of me and said he was the company psychologist.

Addressing me, he said, "Mr. Lowe, our test showed that you are severely depressed. What do you have to be depressed about?"

I said, "Well, I'm at a job making seven dollars, and I'm one of the highest paid in the factory. I just broke up with a girl I've been going out with four years. One of my closest friends was killed in a car accident. I'm trying to make something of myself, and all I want is just one good chance. Let me work here for six months, and if I'm not what you expected, then I can accept that." The physiologist said he wasn't the person who was going to make that decision. He asked me a series of what I perceived as more ridiculous questions.

When we were done, I asked him if I was hired; and again he told me that wasn't his decision. I told him to do me a favor. "Call someone who can make that decision. I have to know right now. If I'm not hired, I will drive from here, pick up my brother and ask him to drive me downtown, give him my car, and join the United States Marines."

He picked up the phone and contacted the people in charge and explained my situation over the phone. He hung up the phone, looked directly at me, and said, "They want you to be here at 8:00 a.m. Monday morning, and you're hired. Tell me, Mr. Lowe. What was your hurry?"

I looked at him and said, "Just trying to make something of my life. I was on the road to nowhere." The Lord made me work for it so I would cherish it. I was given a second chance, not something that happens every day, and it was up to me to make the best of it.

I drove home in complete amazement and couldn't wait to see my mother's face when I told her the news. I pulled up in the driveway and went in the back door, and my mother was cooking dinner. She looked at me and said, "Well, what happened?"

I told her that I would be starting on Monday, and she looked at me with a big smile. She knew this boy was finally a man. She was proud, and it warmed my heart to see her happy. I would do my best not to disappoint her again. I told Big John as soon as he came home. He was happy for me as he gave me words of wisdom, and I listened intently as I felt close to him, after many times being ashamed to be near him. For the first time in a long time, I felt good about myself as I told the news to my siblings and grandparents next door. I couldn't wait until Monday, after thinking about the past few months.

I remembered my Aunt Stella telling me to visit the Our Lady of Lourdes Shrine. I don't know if this was actually a miracle, but it sure felt like one to me. The journey ahead wouldn't be easy, but what in my life was? Thanks to all who prayed and had faith in me even when I didn't have faith myself.

I went to the factory and said my farewells to the owners and all the guys I worked with; they were like family to me. They all wished me well. This was better than any drug-induced high that I ever had. It felt like a big boulder was being lifted from my shoulder, and I finally had some stability in my life. As I drove home, I said a prayer of thanks to the Lord, also asking him to give me strength.

This would not be the last time I would see my friends at the factory. In years to come, I would stop by when I would feel like giving up because my new job was difficult, working for twelve hours a day without a day off. I would look at the sweatshop, and it would snap me back into reality, making sure I would not repeat history and return to the shop.

My New Job

I ran my normal routine on that weekend, preparing myself to start my new job on Monday morning. Things seemed to be different as I ran through the neighborhood, running past the two picnic tables at the park with the same people wasting their lives away. I was no longer chained and doomed to spend the rest of my years there. God was merciful to me. Sometime in the near future, I would try to help some of the partiers by telling them they could do as I did and find a way out. I learned a valuable lesson about people when I talked to them; you can't change people unless they want to be changed. I was no longer one of them, so I decided to put my time and effort into more promising things. I finally let go of my past.

Before I started my new job, I went back to Painesville, to the recruiter's office, to tell him I wouldn't be joining the service. I entered the office and saw the recruiter working on what looked like my final paper work. I greeted him and told him about the job and my future plans at the Nuclear Power Plant. He wished me well and told me I would have made a fine marine, and if I changed my mind or things didn't work out, to come back. I didn't burn any bridges and thanked him for everything. I also promised him that if it didn't turn out like I expected, I would be back. He stood up and gripped my hand, firmly looked me in the eye and said good luck. I didn't see him again, but he will remain in my memory as a positive image of what could have been.

On September 10, 1984, I drove to the Nuclear Power Plant to start class to become a nuclear security officer. I stepped into a trailer where I was instructed to go; I was hired into a group of twenty-six wanting to be security officers. Out of the group of twenty-six, there were two girls and three black guys. Most of the group consisted of ex-military men and people who had been in some type of law enforcement. The Nuclear Power Plant was still under construction, with about three thousand construction workers on site.

For the first week, it was getting to know each other and learning the basic rules. As in weeks to come, we would be given test after test. For some it was a walk in the park; for me, every day was a struggle due to the fact that I had been away from school for so long and decided to get my education from the school of hard knocks on the streets. I wasn't the smartest student, but I wasn't the least intelligent out of all of us either.

These were trying times for me, and I weathered the storm. I had troubles with the written work and to top it all off, I was a bad test taker. We also had some physical testing that I loved doing, and I watched most of the others struggle. Every day was a challenge, but after about six weeks, we completed all the book work and sent to the plant to actually do the job. Although training never stopped, as we found out when we met the first group of officers who knew the job. They started six months before us, and they showed us how to do the job we were hired for.

Some officers, after a short period of time, were released because of drugs in their system. The company would do random drug testing at any time. This kept me on the straight and narrow all the time even though I was never tempted to fall back into that trap again. We worked twelve hours, days or nights, rotating shifts with unlimited overtime. Most of us would work seventy-twp to eighty-four hours a week without taking a day off for weeks at a time. For those who had a life outside of work, this was very hard; but for me, I wanted to forget about my life outside of work. This was perfect for me. I enjoyed my job and liked the people I worked with, but as always, people are different; and with that, came the same old problems. It was literally always black and white. It would never change, so I dealt with it the same way as I did in high school. I ignored it and did my job.

Life-changing Decisions

Things outside of work changed drastically. I wasn't able to see my girlfriend as much as I liked to, and we slowly began to go our separate ways. If that wasn't bad enough, I had to decrease my running schedule but still tried to keep up with it as much as possible. Often right after work, I would run with some of my fellow officers for five or six miles. I also joined a gym to keep fit and often worked out with a couple of guys from work. I never fell back into that deep, dark, depressing state that I was in before. I felt that I was doing something with my life, and I was happy.

After a couple months on the job, I began to find my comfort zone. Things didn't change for a long time until I saw Rhonda Hughley driving past my house one day when I was outside washing my car. I managed to flag her down, she pulled in front of my driveway, and I stepped out to her car on the street. As usual she was in perfect form with a small top on and form-fitting jeans. As I bent down to talk to her, I could smell her perfume. She was a knockout. I asked her if we could go out sometime, and we set a date. She drove off, and I just stood there, watching her car go down the street. I couldn't wait to go out with her. The next few days were a little easier to tolerate because I had something to look forward to. That date was the only thing on my mind.

The next few days went rather slowly, and I counted the minutes until the weekend arrived. I shined up my black Trans Am until it looked like a mirror, and the interior smelled like a pine tree because of the cleaner I used. Everything was just perfect, and I drove up to her house and pulled in the driveway; and her father, Coach Hughley, was outside working.

He approached my car. "Hello there, son, nice set of wheels you got there."

Before I could say anything, Rhonda walked out the door and saved me. For the first time in my life, I was at a loss for words. She quickly hopped in the car. "Bye, Daddy!" And she turned toward me, saying, "Let's go!"

I drove off after a little coaching from Coach Hughley, saying to be careful. I understood him well, and I also understood that he trusted me with one of the things he valued most in this world, his daughter. The coach and I had a lot in common. I also valued his daughter and decided to heed his warning. I treated his daughter like a fragile piece of fine china.

We drove to the movies, and I felt very comfortable with her as we talked along the way. There was never the break-in period with a new date. We knew each other all our lives, and it was if I was going out with one of my best friends.

I enjoyed her company more than any other girl I had been with, and I believed she enjoyed being with me too. We had dated off and on for many years, and each time was better than the date before. Rhonda worked for the phone company as her mother did for many years before retiring. I figured it was a merger between the phone company and the nuclear power plant, two utilities. We often talked about our jobs, but we also talked about everything else more than our jobs.

After working at the nuclear plant for about six months, things were going pretty good for me. I made friends with my fellow employees; we continued to work long hours and rotating shifts. I never complained because I felt like it was a blessing. I had a job I liked. My supervisor was a retired Ohio state trooper. He looked the part, with his gray hair cut into the most perfect flat top I've ever seen, his clothes pressed, and his shoes in a high state of polish every day. Joe Delong ran a tight ship, and for some reason he liked giving me all the hard stuff that came along with the job.

I never complained; but I always checked with the lead officer, Larry, before I took on more than I could handle. Larry was a long, lean country boy who at the time was a real go-getter. I believed he was entertained by my lack of knowledge about the way things were handled in the nuclear world. The three of us had many laughs with each other. The combination of a young green black kid, a young country boy, and a retired Ohio state trooper was actually a mixture that you think could never work well together. We made a hell of a team, with laughs every minute of the day. This was truly the first time in my life I felt like I was part of the team. I learned a lot from these two individuals, and I looked forward to going to work knowing that they would be there. Joe and Larry weren't just guys I worked with; they were true friends. I enjoyed being with them. Despite our differences, we always worked well together, with positive attitudes. The result of this overflowed into the shift, and we all worked well together.

I learned the nuclear ways, and with a lot of training became a useful, knowledgeable security officer. In time I became one of the guys that other officers would come to for help. I was not only helpful to my fellow officers with issues on the job, but officers would often tell me about things that happened at home with their wives and children. Not giving much advice but just listening seemed to help them with many different situations. With all the things that happened to me growing up, I had true compassion for my fellow human beings; and somehow the Lord blessed me with good people skills.

Due to being a vital part of the nuclear plant, we were constantly under the watchful eye of the powers-that-be at the plant. We weren't just regular old security officers that you see on television. The media painted a comical picture of what a security actually was. You know, the guy with one foot in the grave walking around with keys and a night stick, so fat and out of shape, sitting in a chair at a desk, eating every type of junk food known to man. We were highly trained individuals tested mentally and physically every day. The job title doesn't really describe the individuals involved with nuclear security. Often nuclear security officers were terminated for reasons I cannot discuss, so I learned to stay out of trouble inside and outside of the nuclear world. Many others didn't understand this and often lost their jobs due to foolishness off the job or on the job.

Fighting the Devil

Just when you think that everything is going great and problems were far and few between, life throws you a curve ball that rocks your world. Due to working long hours at my job both day shift and night shift, my girlfriend and I saw less and less of each other. My grandfather began to have heart and lung trouble. He would make frequent trips to the hospital. The world outside my job was fading away. I didn't see any of my friends anymore, and I didn't have time to work out as much. If I wasn't at work, I was home sleeping.

When I finally had one day off, it wasn't on the weekend when most people were off. It was in the middle of the week when everyone else in the world was at work. I would do my laundry, get a haircut, or fix my car. I had trouble sleeping, so I would drink a couple shots of alcohol before I went to bed. This was very bad for me, and I began to develop a pattern.

I worked more and more and sometimes worked twelve hours for two and three weeks before getting a day off. My job was my life, and the only people I associated with were the people I worked with. After working twelve hours on night shift, at six o'clock in the morning I would drive home, drink a couple of shots, and go to bed. One morning I went to my stash under my bed and pulled out and empty bottle of the 151 rum I used to help put me to sleep. I felt that I would never get to sleep without it, so I decided to stay awake watching television until the state store opened.

I never drifted off to sleep, and by noon I was in the parking lot of the state store. I had a ton of money in my pocket with every intention of buying a case of the rum I had become so dependent on; I stood in the middle of the parking lot, staring at the state store. I watched people go in and out; I was frozen in place and didn't move for what seemed like hours. I thought to myself, was I becoming an alcoholic? The very thing that I had run away from for so long was entering my life again and taking over in full force.

I turned around and decided that the rum and any other form of alcohol was something I didn't need. I went home and slept for about four hours and went to work for a very long night. To tell the truth, I had only polished off one-fifth bottle of rum, but I was very leery of old habits and decided to err on the side of caution. I didn't need any of these old demons creeping back into my very clean life.

My drink of choice was coffee, and my drug of choice was caffeine, but when I drank too much coffee, I also stayed away from it. Nothing would control my life again. I could turn it on and turn it off whenever I wanted to, even women. I became strong-willed and started lifting weights and running again; these were the things I was good at, and I knew these were the things that were good for me. Once again I was saved; I wondered how many chances I would get. I said a prayer and continued to pray when I woke and before I went to sleep every day.

Maybe there was something to this power of prayer. Was this the glue that kept normal people in the world focused on the good things in life? Was I finally starting to get it? If it was good enough for millions of good people in the world, it was good enough for me. I stayed in prayer and trusted in the Lord.

Finding My Way Back to Church

After a couple of lonely nights at the nuclear plant being alcohol-free and a lot of clear thinking, I made a couple of decisions. I went into the office and spoke to Joe, my supervisor, explaining to him my need to be in church on Sunday. I begged for the next Sunday off. Joe was an understanding believer himself and decided to let me have Sunday off. I hadn't gone to church for more than six months. I entered the church that Sunday and felt I was in the right place. Once again I felt the power of the Lord; once again I felt whole, and my battery was charged. I was ready for all the challenges the world had to give. With God on my side, how could I lose?

For the next couple of months, I managed to have every Sunday off, and I was willing to do whatever it took to have Sunday off to go to church. If it meant getting on my hands and knees pleading and begging my supervisor, I was willing to do it. Somehow Joe understood how important this was to me and did whatever he had to do to make it happen. I felt this was a vital part of my existence; I remained faithful and trusted in the Lord. I was becoming a strong believer, and good things started to happen again. I never turned to alcohol again. I drank an occasional beer every now and then, but I controlled it, it didn't control me. Once again Rhonda Hughley entered my life, and I thanked the Lord for that.

Searching for the Perfect Mate

Despite the long hours at work, I managed to join a local gym; and after night shift or day shift, I would work out for about two hours a day. I began to focus more on my social life. I broke up with my old girlfriend and dated many different young ladies. Every young lady that I went out with seemed to have a host of problems just coping with everyday life. I began to think it was me, maybe I was the one with the problems, so I decided to take home some of the girls I dated, to meet my family. I thought, who would know women better than my mother and Big John?

I was right. Each girl I brought home, I would run them past Big John; he wouldn't say much, just smile or shake his head. Later he would slowly point me in the right direction, provided I would ask him the right questions. The real test for me was how the young ladies measured up to my mother. I would introduce the girls to my mother as she was cooking dinner. I would sit at the kitchen table and strike up a conversation just to hear how my date would respond to my mother. I never really found any flaws with the girls I brought home, they were all very pretty. Later I would sit and talk to my mother, and she pointed out a few key elements to me; and after I thought about it, she was always right.

I dated Rhonda Hughley a couple of times and decided to run her through my series of tests. One evening after going to a movie, I took Rhonda home. She already knew my mother and practically everyone else in my family. She lived up the street only about one hundred yards away. She was also a classmate with my Aunt Linda. Our families knew each other well; I played football with one of her brothers and often played playground basketball with both of her brothers.

I escorted Rhonda up the driveway and through the back door. My mother was in the kitchen, cleaning up after a big meal. We sat down at the kitchen table, and without any effort at all, Rhonda and my mother talked as if they were mother and daughter. I was amazed. None of the other girls that I brought home ever spoke with such ease. I sat and listened, not really joining in the conversation. I watched my mother closely for any signs of disapproval. She had a smile on her face as the two women talked about life, family, and careers. I was very pleased. Rhonda looked very comfortable sitting at the kitchen table talking to my mother. She was very special to me; she also had many fine qualities that all the other girls were lacking.

I drove her home to her apartment. We watched a little television and talked about the movie and our families. Once again, it was a perfect evening; and as I drove home, I went over in my mind how my mother and Rhonda talked. I couldn't wait to talk to my mother when I got home. It was late when I got home; my mother was in bed sleeping. I had to wait until morning to hear her thoughts.

The next morning, I woke up, and for the first time in a long time, I didn't start my day off by running a couple of miles. I could smell the bacon cooking in the kitchen, and I knew my mother was up preparing breakfast before Big John went to work. I quickly took a shower and ran upstairs, taking a seat at the kitchen table. I pretended to look at the newspaper as I waited for my mother to speak.

She continued making breakfast as I finally broke the ice, "Mom, what do you think of Rhonda?"

She slowly turned around as she was draining the bacon grease from the frying pan. "She's a very nice-looking girl with a lot of smarts. Her parents are very good people."

I waited for the usual rundown of all the quirks and perceived problems my mother picked out with the other girls I brought home. She didn't have one bad thing to say. I didn't know what to say, so I sat there silently as I was overwhelmed with pleasure. I decided to be a little more serious with the relationship. Could she be what I was looking for?

Before I could eat anything, I ran downstairs and put on my running clothes. I had a lot to think about, and I hoped Rhonda was as fond of me as I was of her. I knew it long before all this happened; I was in love with her. As I ran, I couldn't stop thinking about her. Did I find my soul mate? I wondered how all this was going to turnout; only time would tell. I called her that day after work, trying not to be too pushy. I asked when would be the next time I could see her. I hung up the phone, and within thirty minutes. I was at her apartment.

Everything was falling into place. Work was going well, I continued working out at the gym; and most of all, Rhonda and I were seeing each other on a daily basis. I was wondering when the bottom would fall out. It never did, and things only got better. I would spend most of my time with Rhonda at her apartment and less time at home. We would go out to dinner and to the movies, but for the most part, we would stay at her apartment, watching television and enjoying each other's company. After about six months together, I wanted to take our relationship to the next level.

The Proposal

One evening after dinner and a movie, we went to her apartment and sat next to each other. We watched the sun go down as a cool lake breeze swept through the room. I was thinking about how perfect things were, and I asked her to marry me. After a moment of silence, she looked at me and said she would be happy to be my wife. For me that was the easy part; it was my turn to pass the test.

I had to ask her father, Coach Hughley, for his daughter's hand in marriage. Her mother was a little less frightening to me. She was a very pleasant lady that I never had a problem with and reminded me of my own mother. As for my folks, I thought they would be very pleased. I believe my mother knew my intentions when I brought her home. We had many family encounters on both sides before it got to this point in our relationship, and it was always the same, they accepted us as a couple.

The next weekend, I took Rhonda home and made the announcement. My parents and siblings were very happy she would be a member of the family. They welcomed her with open arms; I couldn't believe this was happening. When I told my mother, her exact words were, "I think she would be good for you." I also had Big John's blessing without hesitation. The next step was to go up the street and talk to her family. I was very nervous.

I drove up the driveway, and a big knot formed in my stomach. Rhonda stepped out of the car, and it looked like her feet never touched the ground. She was at the front door before I turned the car off. As we went to the door, I could hear her father's deep voice in the distance. We went to her mother first. As we told her the news, she had a big smile on her face, welcoming me to the family.

I went to the dining room where her father sat watching television. He was watching a baseball game, with his legs crossed and very much into the game. I entered the room and pulled up a chair; he always said hello and treated me well. His eyes were on the game but made idle conversation with me. Coach Hughley was never at a loss for words. As we talked, I said to him, "Mr. Hughley, I have something to ask you."

He quickly took his eyes off the game and positioned himself directly in front of me, as if to say you have my undivided attention. He had a slight smile on his face, which was not unusual. He was always a very pleasant, understanding man. He always made me feel very comfortable. Here I sat, looking eye to eye with a man that struck fear into every neighborhood kid with his strong deep voice. I finally realized that it was his voice that actually scared us; looking at him seeing the kindness in his eyes, I had no fear as I said, "Mr. Hughley, I would like to marry your daughter."

He had a big smile on his face as he put his arm around me and said, "Son, welcome to the family!"

I had her father's blessing. We stepped into the other room and told her younger brothers, Kevin and Kenny. We were well received by both families. We had a wedding to prepare for. I found my true soul mate; I had something many men searched a lifetime for, a good woman to love. Once again the Lord blessed me. As I drove her to her apartment, I said a silent prayer, thanking God for all the good he gave me. I was never more sure of anything in my life. I knew I had a good woman.

Rhonda the Wedding Planner

For the next year, we made plans for the wedding. I was still working long hours at the plant, and Rhonda took the bull by the horns as she made all the arrangements for a big wedding with three hundred friends and family to be invited. She was well-organized as she went over ever detail like a jeweler making the final precision cut on a diamond. We worked well as a team, and I thought to myself what a good mother she would be to our children.

It was a storybook wedding; we were married in Wickliffe, our hometown, on September 6, 1986, in Our Lady of Mt. Carmel Church in front of three hundred friends and relatives. I believe we set a record for the largest black gathering in that church, with a Catholic priest and her uncle, Reverend Hilary Battle, a Baptist minister, on the altar gathered in prayer. This was the first black man I saw on the altar of that church after attending many years of school and Sunday mass. We set many records that day; we took pictures outside of the church, and later on in the day took pictures on the bridge over the pond and flower garden at Wickliffe City Hall, which at the time never saw such a diverse crowd. It was a very unique day for the people of Wickliffe as they gathered in the park that sunny day.

Looking through the photo albums, remembering that day, little did we know that that would be the last time our families as a whole would be together. Some would pass away while others for some known reason would go their separate ways and stay away from the family, not being able to settle their differences. I call this the devil's best work, and I will continue to pray for the lost souls of both families who went astray from what was the most valuable asset the Lord gave us, family. I learned this valuable lesson early in life as I watched a man walk away from his four children and wife. I was the second oldest of that family.

My life took on a new meaning. I was not only working for myself anymore but working to start a family. I took on many new assignments at work and enjoyed becoming a radio operator, which was the nerve center of the security force and a vital part of the plant. The long working hours seemed to go on forever, but I never complained because on my time off, I enjoyed being with my new wife. We would often go on trips when we could get away; sometimes we would red-eye to Las Vegas or to Toronto, Canada. For about the next four or five years, we traveled on cruises or took plane trips, enjoying parts of the world that people didn't see in a lifetime.

We planned a big trip to the islands of Hawaii, and for the next few weeks, I worked out hard as Rhonda booked the trip and made all the arrangements for the trip. Life was good, and this would be the last big trip we would take before we would start a family. So not only did we plan to go to Hawaii; but on the trip back home, we would go to Las Vegas for three days before we would go back home to Cleveland. I worked out hard with my gym pals, and my excitement began to build as the weeks flew by getting nearer to the date for the trip.

The Reader

I spent some of the best and worse times of my life working out at local gyms. One of my best friends from work lifted with me every day. Curtis was an ex-marine full of life and was a perfect workout partner. We also had a friend named Kevin, who was one of the biggest and strongest guys I ever met. The three of us spent many hours together working out and pushing each other to the limit. Kevin and Curtis had a great fondness for leg workouts; at first I absolutely hated doing legs. With Kevin's knowledge, we soon became some of the strongest leg men in the business.

We were becoming bigger and stronger with each workout, and Kevin dreamed up more torture for legs each time we entered the gym. We were a team, and on every Saturday at ten o'clock in the morning, some of the biggest and most powerful lifters would gather in the gym to pound out grueling leg workouts that would just cripple me for the rest of the day.

The gym had people from every different walk of life, but one individual stands out vividly in my mind and will never be forgotten as long as I live. I often would tell my friends at work about a strange lady who I became close to, and she would tell me things that were going to happen to me in the future. I never believed in fortune-tellers, but she was the real deal; and it all happened just by chance, as Curtis and I walked in the gym for our morning routine. The events that took place I have no explanation for, and to this day still can't find a reason for it.

One sunny Monday morning, Curtis and I walked in the gym, seeing the regulars and talking to everyone who knew us. As we walked toward the locker room, there sat Mary holding a young lady's hand telling her about her life. Mary walked with a limp from polio when she was a kid. We would laugh and joke with her every day of the week. She didn't come to the gym on the weekends. Mary cleaned the gym and worked out a little to stay fit.

Curtis looked at Mary holding the girl's hand looking deeply into it and tell things that were going to happen to her in the near future. Curtis asked Mary if she was a reader, and she told him she dabbled a little in the process. Mary did more than dabble, and we soon found out how well-versed she was in the subject. Curtis quickly sat down beside her, holding out his hand; she told him of children, a wife, and basically a full and rich life.

I stood silently, and Mary told me to sit down. I reluctantly sat beside her, and she took my hand. Mary was silent for what seemed like a long time, and then she asked me if I was planning to have children. I told her not yet, and she said just be patient. She got up from seat and walked to the other side of the gym. I sat there wondering what Mary saw as she gazed into my hand.

I followed Mary to the other side of the gym, finally cornering her; I asked her what she saw. Mary had a strange look on her face as she said, "Time will tell." She also told me that she didn't see anything in my hand, and her reading came from my heart. I was puzzled but not too curious as to believe anything she said. I thought that it was just some mumbo jumbo, and she was just another quack that played like she was some type of mind reader.

Mary soon proved her validity a couple weeks later Mary stood, silently gazing at a picture on the wall. She asked me if I knew who drew the picture. She told me to stay away from the artist and that he was soon to take a big fall. A few days later, the guy who drew the picture was in jail. The police found a bunch of drugs in his car with two guns. The news was all over the gym, and nobody knew of the conversation Mary and I had. I would just chalk this up as a coincidence, but Mary came up with another super prediction.

Mary was mopping the floor a few weeks after the artist of the picture was in jail. She had that same strange look on her face when I approached her. I told her she looked troubled, her hair was a mess and she looked like she hadn't been to sleep for a week. There was a huge search for a little girl that had been missing for over a month, and the story was in the newspapers every day.

Mary told me she knew where the little girl was. I said why didn't she tell the police, she looked at me and told me she went to the police before and they thought she was nuts. She told me that the little girl was in a field, and she saw the cooling towers of the nuclear plant in the background. I thought it was strange that she was telling me this because I worked at the nuclear plant she was referring to.

A couple of days passed, and some hunters found the little girl's body in a field by the nuclear plant. As soon as I read the newspaper and saw the article about the little girl, I immediately thought about Mary. I don't believe in readers, but somehow she knew things that other people didn't. That very day I went to the gym and looked for Mary. One of the girls said she was sick and wouldn't be back for a couple of days. I worked out and thought a lot about Mary. I couldn't wait to see her to ask her about the events that occurred.

I didn't see Mary for the whole week. She was usually always at the gym cleaning and working out. When Mary finally showed up, she was in no condition to talk to anyone. She avoided everyone, especially me. I believe she knew that I would be full of questions. I felt sorry for her, and I knew when she wanted to talk, she would seek me out. Was seeing things before they happen a curse or a blessing? From the looks of Mary, I was glad I wasn't blessed with this gift.

A few days passed before they got to be normal again, and Mary was back to her old self. I didn't ask her about the artist or the little girl. I felt that when she wanted to talk, she would volunteer the information. What was really on my mind were the things that she said about me a couple of months ago, I believe she also knew that too. It didn't take a reader to figure that out. I tried to treat her as if nothing ever happened and still talked to her as a friend.

Before I knew it, weeks and months passed by, and Mary was feeling her old self after weeks of turmoil entered her life with all the things she saw. Sometimes she would have a strange look on her face, and I knew she was seeing things all along but dared not to discuss anything with anybody. Mary and I were close, and she began to talk to me and tell me things that she saw about me.

She told me I was an easy read because I wore my heart out on my sleeve. I asked her what was in store for me, and she spared me the harsh details and wouldn't give me any information that would hurt our friendship. She also explained to me that it was all in God's hands and to trust in the Lord, have faith and everything would be all right. Mary asked me about children again and also told me that I would be in charge of a lot of people that would trust and believe in me. I was confused, and I did take something valuable from the conversation. I took her advice and trusted in the Lord. I knew it was ultimately in his hands.

Mary often asked me about children, and I was wondering why she was always asking me about kids. Later in my story, I would come to Mary with something heavy on my heart that involved my children. She told me I was going to have children, but there would be a great struggle, and my wife and I would be put through many great hardships before we would have children. I often wondered why she feared to just tell me all the things she knew about my life.

I can tell you that Mary told me three things that would happen in my life, and to this day, two of those things were absolutely correct; I have yet to see the third prediction come true. She told me that I would be in charge of a lot of people who would trust me and believe in me; she told me I would be a great leader one day. I will never forget Mary, and she will remain in my prayers as I often think about her. Mary left the gym, and I never saw her again. Rumor has it that she moved out of state and got a divorce.

Getting Away from It All

Rhonda and I prepared ourselves for a long trip, and I left all the gym with all my friends who continued to work out daily. The memories of the gym would remain with me for a lifetime, and I will never forget all the people who I had a relationship with as we shared a common goal, to be fit and healthy. As we left our house for the airport, I thought of all the strange things that happened to me at the gym. We were on our way to the land people only dreamed about, and I was glad to leave all my worries behind.

We boarded the plane and prepared ourselves for a long twelve-hour ride. We stopped in Chicago's O'Hare airport to board another plane. The plane filled up with passengers, and we were upgraded to first class because of seating. The plane was full of people, older people; we were the youngest couple on the plane. First class was different than anything we had experienced before, as the stewardess treated us like royalty.

We finally reached Hawaii and landed in Honolulu airport for a couple of hours until we were to board a smaller plane and travel to the big island of Kona. We stepped off the plane and immediately felt the hot sun and the trade winds blowing across the island. It was about ninety degrees, and we were dressed for much colder weather. When we left Cleveland, it was barely forty-five degrees. I was dressed in heavy jeans and Frye boots. Rhonda was dressed in winter-type clothes too; we quickly found a restroom where we changed into summer attire while we waited for our flight.

The plane finally arrived, and we boarded it with about twenty other people. The plane took off, and we flew over the ocean, and I peered out of the window looking at all the beautiful landscape of the Hawaiian Islands. It was a very rough flight. The small plane shifted back and forth from the heavy winds surrounding the tiny islands. We saw dormant volcanoes and black beaches where the lava flow met the cool ocean waters. For the first week, we would tour the big island of Kona; and the next week, we would tour the island of Maui.

The islands were full of adventure, but for the most part, we found complete peace as we took advantage of the sunny beaches and walking around the beautiful islands. We decided to take one extreme adventure as we planned to take a trip to see the only active volcano on the big island of Kona. The next morning, we filled up the Mustang convertible and headed for the volcano on the other side of the island. What started out to be a short trip turned out to be eight hours long.

We drove for what seemed like hours, and the terrain changed about every hour. We traveled through a metro park that consisted of two hours of hairpin turns and cliffs with no guard rails. We drove up mountains with an elevation of about 7,500 feet above sea level and traveled back down to the other side, which looked like the big ranches of Texas as we saw herds of cattle and horses. We stopped at the top of one of the mountains at the Kona coffeehouse, which was 8,000 feet above sea level, and a huge lava tube next to it, which looked like a cave. In the back of the coffeehouse, there was a cliff where you could see the rocks below with monstrous waves breaking the shore. We got two island blend Kona coffees to go and continued to drive to the volcano.

As we drove along in the red Mustang with the top down, enjoying the warmth from the sun, the climate began to change as we drove higher into the mountainous area. We were finally in range of the volcano, and as we climbed higher, it became colder. So I put the top up as the sun disappeared and the clouds began to take over the sky. The wind was much stronger, and a slight rain began to fall. We were on the other side of Kona, which was called Hilo.

We were ten minutes away from Volcano Park as we reached an elevation of ten thousand feet. We entered the park and stepped out of the car to feel the cold damp air. As we went into the observatory, the thermometer on the side of the building said forty-five degrees; it was just as cold as Cleveland when we left. We had no idea it would be this cold in Hawaii. A little bit more research before venturing out on a big trip would have helped us discover the rapid change in temperature. A valuable lesson learned, as we shivered approaching an area map of the park.

We also found out by looking at the map that we were twenty-six miles away from the volcano, and you could hike along the trail into a heavily wooded area or take a horse to reach the volcano. Well, we never saw the volcano. We got back into the car and turned on the heater as we drove around the park, settling for a view of a sulfur pit, which smoked and had bright yellow sulfur around its opening. The sulfur pit was a bleed-off from the volcano and definitely not one of the big tourist attractions. We drove out of the park and headed back to warmer weather and our comfortable condo on the other side of the island. Not seeing the volcano didn't ruin our day, and we vowed to come back to Hawaii to see the volcano with our future children.

The next day we traveled to Hana, the place songs were made about. The island was full of life with people from all over the world. There were little shops and island music playing throughout the tiny shops we entered. We would see hula dancers and huge Samoans walking around in their native garb. I wondered what it would be like to live in Hawaii with beautiful weather and the ocean breeze blowing through the massive palm trees. For me this was truly heaven. For others, this was their normal way of life. The only way some of these people ever experienced snow was high in the mountains. I knew that in a few short months, Rhonda and I would be facing Cleveland's harsh cold winter with the bite of the wind cutting across the land from Lake Erie. I vowed that if I ever hit the big time, this would be the place where my family would spend our winters. For me, the Hawaiian Islands were as close to heaven on earth as possible.

Our next phase of the trip, we ventured to the small island of Maui and stayed for one week before we departed for Las Vegas. Maui was full of beautiful beaches and flowers we only saw on television back home. The islanders were a quiet people but very proud to show us their heritage and many beautiful parts of the island. We drove around and settled on another beach with very few people and warm island breeze blowing continuously across the hot sand. We went to the beach daily and enjoyed the warm, hot sun and seclusion away from all the problems of the real world. Maui was the lifestyles of the rich and famous with people driving around in cars that cost more than my house. Our condo faced the ocean shore, and the trade winds providing a cool breeze and we watched the sun go down on our balcony.

The first day on Maui, we had to get another condo. Rhonda noticed a thin black line of ants crawling over our countertops in the kitchen. We were moved to another nice condo and settled in for the night. We went to dinner and returned to the condo that evening just in time to watch the sun go down, to end a perfect evening. Later that night, Rhonda woke me up screaming about a lizard in the room. I turned on the lights just in time to see the small gecko sprinting across the room for more cover. The native islanders say if a gecko enters your room, you'll have good luck for the rest of your life.

I knew that if the gecko wasn't out of the room, Rhonda wouldn't let me sleep all night, so the chase was on. I chased him under couches and turned over chairs, and we had a standoff in the dining room. He stood his ground, panting in a corner of the room. I stood in front of him panting and completely covered with sweat from chasing him room to room. He was tired, and I was tired, and I managed to catch him in a water glass. I took him out on the balcony and let him go. Finally I could get some rest, and my wife was on gecko watch for the rest of the night as she curled up next to me as close as possible.

Early one morning while watching the news after the shark report on the local news channel, we watched O. J. Simpson driving down the freeway with about a dozen police cars following him. Suddenly we were brought back into reality. While we were on the secluded islands of Hawaii, the real world went on with all of the real world problems. Somehow that longing for home seemed to dissipate as I watched the police chase on the television. We packed our things and went to the beach for a couple more days of the good life before we had to go home.

After a few more days of fun in the sun, we packed our things and prepared for the final leg of the trip, Las Vegas, for three days. We boarded the plane.

Rhonda and I were very quiet, and I could feel sadness in the air as we looked out of the window of the plane. I finally said, "At least we had a chance to experience something very beautiful and peaceful together." She agreed, and for the next eight hours, we were in the air on our way to Vegas.

It was pitch-black outside as I heard the announcement that we would be landing in Las Vegas in the next twenty minutes. I looked out of the window and saw the City of Lights. Rhonda and I were very excited, and we were still on vacation. Somehow the Hawaiian adventure faded as we thought of all the activity in Las Vegas.

I wish I could say we were big winners in Las Vegas, but that wouldn't be true at all. We did win enough money to see the Siegfried and Roy show and take a bus trip to Hoover Dam and Lake Meade. We stayed at the Mirage Hotel, and we did see a volcano. The hotel had a man-made volcano, which flowed lava every fifteen minutes of the day and night. The weather in Vegas was much hotter than Hawaii as the desert reached about 115 degrees in the middle of the day. We stayed in the casinos and out of the hot sun, spending money and watching people spend more money than we could earn in ten years. Our big trip finally came to an end; after fourteen days in Hawaii and three days in Las Vegas, we were completely exhausted and ready to go home.

We took the final four-hour flight back home to Cleveland, and when we touched down at Cleveland's Hopkins airport, the pilot made an announcement saying it was forty degrees and cloudy. As we went to the baggage claim, people stared at us, looking at our deeply tanned bodies, knowing we came from somewhere extremely sunny. I was actually thrilled to be home, wanting to share our experiences with our families.

We settled down when we finally reached our home. We still had a couple of days before we went back to work. We hung around the apartment and enjoyed each other's company before we got back to our normal routine. I couldn't wait to get back to the gym. After about a full month away from the gym, I could see the heavy toll it took on my body, and my clothes were kind of snug. I walked into the bathroom and faced the scale. Stepping on the scale and looking down to see I gained about twenty-five pounds, I knew I had a lot of work to do.

The Gym

The next morning I went to the gym and met my workout mates, and they were less than kind as they noticed my drastic weight change. As the fat jokes began to fly, I became very depressed and went to the locker room to collect my things to go home. Before I could leave, Kelly, who owned the gym, called me into her office.

She told me to take a seat; she could see I was very upset due to the greeting my friends gave me. She said a few kind words and told me to ignore the ridicule and get back to my diet program and workout routine. She also gave me some of the most solid advice I ever heard. She told me to do my own thing and workout to achieve my goal. She knew me well and what I wanted as far as bodybuilding was concerned. I also considered her very knowledgeable and one of the most honest individuals I ever met. Kelly was also one of closest friends I had. Before I talked to her, I was ready to quit the gym, vowing never to return again. Instead I walked out very angry, mad at my pals; but I had a game plan, and I was determined to see it through.

The very next morning, I walked into the gym wearing a thick hooded sweatshirt and sweatpants. I walked past my workout pals and went directly to the stair machine known as the gauntlet. My workout partners called out to me from across the gym, laughing, telling me to get off the crazy machine and come lift with them. I mounted the machine and put my Sony Walkman headset in my ears, ready to do battle with the gauntlet. My friends were big thick power lifters, and at this moment in time, I was also a big thick meaty power lifter weighing in at about 230 pounds. They bellowed with laughter, telling me I would never last; Kelly just looked over at me with a slight smile on her face, knowing how serious I was. It was if she knew all the time that I was determined to change.

The machine got the best of me in the first ten minutes of exercise, at the easiest level possible. I pulled the hood of the sweatshirt on my head and got back on the machine for another ten minutes of hell, and I continued this madness until I completed a full sixty minutes, which actually took me a full two hours to complete. The laughter from my friends only fueled the fire in my heart; the more they laughed, the more determined I became. I knew this would be no easy task. I drove home stopping a couple of times on the side of the road to throw up. I woke up every morning repeating the same process, determined to succeed. I followed a strict bodybuilding diet and did as much cardio exercises as possible, sometimes doing the whole process twice a day. I was focused and never cheated on my diet or routine, and all I could see were my friends laughing at me. I was a man on a mission. For at least the next eight months of my life, I would beat myself up every day and weigh my food, not eating one thing that would set me back. I religiously went to the gym dressed in my hooded sweatshirt and sweatpants to match, never revealing my body under the thick clothing.

After a couple of months, I would have to buy smaller-sized sweat suits, but they were always pretty much the same—a hooded sweatshirt and sweatpants to match. The stair machine was much less of a challenge, and I was able to stay on it at the top level for a complete hour. I incorporated a heavy rep routine with light weights and abdominal exercises. Everyone in the gym wondered what exactly was going on as I became a loner, never working out with my partners, and living on the stair machine. Sometimes after a grueling workout, I would go into the aerobics room, turn on the stereo and jump rope, and hit the speed bag like a boxer.

After about a solid eight months of serious training, I stepped on my bathroom scale and weighed in at a cool 165 pounds, finally realizing that I achieved my goal and then some. I looked in the mirror and counted six defined ab muscles. I put on my baggy sweat clothes and drove to the gym.

One Saturday morning, I walked into the gym, and Kelly gave me a bodybuilding tank top with her logo on it and a tiny pair of spandex shorts, telling me it was time to show the finished product. On Saturday mornings, everyone that belonged to the gym would come in early to work out, so they could spend the rest of the day with family or just relaxing. I went into the locker room and stripped down to my underwear to put the clothes on. Two of my friends who were local gym rats and policemen stood there, looking at what I had accomplished in the few short months. They praised me and told me that I was in the zone, which meant that I was in the bodybuilding zone, with my body looking better than it ever was.

I felt good as I walked out on the gym floor, getting ready to go on my stair machine. Kelly suddenly looked up and started to clap, and then the entire gym started to clap, and everyone came up to me to ask about my program and tell me I looked like I belonged on a fitness magazine front cover. My power-lifting buddies, that had made fun of the fat guy that came back to the gym from his Hawaiian vacation, looked up and saw me standing there, raised their hands in the air, and yelled, "Way to go, Tim!"

I believe this was one of the high points in my troubled life, and I felt like a king. Something that eluded me for years finally came to fruition that morning. People began to ask me how I did it, and would I be willing to train them? I kindly declined their offers and remained a loner, keeping fit and sticking with my program. I still felt good as I gained the respect of the bodybuilding community in my local gym with the help of my friend Kelly and my understanding wife, who put up with my crazy workout routine and even more bizarre eating habits.

Finding a Home

Life didn't get any easier from this point. I had a weight problem all of my life, and trying to maintain the ultralean body and keep up with the workouts while working rotating shifts and trying to find a decent house to buy began to take its toll on me. I wasn't getting enough rest working long hours and going house shopping almost every weekend. I began to miss workouts and eat fast food again. I kept physically fit for many years after but put on a couple of pounds here and there along the way.

Rhonda was a very understanding wife, but I would much rather spend my day with her than be at the gym every morning trying to live the life of a bodybuilder. Besides, living in the apartment with rent going up and never really having a place of our own, just didn't seem right to me. We had many discussions about buying a house and starting a family. I felt this was much more than having the perfect body. I was much happier being with her. So I backed off the gym and spent more time enjoying life with her. We began to pursue a common goal, looking for a house, and talked about having children. At least I satisfied myself and realized what was important in life were my wife and future children. The following Sunday, we went to church and spent time with family and friends.

Living in the apartment had many different challenges; it was a nice place that was on the shore of Lake Erie. In the summer, we would open the balcony doors and bedroom windows to listen to the water hit the shore. At night the water had a calming effect that would put you to sleep. We moved from her one-bedroom apartment to a two-bedroom apartment on the lakeside. You could look out the bedroom window and see the lake; it was about fifty yards away.

Life was not always good at the apartment. We shared the laundry room with other tenants on the same floor. Also many times at night, we could hear the people that lived above us at night, which was very annoying after a hard day's work. We would wake up three and four times a night from the noise above, sounding like big-time wrestling matches. We would often complain to the management, and it would stop for a couple of days and start all over again.

We longed for a place of our own. I believe the determining factor was when the rent went up making it about equal as a house payment. The decision-breaker for me was when my prized possession, a 1983 limited edition Hurst Oldsmobile, was stolen from the parking lot of the apartment.

One night we were going to a concert, and I went outside to start my car. After searching the parking lot over and over for my car, I remembered parking my car close to the street for lack of parking spaces. The next day, my car was gone. I filed a police report, and a few days later, the car was found. It was in a Cleveland impound lot, stripped and sitting in two feet of mud with no tires, the column peeled back like a banana, and the windows open, letting the snow and rain mix and complete drench my once pristine interior.

As we approached my car, I began to feel physically ill as I looked at what was left of my once showroom vehicle. I knelt in the mud next to my car, crying like a baby, Rhonda by my side, looking down at a broken man and helping me up. We walked up front only to find out I had to pay seventy dollars and have the car towed to the repair shop. The lot was filled with about three hundred broken-down heaps of metal that nobody cared about. My car was completely ruined, and I felt like someone close to me in my family just died.

On the way home, I told myself that I would never feel this way about something as insignificant as a car. I told Rhonda that the next car I would own will be nothing special and look like every other car on the street. No thief in his right mind would even look at my next car, and it would be strictly used to go to and from work. With all the events that took place, this was what set the wheels in motion to find a house of our own. We decided to contact a realty company when we got home.

My car was towed to an Oldsmobile dealer in Mentor, and I was given a little red "Shit-vette" to drive around in for the next six months while my car was being repaired. I went from one of the coolest cars on the street to driving something that looked like a car from the movie *Revenge of the Nerds*. All of the guys I worked with loved to make fun of me as I drove the humiliating little piece of crap to work. I begged the car dealer to finish my car early. I even offered the guy working on it a thousand dollars to get it done right away. No one listened, and I continued to drive that little red car until it hurt.

Good thing Rhonda had a respectable neat-looking Volvo that I drove any chance I got. She would drive her car to work, and of course that meant I would have to drive the embarrassment on wheels to work. It was a humbling experience for me. I remember pulling up next to my brother at a traffic light, revving the engine as if I wanted to race him. He looked over at me, exploding with laughter as he sat in his midnight blue Cutlass Supreme.

In the meantime, Rhonda and I would spend all our efforts going to open house after open house, looking for our first home. We went back to Wickliffe and decided we didn't want our kids to be subjected to the same type of childhood we had with the four streets of black people and prejudiced, narrow-minded people we grew up with. We visited other communities and found that some of them were just as bad as Wickliffe, if not worse. Some of the houses we went to weren't fit for a pack of dogs to live in also. We were shown houses in dire need of repairs, and some of the owners were in worse shape than their houses.

We searched for almost a full year trying to find the perfect home. We looked at century homes, new homes, and everything else in between. Every day we looked at a couple homes, and things began to get ridiculous when we were shown homes with no doors and children running all over the house, or dogs that were cleaner than the kids. Mother's screaming at dirty snot-nosed kids while making dinner, and Father's half dressed, watching television with a six-pack completely oblivious to what was going on. We even looked at a brand-new home we named "Sloppy's house" because it looked like the family just got up and left the house before we came. With dishes piled a mile high and dirty clothes in every room, the place looked as if it hadn't been cleaned in months. The family had nice pictures on the walls and expensive furniture with dust and dirt everywhere. We decided with a little work, this might be the house for us. We continued our search, hoping something else would show up, and in the crazy mixed-up business of finding a house, my car was finally completed. The repair shop called me to pick it up.

My car was finally repaired. Nothing was going right. I went to the dealer and got my car. It wasn't the same. As I looked it over, the paint had been touched up, and it looked like black house paint. I drove the car home and decided that now it was just a car, and I would drive it to its grave. I no longer treated it like something special. I just kept it clean and drove it back and forth to work. Until one day, it failed me, and I nursed it until the weekend and went to a car lot to find another car. The dealer told me he would give me three hundred dollars if I wanted to trade it in. I declined, but I did buy a little midnight blue Saturn from him and drove my car home where it would sit until I found a buyer. The Saturn was nothing special, and in fact looked like every other car on the street. I was completely satisfied, and Saturn was everything that I heard about. I would form an everlasting love for the little car as well as the dealership.

Finally after a long search, we found a house on the edge of Euclid, a suburb that bordered East Cleveland on a big hill that was actually hidden from the outside world. The name of the community was called Indian Hills, and each street was named after some of the great Indian tribes of native America. The community was tucked away on a big hill with a huge metro park on one side and the tough streets of East Cleveland on the other side at the bottom of the hill. This quiet little community never had any problems because of the way it was situated, practically hidden from the outside world; and if you didn't know where it was, you would pass right by it, never realizing it was there.

The house was an older brick bungalow with a huge finished basement with a fireplace and wet bar. The main floor had two bedrooms, a bathroom, and a living room with a stone fireplace. The upstairs had another bedroom and bathroom with a huge cedar closet. The house also had a long driveway with an attached garage that faced the backyard instead of the street. It was on a half-acre wooded lot with two apple trees, one pear tree, one cherry tree, and too many old maple trees to count. Our neighbors on each side were two old widowers that never bothered anyone. The community consisted of mostly old people and was considered one of the best neighborhoods in Euclid. Rhonda and I were very happy. We both agreed this was the perfect place to start a family.

Marriage,
Till Death Do Us Part?

After we were situated, our house was turned into a home, with all the things that made us comfortable. I thought it was smooth sailing for a while until we were faced with another tragedy. We were in our new home for about three months when Rhonda's parents decided to get a divorce. This would absolutely crush her; I knew divorce well because my parents went through the same thing when I was just a child. I hoped it wouldn't be as traumatic for her as it was for me and my family.

After the separation, we were given boxes of all the memories of a once happy family. We unpacked boxes of memories that came from her parents' house; I watched the tears flow from her eyes as she held each precious item that reminded her of all the good times the family had together. Divorce is such an ugly thing for two people that vowed to spend their lives together, "till death do us part." At least that's what you say when you get married; once again some of the devil's best work. As I watched my wife with her hands shaking and tears rolling down he cheeks as we unpacked a lifetime wrapped up in a few neat boxes. I thought to myself, saying, *I hope this will never happen to me and my wife.* I said a silent prayer asking the Lord to bless our marriage and give us everlasting life together. We unpacked all the things and went upstairs for a quiet evening together.

With my usual pattern, when things troubled me, I worked out harder and harder, trying to justify all the wrongs. I would work out and go home to help Rhonda get over the hurt and pain of the separation of her parents. I thought after time heals these wounds, everything would be back to normal for us. I didn't know how wrong I was; the next series of tragedies in our lives would shake the very core of my faith as we tried to start a family.

Trying to Start a Family

We went to work every day, and life was as normal as it could possibly be for Rhonda and me. One sunny beautiful Saturday morning, we were eating breakfast when Rhonda told me we were going to have an addition to the family. I was never happier, and for the next few weeks, we went to the doctor's office together with happy thoughts of having a child. Later on, we told our families and friends. We were busy making plans, preparing ourselves for one of the biggest steps in our lives, parenthood.

One day I was at work when I received a call from home. It was my mother-in-law telling me to come home immediately. I had ridden to work with one of my friends and left my car at his house. Larry, my lead officer, drove me to my friend's house to get my car. It was a very quiet ride home; Larry tried to soften the blow by gently telling me that things had a way of working themselves out. I knew something was terribly wrong, and I sat silently, not knowing what I would face when I got home. As soon as I got in my car to drive the rest of the way home, all I could think about was my wife and unborn child.

My mother-in-law met me at the door. I went into our bedroom where Rhonda lay on the bed resting. She held my hand and told me the baby was gone. I held her tight as I sat silently on the edge of the bed, to feel joy and then the tremendous pain of losing what I thought was a sure thing. How could this happen? How could I make my wife feel better? Why did God do this to us?

For the next few weeks, I went to the gym after work and before my wife got off work. I worked out harder than ever. In order to deal with so much pain in my heart, I used working out as an outlet. The moment I entered the gym, I saw Mary at the other side of the gym. She immediately looked up and saw me at the door. As I got nearer to her, I could see she was in a state of complete panic, and I could see the tears falling on the ground as she quickly mopped them up; she was cleaning. I walked over to her, and she reached for my hand, hugging me and telling me how sorry she was.

I sat down on a step, and she sat beside me, I asked her how she knew. She said she felt it as I entered the room. Being the kind of person she was, she told me to keep praying and trust in the Lord, my wife and I would be good parents. I was totally confused, but I remembered our conversations about children many months ago. The Lord works in mysterious ways. Kelly, the owner of the gym, and all my friends helped me through this difficult time.

I wasn't the only one suffering. There was a girl who also had problems with her pregnancies. She had lost two babies, and I was close to her older sister. Somehow we connected, and we helped each other. I think talking to each other helped ease the pain. I prayed for her, and she prayed for my wife and me. We became good friends. Mary kept reassuring me, telling me good things happen to good people.

I also had to help my wife, if my mind wasn't clear how could I be of any use to her. We went through these tough times together, feeling the pain together and dealing with it together. I believe the struggles we shared together made our marriage stronger. We suffered a second time when we had another complication, and again we were denied a child. I never really showed it on the outside, but I was dying on the inside. Rhonda and I stayed close as we searched for answers. She helped me to stay strong. We went to church every Sunday and prayed together.

To complicate things more, I took three days off work to be with my wife at a time of need. The powers that be told me that I had to use personal days to cover the time I missed. I really didn't feel like arguing about the time, but my coworkers fought for me with managers and supervisors. Finally I contacted the board of directors, and my time was given back to me. Once again I fought for everything that I had; most of all, my wife and I fought with everything we had to have children. Nothing in my life ever came easy. Together we trusted in the Lord, and we became stronger as we were blessed a third time. We cherished the opportunity, and somehow we knew through God we would be parents.

Our Son

With every blessing comes some heartache along the way. In that busy year of preparation, Rhonda's grandmother passed away. I felt very blessed because I knew her grandmother Alice very well, as we spent a lot of time visiting her. She was a pleasure to be around as she would laugh and joke with us. She told us many stories about the family's past. To this day, I can still see her very loving face and smile. Rhonda was deeply saddened by her passing, and to tell the truth, so was I. Grandma Alice Battle will always live in my heart along with my grandparents Louis and Gwendolyn Massey, whom Rhonda knew well. She also spent time over my grandparents' house with me. I thank the Lord for the time we had together with them.

For the next few months, we practically lived at the doctor's office. It wasn't easy, but the closer we got, the harder it became. Rhonda had many complications; and on December 9, 1994, we had a son. He would be a junior with my name. He was truly a miracle, and we were grateful after a long hard-fought battle, we were parents. The struggle for life made us strong, and together we would strive for excellence to become the best parents we could be. With God all things were possible; we were finally a family as we showed our newborn son to the world.

Things were pretty normal for a while in 1994. I was in my tenth year of employment at the Nuclear Power Plant, and Rhonda was at her job with the phone company for about fourteen years. We were very happy. We found a neighbor that ran a day care center two houses down the street from ours. Sheila Ashby was more than just a baby sitter. She was a very religious lady who had had some tough times of her own. We had a lot in common and would often talk about the similarities of her ex-husband and my own father.

Sheila had two children of her own, and her mother would also help with the day care. Sheila was also working a day care center for her church on Sundays. Olivet Institutional Baptist Church in Cleveland had over three thousand-strong members, and Sheila was taking care of the small children while people attended church. Little did we know at the time that our lives would run the same course, and our families would be forever together. As I said before, life is one big circle.

Rhonda and I would go to work, and Sheila would watch little Timmy as we went to work. Sheila not only watched the children but also taught the children how to read and write, preparing them for school. We never had a problem, and Sheila ran a tight ship.

One day when Timmy was about three years old, he walked across the backyard to our home. Everyone was in a panic until we found him sitting on the back porch waiting for us to arrive; he was very independent and had decided to venture out on his own as the other children played in the backyard. When I came home, I went directly to Sheila's house. She was in the backyard when I arrived. She looked up at the children, and Timmy wasn't there. She quickly ran inside looking for him. I checked the area and ran across the backyard. He was sitting on the back step, calmly waiting for his parents. That was enough excitement for a while. It never happened again, and Sheila was out of her mind with worry.

Building a New House

One night around the fourth of July, late at night we heard what Rhonda thought to be firecrackers and someone starting their holiday early; but I knew the sound of gun fire well. We listened as a series of bangs sounded off and then a couple of louder bangs, which I knew the sound of the shotguns as the police returned fire. Being so close to East Cleveland, which was a war zone, I told her we better start looking for a safer place to live; and the city of Euclid was no place to raise a family or send our children to school. That night we decided to look for a new place to live, and in the next few months, we would start the process of looking for a new home.

With two good jobs and our first home almost paid for, we decided to look at newer communities, and we looked at our options. We even went to a new place in Painesville where new homes were being built. One of my friends from work told me he lived in the new complex, and it was very quiet, and new homes were being built every day; we decided to give it a try.

The next weekend we had and appointment to go to Painesville to view the new homes. We drove down the street and saw many brand-new beautiful homes. We pulled in the driveway of the model home and met the builders there. We went into the model home, and there sat a blonde-haired middle-aged woman who greeted us and began showing us the home. She wasn't very friendly and showed us the home very quickly as if we were wasting her time. After the brief encounter with the builders, we decided this wasn't the place for us.

Later in the week, we received a call from the same builders in Painesville, telling us they would like to show us the homes again. The woman on the phone was the same woman that showed us the model home. She kindly told us she didn't think we were serious about buying a home, and she said that last week they were visited by the NAACP. She also told us that she thought we were from the NAACP sent to prove that blacks weren't being welcomed to the new complex. She offered to give us a second viewing.

We declined the offer. If we were treated in this manner, why would we want to live in a place that showed extreme prejudice right from the start? The search for a new home and neighborhood would take more time than I expected, as we searched for many more months only to find poor quality in the freshly built homes and poor representation also.

In 1996 we looked at a new neighborhood in Richmond Heights, and the builders were very friendly. When we entered the model home, I saw a familiar face. A young man greeted us, and it was someone I saw at the local gym every day. He was quite surprised, and so was I as he showed us around his well-built home. He also told us that this was his family's privately owned business, and the Casablanca Builders were a quality outfit. We were very pleased, and he didn't rush us around like the others did. He was very proud of his family product as we spent most of the day viewing different homes that Casablanca built. He was right, and the homes were built very well. That day my wife decided she wanted Casablanca to build our new home. Of course I agreed.

The next year would hold many different new adventures for me and my wife as we worked with Casablanca designing our new home. We picked the plot of land, which was on a cul-de-sac, and our house would be in the very center. We designed the new home from top to bottom, and Rhonda showed very expensive taste but showed a lot of restraint as she tried not to go overboard. She knew just what she wanted, and I sat back and watched until it came to the kitchen. I figured that this would be where I would spend most of my time. Rhonda was a looker and definitely not a cooker.

The house had many ups and downs, with time being on the down side. Sometimes it would look like they were building it quickly, and other times the hole in the ground would sit for a long while with very little progress. Casablanca builders were actually building three or four homes at a time and did all the work equally at each site. In the meantime, we were preparing to sell our first home. It went on the market quickly, and it sold even quicker. We had very little showings, and our home was sold to an iron worker that wanted us out of the home as soon as possible.

Things were beginning to get very hectic as our old home sold faster than our new home was being built. Rhonda had to go to Chicago on business, and we had to move. Suddenly we needed a place to live until our new home was ready. The old house and all our belongings had to be packed and ready to go, and I was the only one to do it with Rhonda away on business.

The next week would prove to be one of the most trying times of my life. I woke up early that morning as Rhonda left for Chicago, and I took Timmy over to the sitter's house. I was at home drinking a cup of coffee looking at all the things in the house—ten years of accumulation. Three floors with furniture, closets full of coats, and everything we owned, to be boxed and moved. I drank my coffee and headed out the door to Willoughby Box Company about eight miles away. I was there as soon as the place opened; they had every kind of box under the sun. I quickly decided what type of box I would need. I ordered fifty boxes, loaded them into my car, and drove home.

I drove up the driveway and emptied the boxes in the garage. I went into the house and turned on the stereo so music filled the house. I started room by room, loading the boxes and labeling each one. It took me about three days to have everything completely boxed and loaded in the garage for moving. The boxes filled up a two-and-a-half garage from top to bottom, with only room enough to walk in the door. When Rhonda came home from the airport, she pulled around back, hitting her garage door opener and seeing all the boxes. She stood in amazement, looking as I walked outside to greet her.

She walked into a practically empty house with only the things needed to stay the night and prepare for moving in the next few days. Our bed stayed intact, and Tim's bed with the television and couch in the living room; everything else was boxed and ready to go. We ate from carry-out for a few nights as we prepared for the moving trucks to arrive in the next couple of days. We called a moving company along with her brothers and my brothers to help with the move. She also found a completely furnished apartment that we rented until we could move into the new house. Moving into our new home would turn out to be one of the most trying times we would ever encounter in all the years of our marriage.

The day of the big move, rain poured down and would not stop for the entire day. That didn't stop us as we moved all the boxes onto the moving trucks. The once clean floors had tennis shoe prints through the entire house, with the kitchen floor taking most of the dirt tracked in from the outside. We continued moving every piece in the house. The two trucks were completely filled with everything we owned, soon to go to a big warehouse for safekeeping until we were ready to move in our brand-new home.

After everything was done, we fed our helpers and headed to the apartment about six miles away to Beachwood. This would be where we would stay for the next six weeks until our new home was ready. Completely exhausted from the long day, we entered the beautiful apartment, which was fully furnished and very clean. We turned on the television, and I picked up Timmy and put him in his room. He was also completely worn out from all the activity that day. We talked a little, wondering what could possibly happen next.

For the next couple of weeks, we lived in the apartment, which was actually kind of nice, no more yard work, no more patching up an older home that had its up and downs. I would miss the place that I worked on daily to make a house into a nice livable home. The only thing we really had to worry about was when we could make the final move to our new home. We would come and go each morning, dropping Tim at Shelia's house in the old neighborhood.

The next thing would be the finance company that we were dealing with. For months I thought they would have all their ducks in a row. What a disaster that turned out to be. This was the final straw; the next series of traumatic events would leave us lifeless, without hope.

The Final Paperwork

We went to work as usual and later in the day went to Orange Village where the finance company was located. We entered the office and sat down and were greeted by a host of financial officers, to discuss the final closing of the house. The house was finally ready for us to move in. The only thing left was the closing details with the finance company. As we looked over the papers and signed about a billion pieces of paper, Rhonda had this puzzled look on her face as she scanned the paperwork. I knew something was wrong by the look on her face. We continued to sign the papers, and the financial officers never gave any indication that something was wrong.

Later on the ride home, Rhonda told me the numbers didn't match up. I said, "They have been working on the project for over six months. This is their business. How could they be wrong?"

We had about a week before we would sign the final papers for our house. On Monday evening, I picked Tim up from Sheila's house and went to the apartment. I began making dinner while Tim watched television, waiting for Rhonda to come from work. I received a call from the finance company, telling me that the final figures for closing were incorrect. Somehow they had made a six-thousand-dollar mistake, and before they could turn over the keys to our new home, we would have to come up with the money. I asked them how such a mistake could be made when this was their business. No matter how angry I got, they said the payment would have to be made. I hung up the phone, thinking of how Rhonda would feel when I told her the news, and also thinking how could we come up with that kind of money in such a short period of time. I sat next to Timmy on the couch with the feeling of defeat; I picked up the phone to call Rhonda on her cell phone.

She answered her cell phone, and I told her the news. I could hear the despair in her voice. Finally we were delivered a blow that sent us both into a panic. How could we come up with six thousand dollars in about four short days? After all the hard work and effort we put into building what was a dream come true, all our money was tied up in building the home. What was once a dream come true turned into one of the worst nightmares staring us right in the face. We could stand to lose everything and still be out of our new home until six thousand dollars would magically appear and fall in our laps.

Rhonda finally entered the apartment, and we stood in silence, wondering what to do next. She took a seat between Timmy and me on the couch, with her head hung low from a hard day at work, only to come home to an unsolvable costly mistake that we had no control over. She slowly began to work our next move. I wanted to sue the finance company, but we both knew that would only tie up our house in the court systems and turn six thousand dollars into a much larger amount of money that we didn't have. Somehow we would have to pay the fee.

Rhonda was upset and called her mother and talked for what seemed like hours. When she hung up the phone, she told me her mother would give us the money to close on the house. My mother-in-law was a financial genius. She was very frugal with her money, and by the grace of God, she had enough money to help us out. I agreed, on one condition that we would pay her back as soon as possible. With only two days left, we went to the finance company and made the payment as they reworked the papers. Later in the evening, the finance company called and told us to come in tomorrow to get the keys to our new home. We looked at each other as tears began to flow from our eyes. This was a special moment that we would always remember, and we knelt down with Timmy between us, holding our hands as we said a prayer of thanks. This was truly a blessed day. Once again, through God all things were possible.

We moved into our new home on the weekend without incident. We had champagne and a big cake with our families that evening. Once again thanking the Lord and asking him to bless our new home, we all joined hands and prayed as one big happy family. That night after putting Timmy to bed in his new room, we sat on the couch discussing all the things to come in the next few weeks. I looked around thinking about how each box had to be unpacked and all our possessions had to be put in their proper place. We were very tired after a late evening, putting together only the things needed for the night.

We went upstairs to our empty room, with our bed ready for sleeping in the middle of the room. Our heads hit the soft down-filled pillows as we listened to the pure silence of the night and slept through the calm night, with the night air softly blowing across the room. A feeling of great accomplishment touched my soul as I looked at my wife, thinking what a wonderful woman she was and how well we were together. She was sound asleep, and I wasn't far behind as I drifted off to sleep.

Making a House a Home

The next morning came quickly, and we woke up early in the morning, starting off with a big breakfast from McDonalds, which was less than a quarter mile away, practically in our backyard. We ate and started unpacking boxes, going from room to room, putting things in their proper place. For the next couple of months, we unpacked box after box; and to this day, we still have pieces to the puzzle that remained in boxes. We soon learned that a new home didn't come with all the things needed for day-to-day living like towel racks, soap dishes, toilet paper holders, mirrors, and many other things that you just assume are supposed to be there.

Our big appliances began to show up and put in their proper place. Some things were just perfect and fit like a glove. On the other hand, when our refrigerator arrived we tried to slide it into the spot in the kitchen. I had to remove some molding from the wall before I squeezed it into the very tight spot. The gas fireplace had piping and the burner setting in its space just waiting to be put together. I had no idea how to tackle this project. I went down the street, seeing a couple of Amish guys working on a house. I asked them if they might be interested in making a few extra dollars on their lunch break. I told them about the fireplace, and one of the guys walked to my house with me.

In less than fifteen minutes, the piping for the fireplace was in working order. I asked him how much I owed him. He smiled and looked at the cake on the kitchen table and kindly asked for a piece of cake and some milk. He said that would be a fair payment. I cut the sheet cake in half and gave him a gallon of milk, telling him to share it with his buddies. He was very happy and walked out the door with a big smile on his face and plenty of cake and milk to share with his coworkers.

For the next couple of months, we managed to put all the things in order, and the interior of our new home was beginning to take shape. We put things together and bought household items almost every day. We didn't have much money for a while but managed to make things work. I bargained with every worker that came to the house. They all seemed to want something other than money or added a little extra as I talked to them with kind words and helping them.

The cable television guy was the most impossible to deal with as he missed several appointments and never bothered to call. Finally after about three weeks, he walked up the driveway. He had a style all his own, with long hair and a tool belt slung low around his waist. The guy looked like someone from a rock band.

He entered the house, and I was already in a bad mood waiting for two hours for him to show up. He was real cool as he pulled a twelve-way splitter out of his tool pouch and offered to put cable lines in every room in the house for an extra twenty dollars. I agreed, and he was happy as he put the fresh twenty dollar bill in his pocket. I knew the cable company would never know about the extra money or the splitter he installed. Within the hour he was gone, and we scanned the television with all the new channels we had.

Mrs. Ann Lukek,
One Fine Neighbor

Waking up and walking around my unfinished yard of rocks, hard clay, and weeds, thinking of all the hard work that was ahead of me, I saw an old woman, who lived directly behind my next-door neighbor's house, walk across the barren land. She looked to be about eighty years old; in her right hand, she held a fancy plate with a white doily and some old-style German passel cookies on it. She told me her name was Ann Lukek. She pointed to her house as she handed me the cookies.

Timmy came running through the backyard, and as she spoke to him, I could see the delight in her eyes. He was just as excited as they talked like she was his long-lost grandmother as he ate one of the cookies. They were friends for life, and every morning Timmy would wake up and look out the back window. Seeing her, he would beg me to go outside to see her. Little did I know that she would be one of the greatest people that I would ever meet in my life.

Ann Lukek was the salt of the earth. She would bring cookies to the house, and on special occasions give us things from her past such as very old books that provided us with a history of Richmond Heights. She would also bring old coins for the children on their birthdays. She would also bring Rhonda and me gifts from the past. Ann never forgot a birthday or our wedding anniversary. She was a wealth of knowledge, and I listened to her every word as she told me of her deceased husband, who was a soldier in the army. She lived in her house by herself, but she was never alone; each day many neighbors and friends would come over her house to visit. Timmy would spend as much time as possible playing in her yard. She would toss the football at him and sit at her picnic table, eating cookies, laughing with her.

Shortly after we met, she was in her yard cutting grass on her half-acre lot. I offered to help her, but she insisted on cutting the grass herself. She told me that I had enough to do and said this was one of her forms of exercise. I would often see her in the early morning walking for miles. She always had time for my son, and later she would watch my son and daughter while I did my yard work.

After many years of friendship, one morning before work I was outside working on my lawn when I saw her struggling to start her lawn mower. I walked over to her to see what the problem was. She told me there was nothing wrong with the mower, she just didn't have the strength to pull the cord to start it. I started the mower, and as always I offered to cut her grass; and as always she refused to let me help her. I walked back over to my yard as I watched the frail old German woman walk up and down cutting her grass. She threw up her right hand and waved me off again.

There wasn't a thing that I wouldn't do for her, but the only thing she ever asked me to do was help her re-cover her old piano bench. As I tacked down the fabric, she told me what a fine job I was doing. In her basement there were tons of old World War Two tools. She told me her husband had been a mechanic, and he bought a new tool or two every time he got paid. She also told me to take anything I wanted, but I didn't feel right taking anything from her. I just enjoyed her company and her history lessons about the war, her family, and how Richmond Heights came to be. The history and the knowledge I gained from her were worth millions, and later on in life, I would tell her family things about her family that they didn't know.

One bright sunny day I was in my backyard planting flowers when Mrs. Lukek walked over to talk with me. She asked me to sit down with her; she asked me if I had time for a little idle chatter. I knew that with the seriousness in her voice and the look in her eye that it wasn't just idle chatter. Besides that, she never stopped me from doing anything. As the sun beat down on bodies, she began to tell me she had cancer, and she knew that it would be the end of her. She also said she would fight it with her last dying breath. I believed every word she told me.

For the next few years, I watched her slowly fade away as she became thinner and pale-looking but she never let it get her down; and she continued to laugh and play with the children as if nothing was wrong. Ann also attended every Christmas party and family function we had, bringing her homemade cookies and gifts from her past. She would pick up my daughter and say an old German word, "*Vivalaisa.*" Later one I found out that the word meant baby, something that my family would never forget.

As we started our landscaping project, Ann would stop by and with great interest, asked the details of the project, also telling me that she and father planted over three hundred evergreen trees and had livestock that used to be where my house now stands.

For many years, Ann Lukek would continue as if nothing was wrong. Little did I know that Mrs. Lukek would walk to the bus stop to go to the hospital to receive cancer treatments at the hospital. Truly no one knew the strength this old woman had. She would spend hours waiting for the bus to arrive, and she didn't want to be a burden to anyone. I didn't know of the bus trips until after her death.

In the year 2004, Ann would miss the family Christmas party, and I knew things had gotten worse for her. Every year I would shovel a path through the snow in our backyard so she wouldn't have to walk through the two feet of snow.

That year as the entire family gathered at the Christmas party, we said the prayer before the meal and a prayer for our eighty-six-year-old friend.

In the spring of 2005, Rhonda became concerned and sent me over Ann's house. I hesitated to go, but I walked across my backyard in fear of the worse. A middle-aged woman answered the door, and I looked up and asked her if I could see Ann. She told me things were bad, and Mrs. Lukek was resting in her bed. She told me I couldn't come in. I looked the woman in the eye and said, "You don't understand, I have to see her." She must have seen the expression on my face and kindly opened the door for me to enter.

I sat at her bed as she grasped my hand, telling me to take care of my family and she loved us all. She said to me she was dying, and her struggle was over. I felt the tears roll down my cheeks, and she said, "Don't cry for me, I'm going to be with the Lord." And I felt sad, but at the same time, I knew that the Lord would gladly accept this strong God-fearing woman into his kingdom. She sat up for one last time and kissed me on my cheek, saying that she loved me and my family, I kissed her on the cheek and asked the Lord to be merciful as she fell back to sleep. I thanked the woman who had let me in, and without a word spoken, she knew what it meant for Mrs. Lukek and me to see each other one last time.

I slowly walked across my backyard saying a prayer for her; I also knew I would have to tell my family. I sat outside on my deck for a long time. Rhonda came outside and sat with me as I told her the news. We both knew that this would be a devastating blow for our children. This would be the first time they would have to deal with losing someone closer than any family member. Ann Lukek was someone who was in their lives every day, and they expected her to be around as long as they were around.

As I came into the house, I knew what had to be done. Death was a part of life, and it literally tore me up to tell them. Victoria, Timmy, and their Cousin Tyler were gathered on the couch. We told them that we didn't think Mrs. Lukek would make it through another night and that she would be in heaven with God, and no one wanted to see her suffer anymore; God wanted her in heaven.

Victoria was about four years old, and she didn't understand, but she began to cry; and she yelled, "Dad, she is my best friend in the world. I don't want her to go. You tell God to take someone else. Dad, do something!"

Timmy put a pillow over his head, and Tyler sat in silence with tears rolling down his cheeks. They all knew her and loved her, and I explained that there was nothing I could do, as Rhonda held Timmy's hand and hugged Victoria closely. I sat next to Tyler with my arm around him. The rest of the night was very still and silent, and we took them to their bedrooms. We all knelt down and said our prayers, asking the Lord to take care of our friend.

Mrs. Lukek lived for a few more nights and died one morning. We watched her family come to the house; they had driven from Florida. I walked across the backyard and greeted them; we knew each other because they had visited before.

I talked to her nephew, who was a well-dressed business man at least ten years older than me. I told the family of all the things she had done for my family. I also told them some of the things about their family Ann told me. I knew their story better than they did, and they thanked me for the memories. They also knew everything about my family. Mrs. Lukek had talked to them about all the great times we had together.

We went to the funeral, and I said a few kind words about her, and what a blessing it was to know her; and before I could sit down, Timmy stood by my side as he told his most fondest memory of her. He stood proud in his best suit, telling how he came home, and no one was home. How he walked across the backyard and knocked on her back door. He told everyone how they spent the day as she gave him something to eat, and how they laughed and ate lunch together. By the time he was finished, I don't think there was a dry eye in the entire place. I felt proud of my son as he spoke telling how he would miss her, and the family could see Ann Lukek spent the later years of her life with more love than anyone could ask for. She also gave more love to my family than we could ask for.

Later in the week, Ann's nephew walked through the backyard handing me three envelopes for Tyler, Tim, and Victoria. Each envelope contained a letter from her with what little money she had left in the world. The letters told them how much she loved them and some of the memories of them being together. We kept all the letters she wrote us; and from time to time, we read them, refreshing the memories in our minds of all the things she done with us. Each Christmas we say a prayer with our entire family and friends celebrating the time we spent together. God puts people in strange places, and I believe her strength and wisdom live on in my family today.

The Landscape Project

Things began to slow down, and as soon as we completed one project, another one would be started. Rhonda got very tired of cleaning the floors due to our entire yard consisting of mud, rocks, and weeds. The next step was calling a good friend from our old neighborhood; John Polito owned his own landscaping business and was up to the task of making us a beautiful green yard. John was a man of many talents. Not only did he do our landscaping, but he also put in an underground sprinkler system, deck, gazebo, and a small ornamental fish pond. He also worked a deal with our neighbor, putting in our back lawn and our neighbor's back lawn at the same time. He worked out well, and we never called another landscaper. To this day, he remains a loyal friend and is still called upon for minor details with my yard.

Timmy's Little Sister

One evening Rhonda sat down with her two men and told us we were going to have another baby. Timmy was excited and hoping he would have a little brother. We soon found out that the baby wasn't going to be a boy. I believe the news of a daughter made me the happiest in the family, and as before it wasn't going to be easy. Why did I expect anything different? As a family, we went to the doctor's office to be told that there were many complications. Rhonda was suffering from pregnancy-induced high blood pressure and something called toxemia, which had something to do with toxins in the blood.

The pregnancy wasn't going well, and every day closer to child birth was a blessing as we prayed every day for our little girl. After a series of tests, the doctors told us that the baby wouldn't go to full term as her condition had gotten worse. Rhonda was about six months pregnant and confined to her bed only allowed to get out of bed for bathroom breaks and doctor's visits. I stayed by her side as much as possible. When I went to work, her mother would take over guard duty. We were in constant fear of the unknown, and the doctors were straightforward with what could happen, and the bad news outweighed the good news. I really can't recall any good news at all.

On one particular day, Rhonda and I went for a routine ultrasound at the doctor's office. The checkup took longer than usual. After the test was completed, we were escorted to a room to speak to the specialist. Sitting in the cold room with no windows, waiting for the doctor to arrive, it was as if the outside world didn't exist. The doctor finally showed up, taking a seat at his desk. The seriousness in his eyes and his demeanor sent a cold chill through my entire body as I held my wife's hand firmly. This wasn't our first ride on the merry-go-round, and we discussed with each other that whatever happened or the doctors said, we were willing to accept; it was God's will, and we would love our child no matter what happened.

The young doctor began to tell us that due to my wife's condition, they would induce labor the very next day. He also told us the baby was a little over three pounds, and her lungs weren't fully developed, which would complicate things more. We listened very intently as he told us all the things that could happen. He also told Rhonda that she would have to stay at the hospital to be watched. She asked the doctor if she could go home to tell our little boy why mommy wouldn't be coming home; Timmy was almost four years old and didn't like the cold feel of hospitals.

The doctor paused for a moment. "Mr. and Mrs. Lowe, I'm afraid you don't understand. Mrs. Lowe, with your high blood pressure, you could die on the way home. That's why you can't leave."

At that moment, my world went into a tailspin, and I tried not to show my feelings; but my wife and I had just been told the worst-case scenario. The room was silent as the doctor calmly got up from his chair and left the room. We waited in the office as they prepared a room for Rhonda. I couldn't believe this was happening as Rhonda put on the hospital gown in the cold white sanitary room with one bed and a television. She cried as I left the room, promising her a call from little Timmy. I felt great despair as I prepared myself for the lonely ride home, which was only six miles away but seemed like eternity.

I drove to our house, and my mother-in-law sat on the couch as I explained in detail what the doctors told us. She was in complete shock when I entered the room without her daughter. Timmy was in his room sleeping. When Rhonda's mother left, I sat on the couch thinking of all the things that happened that day; and for the first time in our marriage, I felt all alone. I turned off the television and got down on my hands and knees to pray and pray and pray and pray. With a huge lump in my throat and a sick feeling in my stomach, I prayed. I got up and went upstairs and sat in Timmy's room, watching him sleep as I sat silently in the big rocking chair my mother bought us to rock him to sleep. The sun went down, and Timmy was finally awake, and the first words from his tiny little mouth were, "Where's Mommy?"

I took Timmy downstairs and started making dinner; he had a puzzled look on his face, knowing I owed him an explanation. And again I heard the tiny little voice say, "Where's Mommy?" It wasn't as if I was avoiding the question, but finding the right words to tell a three-and-a-half-year-old his mommy was in the hospital, trying not to alarm him. I reached for the phone as I explained that his mommy was in the hospital getting ready to bring his sister into the world.

We called the hospital, and Rhonda did all the explaining for me. She always had the right words to make him feel comfortable with whatever was happening. Timmy hung up the phone, asking me if he could see his new sister tomorrow, and could he sleep in my bed because he knew I missed his mommy. I smiled at him, telling him I needed him to help me make it through the night. He assured me everything was going to be all right, and somehow I actually believed him.

Timmy finally drifted off to sleep, and I lay their staring at the ceiling, actually speaking to God in my mind, asking him to give me strength and protect my wife and unborn child. I went downstairs and looked out the front window of our beautiful home meant for a complete family, which to me included a wife and children. I picked up the phone and called my mother, telling her that I couldn't live without Rhonda and how my whole world was caving in. The doctor told me I might have to choose my wife's life or the baby's life. How could this decision be made by any husband or father? I cried uncontrollably as my mother could hear my voice trembling as I gave her the details. She listened, and just like little Timmy, my mother could always find the right words to calm her once little Timmy.

Asking God for One More Miracle

The next day came quickly, and it was a very restless night for me. I never really went to sleep, just thinking of all the things that could happen. I never considered myself lucky, so why should it start now. I really didn't know how lucky I was; if you think about all the hardships in my life, I was the luckiest man on earth cheating the devil from one more soul to add to his collection. I had been truly blessed by God who gave me a second chance at life, taking me to this point. As usual I was asking God for one more favor; and as usual it was just one more favor. I prayed the entire night as I watched my little boy sleeping peacefully beside me.

I fed Timmy and packed a few of his things; we got in the car and drove over his grandma's house. I entered my mother-in-law's house, and she hugged me and told me everything was going to be all right. Timmy was in for a long stay at his grandma's house, and I was in for even a longer stay at the hospital. I kissed Timmy good-bye, telling him he would soon have a little sister. I drove down the street; and before I knew it, I was at the light, ready to make the right turn into the hospital parking lot. Time has a funny way of slipping away when your mind is full of thought.

The Parking Space

I drove up and down each side of the parking lot, looking for a space. The entire lot was full. I watched an old couple move their car, and I turned into the available space. Just as I was about to get out of my truck, a stout older man knocked on my window. He told me to move my truck because he had been waiting at the end of the parking lot for about an hour for the next space. I told him in so many words to get lost, which only infuriated him more. He told me to move my truck, or he would move it for me. I was thinking this guy must be crazy, and I wasn't going to move my truck.

I reached for my cell phone and called the police. He knocked on my window, telling me to get out of the truck so he could whip my ass. I was getting madder by the second, and I was just about to get out of my truck and do battle with this idiot. When I thought about what was happening, and my wife inside ready to have our child, would I be inside the hospital watching my daughter being born, or in jail for beating the crap out of some fool over a stupid parking space?

It took every ounce of restraint in my body, but I started up my truck and moved out of the parking space, never looking back. To top it off, the hospital had a huge empty parking garage with six floors; I drove over to it and parked my truck on the top level, hoping I wouldn't run into any more idiots.

I walked into the hospital hoping not to see the same guy that was in the parking lot looking for a parking space; I shook my head and waited for the elevator. As I was waiting, the same moron came in the hospital, screaming and yelling at me, calling me a nigger, telling me he was going to whip my ass. I just stood there in total disbelief; then security showed up and handcuffed him, taking him out to the police car in the parking lot. The elevator arrived, and I stepped inside, wondering what in the hell just happened.

I entered the room where Rhonda was in the bed waiting. She said, "What took you so long?"

I said I had trouble finding a parking space. She had a puzzled look on her face; later I would explain the whole crazy thing to her. Right then my only concern was her and the baby inside her. This was the calm before the storm as we talked quietly as if it were just a normal day. We both knew that wasn't the case at all as the nurses did blood pressure checks and IV work.

The Team of Experts

The nurses made sure Rhonda was comfortable. With good bedside manners, they made sure that we knew step by step what was going on. In all my concentration, as I focused on what was about to take place, I failed to realize that one of nurses waiting on us hand and foot was Orella Delgado, the wife of Mike Delgado, a close friend of mine who was a fellow officer at work hired on the same day I was. Orella Delgado was one of the nurses at the birth of our son; it seemed very strange she would help with the birth of our daughter. I believe she was our guardian angel. As I said before, the Lord works in mysterious ways, and life is one big circle. As she swiftly moved around the room, she called me Tim, and I finally realized who she was. She was a blessing in disguise, and I felt very confident after talking to her. The Lord sent in the first string of medical people, and to top it off, after a couple of hours of preparation, my mother entered the room.

As my mother spoke to Rhonda and me, contractions were coming closer and closer. The nurses began to gain sense of urgency, and my mother and I watched in anticipation. The nurse left the room and told us we had a little while before anything happened. My mother watched Rhonda with a trained eye. She had been a pediatric nurse for over twenty years, and she knew it wouldn't be long. She told me to call the nurse back. The drugs that induced labor were in full force. Rhonda began to feel the pains of childbirth as she let out a painful small scream. The nurses rushed into the room, and we were on our way to the room prepared for delivering babies. With my mother right by my side, we were all in the room with the nurses and the doctor en route.

Victoria's Early
Entry to the World

We weren't in the room long, about ten minutes. The nurses were preparing everything for the doctor, and I held Rhonda's hand as she winced in pain again. I guess our daughter didn't want to wait for anybody, and before anyone knew anything, our daughter entered the world and into my waiting arms. I literally caught her as she arrived with my mother standing beside me, watching. One of the nurses turned around. To her surprise, I was holding our daughter.

She was under a foot long and weighed only three pounds and three ounces. I held her tiny body in my arms; she was so small it was like holding a tiny doll only the length of my forearm and her head smaller than my fist. Our daughter entered the world after only developing only a short seven and a half months.

The nurse took the small baby, cleaning her off and making sure she was breathing. She let out a tiny scream, letting everyone know she was alive and well. The doctor entered the room, taking the baby into her arms and making sure the young preemie showed all the signs of survival. I cut the umbilical cord separating her from her mother. Besides being so tiny, she was perfectly healthy. She was put in a fully enclosed incubator and taken to a room for further analysis.

Rhonda was doing well as the nurses checked her vital signs. I was very fortunate to have my mother witness the birth of her granddaughter; and the world seemed perfect with mom, wife, and new daughter, Victoria Alyse Lowe, born on September 23, 1998. As for the name Victoria, depending on who you talk to, as for her mother it meant victory. I will tell you I picked that name because every Victoria I knew in the world was a strong-willed forceful woman, and I wanted my daughter to be just that. Anyway the next few months would be hard for my family, and we had to join together praying for our preemie, asking the Lord to put his arms around her and help her grow in to a normal baby mentally and physically.

The Long Hospital Stay

Rhonda rested in the hospital for the next few days; Timmy and I would come and visit her and Victoria. He wondered when they would be allowed to come home, and so did I. This was a very trying time. Rhonda would leave the hospital, but as for Victoria, she would remain in a room with about half a dozen premature babies under constant observation. Mothers were allowed to come in daily to breast-feed their tiny babies. Mother's milk was one of the major things to fatten them up.

I believe this was among one of the hardest things in our lives. Young Timmy not understanding why his little sister wasn't home with her family, Rhonda leaving her baby in the hospital. As she would go home, she felt an empty feeling longing for her daughter. She would spend many sleepless nights worrying about her tiny daughter. As for me, I tried to be the glue that held us together. I hid my feelings and tried to remain strong, telling my family to keep praying. Each night we would join together praying for Victoria to come home. I also spent many sleepless nights wondering if she would be a normal child. Before she was born, the doctors warned us of all the things that happened to a baby that didn't go to the full term of the pregnancy. Just like Rhonda, I prayed for our daughter every waking moment and longed for the day she would go home with her family.

We would go to the hospital every day and stay for extended periods of time as Rhonda breast-fed the baby. The nurses were very helpful as they explained in detail Victoria's progress. I learned a lot about preemies and often prayed for all the babies in the room. Victoria looked like a little featherless bird just hatching from an egg. I looked at her belly button poking out of her stomach, curiously asking one of the nurses about it being an outie. The nurse told my Victoria didn't have enough body fat, so her belly button would remain an outie until she fattened up, and then it would be an innie. Each day was a lesson, things that only parents with premature children would know. This is the case in life that if it affects you, learn as much as you can to help deal with the problem; knowledge is power.

For the next four to six weeks, we would go to the hospital every day, watching little Victoria grow, waiting for the day they would release her. The nurses said she was a strong little fighter, and she was always the one making the most noise out of all the little preemies. She was getting stronger and bigger every day; I would often walk around the room looking at all the doll-sized babies.

After a few weeks, things were getting better. We got to know the nurses well as they would see us and give a progress report daily. As Rhonda would go into a private room to nurse Victoria, I would often see other parents taking care of their children. I met an Indian guy, a first-time father who had preemie quadruplets. He watched little Timmy run around the room and asked me for advice on how to be a good father. I told him with the four new children he had, my advice for him was to go home and get plenty of sleep; I couldn't imagine dealing with four newborns at the same time.

As I walked around the room, I noticed one of the babies lying very still in the incubator. He was a lot bigger than the rest of the babies; he was bigger than any newborn. He never moved or cried every time I came for a visit. My curiosity finally got the better of me, and I asked the head nurse what was wrong with him. She told me the twelve-pound baby boy had problems being born because he was so big, and they didn't know if the complications of lack of oxygen and other problems while being born hurt the chances for the big boy to lead a normal life. The nurse also told me that the father never came to see the boy; he was going through problems dealing with all the things that happened to what was supposed to be a big healthy baby boy.

I looked down at the nameplate on the incubator; his name was Chad. When Chad's mother wasn't there, I would often stand over the big boy, thinking about him and his parents and all the things they were going to go through raising him. I said many a prayer asking the Lord to help this baby lead a normal life and to help his parents and family. I couldn't imagine being one of the parents thinking everything was going right, and life throws you a big curve. I thought of my little girl getting healthier every day and a 99.9 percent chance for a normal life, soon we would be taking her home.

The Homecoming

Finally, after weeks of going to the hospital to visit our daughter, she gained a couple of ounces, which brought her up to a whopping three pounds and 13 ounces. We were allowed to take her home; she showed no signs of any problems. The hospital provided her with a special car seat, which she would be in a lying position; she wasn't strong enough to sit up yet. The hospital also supplied us with diapers for preemies until she reached normal size; the stores didn't carry diapers for preemies due to demand being so low.

Victoria came home just days before her mother's birthday, which was on October 21. She spent a little more than a month at the hospital; she was born on September 23. For the first time, my family was whole, and this would be one of the best birthdays for her mother. We felt truly blessed and continued to pray for all the babies still in the hospital under special care.

As we loaded up the family truck, the nurses came outside to witness the event and wished us well. One of the nurses said, "We will continue to pray for your daughter." I looked back at the door with all the nurses standing there.

I paused for a moment, thinking how the Lord had truly blessed my family, and I was taking my daughter home. As I looked at the nursing staff, I said, "Thank you for your prayers. Please say your prayers for those less fortunate than this family. Say your prayers for Chad and his family." As we drove off, I looked in the rearview mirror at what would be an everlasting memory: the hospital, the nurses, and all the babies fighting for life.

For the next couple of months, Victoria would continue to grow bigger and stronger without any problems. After a couple of months, she was a normal-size baby, and we no longer needed the special car seat from the hospital. We filled the car seat full of candy and returned it to the hospital. My family and I went back to the special care unit to return the car seat. We brought Victoria in so the nurses could see how big she was.

I peeked in the room full of new preemies and couldn't believe that only months ago, we were in that very room. Victoria looked like a giant compared to all the newborn preemies. We no longer needed the special diapers the hospital provided. As we left the hospital, I thought of Chad and said a silent prayer for him and his family, wondering how he was doing. I would never see Chad again, but as I scan through pictures of Victoria, I always think of Chad and say a prayer for him and his family.

Learning How to Be a Father

The freedom we once had of traveling light disappeared; what used to take less than an hour preparing to go out would now be a big event. Women would naturally take longer getting ready, but mothers would take hours. We had two car seats, and we packed a diaper bag and toys to keep Timmy occupied. While Rhonda was upstairs getting ready, I would pack bottles, diapers, and everything else we needed. I would often spend most of my time getting Timmy ready to go out.

Now depending on whom you ask, my wife or me, the story would be told differently. I am sure after she reads this, she will have a completely different view on the whole affair. If you really want the truth, you can ask my children; they are at the age of tell-all now. I'm quite sure their story will be close to mine. I would put two children in car seats and open the garage, pull the family truck outside, and wait for my queen to arrive. Sometimes fifteen to twenty minutes later, she would be ready to go.

All the fathers with small children can relate to what I am saying. Often we would go places, and I would drop them off at the door. It was like being at a loading dock. I would put on the flashers, and it didn't matter if it was raining or snowing: my wife would stand underneath a nice dry shelter, and I would hand off the car seats with kids strapped in them, put blankets over their tiny faces, carefully not exposing them to any type of adverse weather conditions. Rain would trickle down my back or snow, and wind would chill me to the bone while I unpacked the truck. Once everyone was inside, I would search the parking lot for a space. Sometimes I would have to walk from Egypt exposing myself to what Mother Nature had in store that day. Once inside I joined my family, sitting in wet clothes or freezing to death as we waited for our food.

The best is yet to come. When the food finally arrived piping hot, we would say our blessing, and everyone was about to eat. Timmy, being a little boy around five years old, was my responsibility. I would take two bites of the food, and he would say he had to go to the bathroom. I would get up from the hot meal and take him to the bathroom, which would take about a good ten minutes depending on number one or number two, then come back from the bathroom and sit down at the table to the cold meal. Rhonda would be halfway through her meal as she held Victoria comfortably in her arms.

I even tried to beat the game by taking Timmy to the bathroom before the meal arrived, but he would say he didn't have to go. But soon as the hot food arrived, it would be the sign for his potty break. After paying for the meal and tipping the waitress, I had the joy of repeating the whole process of the parking lot detail again. The absolute joy of being a father—I wondered how many years this would last.

Visiting Family

For a few years, things were pretty normal. I would often take my children to my grandfather's house and sit with him for a couple of hours. His health was failing him, and I wanted my children to know their great-grandfather. He would smoke cigarettes and suck on his oxygen before or after he would smoke, and eat eggs and bacon every morning—all the things the doctors told him not to do. The old man was pretty lucid as he talked to me about my job and asked me how my wife was doing. He would give me advice and tell me to hang in there. He knew how important a good job was to a family man. Rhonda would visit my grandfather. She enjoyed his company, and he knew she was a good woman.

His days weren't long for this world. He was eighty-four years old, dying from a lung disease due to smoking, and his wife, my grandmother, died at the age seventy-eight of Alzheimer's disease many years before. My grandfather would always have a story to tell, and I learned many lessons from him. Before I got to this point, I remember him telling me I was a piece of shit, just like my father. I gained his respect many years after, and before he died, he told me I was a pretty good piece of shit!

He also knew that I was doing things right, and I got my work ethics from him and my stepfather Big John. The day he died I was at peace because I could hold my head up high and look him in the eye, and I thank the Lord for letting him see that I was going in the right direction. He told me he was proud of me, and I had all a righteous man could ask for: a good wife, two fine children, and a decent job.

As all families have, we had our share of tragedies. Rhonda's aunt went into the hospital after taking a fall and passed away days later. Aunt Retha was a good woman and always had a kind word for everyone. She would be sadly missed by all family members; I had the pleasure of knowing her for a few memorable years before her passing. Her daughter Michelle would carry on family traditions, and often I see a lot of her mother in her when she comes to visit. I often say a prayer for her mother. I could still see her sitting at our table, laughing and joking with all the family members. Life teaches you a valuable lesson; cherish the times spent with all your loved ones, they might not be around tomorrow as they join God's army in heaven.

The family would suffer another tragedy with Rhonda's Aunt Wenzel, who was diagnosed with colon cancer, her older sister having passed away only months before. Aunt Wenzel was a tough woman who was known for telling it like it is.

I had the pleasure of knowing her for a short time when I married my wife. We watched her condition worsen as the months passed by. Aunt Wenzel told me I must be very special because I had her first son's name and her youngest son's name for my middle name. For the first time in my life, I was proud of my name Fred Timothy.

Aunt Wenzel had four children, two boys and two girls, and they were all good people; she raised them well. Our families meshed very well together. My younger brother, Danny, dated one of Aunt Wenzel's daughters, Lisa. When the two families got together, a good time was had by all. Both aunts were loved by all, and when the families get together, we join in prayer to remember all the ones who aren't with us anymore. My children had a short time with some of these family members and sometimes surprise me with how much they remember.

Brothers

Soon my younger brother, Danny, would get married; and for the first time in our lives, my brother and I would have one of the biggest disagreements in our lives. For a long time, we weren't as close as we were growing up, and we tried to patch things up. But finding the right words were too difficult for both of us. We tried to be one big happy family, but there was always something in the background, and we both felt it when we got together. While we were having our problems, my older brother, Bill, was getting a divorce after years of marriage and two children. I'm sure other families went through trying times, and we were no different. The love was still there, and whatever was done in the dark would come to the light of day.

My brother Danny and his wife would have a son together, a few years earlier than me and my wife. His wife also had a teenage son from a previous marriage. For many years, it seemed as if they were happy together until she decided they needed to go their separate ways. Danny would go through one of the nastiest divorces in history. She was meaner than a rattlesnake, but she didn't count on Danny being meaner than a whole nest of rattlesnakes. As always the children would suffer; my nephew Tyler and his older stepbrother were thrown in the mix.

My brother would go to jail for a trumped-up charge of domestic violence, and his entire house was stripped of every ounce of furniture and anything else useful. He managed to keep his son Tyler, which was a true blessing for all of us. After many thousands of dollars to the court systems, they were finally divorced; but it was far from over, it's still an ongoing battle today.

Tyler's Turmoil

One fine afternoon after a hard workout in my basement, I ran upstairs to take a shower before I went to work. Timmy called me while I was getting dressed. I ran down the steps and found Tyler sitting at the kitchen table, crying and upset. He told me his mother was outside. Before I went to the door, I reassured him everything would be all right. I opened the front door, and she was standing beside her new car screaming she had enough and she was through with her son Tyler.

I told her that she did a good thing bringing him to my house. I also said, "If you're leaving him with me, do me a favor and don't come back."

She said, "No problem," and backed her car out of the driveway as fast as she could, peeling rubber and moving like a bat out of hell.

I went inside and talked to my nephew, who was about eleven years old and more of a man than most. He explained that he had wanted to spend Mother's Day with his mom and treating her special. Tyler went to her apartment building to spend the day with her. He met her at the door, and her friends were in the apartment smoking dope and drinking. He was very disappointed as she told him to do her laundry while she was with her friends. Tyler put up such a fuss that she put him in the car and brought him to my house. He also explained that just last week he was given and award at school from D.A.R.E, the drug abuse restriction education organization. He was very smart and decided he didn't want to be with his mom and her friends while they were indulging in the very thing he was dead set against.

I called my brother and told him what happened and that Tyler was with me and my children at my house. Danny knew that Tyler was in a very safe place. Rhonda and I would take good care of him while he was at work. That day Tyler was very comfortable playing with Tim and Victoria. Tim was very happy that his older cousin was with him. He worshiped the ground Tyler walked on.

For the next couple of years while Danny was at work, Tyler would stay at our home. Rhonda treated him just like our son, and she said that no child would be left alone while we had a place to stay. Of course, things weren't always good as the two boys tried to establish which one was the man of the house. I would often come home to find two boys ready to do battle and Rhonda in the middle of it. We would have our ups and downs like every family, but there was a lot of good that came from this relationship.

Danny and I became close again, and we made up for lost time. We amused our children with stories of our childhood and laughed at all the things we thought were insignificant when we were growing up. Once again the Lord blessed me by bringing back my brother and adding my nephew to my home, also for an understanding wife who dealt with a new son in the family. Tyler considered Rhonda to be his mother figure for the time being.

The following year on Tyler's birthday, we received an unexpected visitor at our door while the family celebrated his birthday with cake and ice cream. His mother showed up at our door. Tyler was downstairs trying some new gifts that his father had bought him; Danny was at work at the time. I was surprised to see her standing at my door with gifts for her son. I yelled to Tyler from the top of the stairs, telling him his mother was at the door to see him. He yelled back that he didn't want to see her and said if she had anything for him, to leave it or take it back with her.

She was very upset, and Rhonda and I stood at the door, not knowing what to say as she handed the gifts to me. I could see the tears rolling down her cheeks; she said good-bye with her head hung low as she got in her car. Rhonda said she felt very sorry for her, and even though we weren't always on the best of terms, I also felt very sad for her. I remember the day my own father walked out of our lives, and I still wonder how he felt. Later I would talk to Tyler, and he said that his Aunt Rhonda was the closest thing to a mother he had.

My wife and I agreed that we would say our prayers for her; and when we would get on our knees at night with Tyler and our children, we always included her in our prayers, saying her name out loud so that Tyler could hear us. It's easy to say prayers for loved ones but hard to say prayers for the ones who really needed it.

As my children and nephew grew older, we would explain to them that things didn't always go the way you wanted them to and you must make the best out of situations that you had no control over. A little knowledge goes a long way when you channel it in the right direction. I would often talk about the good things Tyler's mother did and also explain it in a way that might make them understand life a little more. We were a good, God-fearing family, and we tried to teach our children that life was too short for hate. We taught them that there was good in all people, and you just might have to dig a little deeper to find it in some people.

My Uncle Dennis

Soon the family would face another tragedy. My Uncle Dennis was in the hospital. My mother called me one morning before work and gave me the news. Dennis was one of my mother's younger brothers. He was a hard man that lived a hard life. He was drafted by the Marine Corp during the Vietnam War in 1969. After he served his time, he had small-time jobs that never amounted to anything. He would spend most of his time with the party people at the top of my street. Dennis would use drugs and drink continuously in order to dissolve bad memories of his past; he had a son and beautiful wife. I believe his demise was when he got a divorce from his wife and was only able to see his son when the courts allowed it.

Dennis was always fun to be around, and we spent many days fishing with him and my grandfather. He was a lover of salmon fishing on the Chagrin River. Dennis was always strong and a well-rounded individual that impressed me with his strength and knowledge of many different things. I will always remember him for all the good things he brought to the world.

After about a week had passed and I finally had a day off work, I planned to go see him at the hospital. I woke up and took a shower preparing to go to the hospital. As I sat in my room putting on my shoes, the phone rang; it was my mother. I wasn't prepared what she told me. My Uncle Dennis had passed away that morning. I was devastated, and I called Rhonda and told her the news. It was finally over, and Dennis would suffer no more; the \lord was merciful. My mother told me before he died he saw a priest and made peace with the Lord.

Dennis will always be remembered in my heart as a great man that I loved. Remembering every detail of the things we did together when I was growing up, I will never forget all the good times we shared together. Each person taught me a few things along the way. Every time I go fishing with my brothers, someone always brings up Dennis's favorite line. As he hooked a big salmon, he would yell, "Tuna," so loud that everyone in the world could hear him. With a huge smile on his face as he splashed down the river and grasping the big fish, raising it high over his head with pride, he was truly the best fisherman on the river.

My Uncle Walter

As I grew older, I would lose many friends; and each time it was no different. It would just destroy me. To me most of them were untimely deaths, some from freaky accidents but most of them were from drugs and alcohol abuse, the very thing that I no longer had any use for. Somehow I was blessed and given a second chance at life.

Later on in life, I would talk to my children and tell them about my childhood and my battle with drugs and alcohol—the battle with good and evil. I would leave nothing out as I prepared them for their journey through life, hoping that I tell them enough so they wouldn't venture down the same road. As they grow a little older each year, I give them more details about the things I did and how I escaped a life of misery, cheating death by staying close to God and listening to good and bad from people that knew what life was all about.

Not long after Dennis's death, his brother Walter would be diagnosed with cancer from Agent Orange, a chemical they used in Vietnam during the war. Walter went to Vietnam in 1969, wartime, and served in the army. He was a tunnel rat, a job for smaller soldiers who would crawl through tunnels that the enemy made for escape and shelter. My mother told me he fought at a battle in the Black Virgin Mountains in Vietnam, crawling through tunnels and commanding the troops.

Walter was one of the most intelligent people I would ever know in my life. I was only nine years old when Walter and Dennis got drafted at the same time to serve our country. After Walter served his time, he got married to a girl from Painesville and moved to California. Walter and his wife drove his 1966 Corvette from Ohio to California and remained there to start a family. Walter became a Los Angeles County Marshall and lived in Englewood. At that time it was a nice place to live; but soon it would be known as one of the toughest places to live in California. Walter and his wife had two children, a boy and a girl who I barely knew because of the distance between us. My Aunt Linda would follow her older brother Walter to live in California after she graduated from high school in 1977. Soon many members of the family would visit California and spend time with Walter and his family.

The news of Walter's illness spread through the family like wildfire. I didn't think my mother could handle any more bad news. Walter's son, Chris, was playing football for the Washington State Huskies. The last time I saw him, he was just a toddler. His older sister, Nichole, was planning her wedding; and her father was too ill to give his daughter away. My Uncle Tony would give Nicole away at her wedding. Her daddy passed away before she got married. My mother didn't make the trip to California to see her brother, but she talked to him and his wife daily. Actually I believe my mother stayed away because she loved her brother, and it would just destroy her seeing him that way.

Walter was someone you just couldn't get enough of, and when he was around, I wanted him to stay around. He would always be thinking, and I would often look at him and say to myself, *I wonder what he is thinking.* I'll never forget the air show we went to; as the jets would fly over our heads, he knew a little something about every aircraft. That year was one of the first times the public got a look at the Harrier jet, and my uncle was really impressed with the new technology of the jet. He had stood in amazement; and as I looked into his eyes, I could tell he was in deep thought, taking in every inch of the plane as if he were building it himself.

Walter had everything to live for, a great wife and two children that I'm sure he was very proud of. To suddenly find out he was dying of cancer from Agent Orange, I can't recall anyone in the family saying he was ever sick. Then again, knowing what type of a person he was, I doubt he ever told anyone until he had to. I cried when he went to Vietnam, and I cried when he left for California, and I cried when I was told of his death. I know if there is such a thing as an angel, Walter would be one of them. Walter lives on in the hearts of the ones he left behind; and as I am writing this story and thinking of all the good times we shared together, with tears in my eyes, I say a prayer knowing he is in a good place with God by his side. Walter was loved by all, and I can't think of anyone that didn't like him that met him. God rest his soul.

09-11-2001, or 911

Life seemed to go on as normal, and many of my old-time partying buddies and classmates passed away in the year 2001. I was still working at the Nuclear Power Plant. I was in my seventeenth year at the plant. My fellow officers and I knew each other better than our own families, putting in as much as seventy-two hours a week at work, and at that time, we could work eighty-four hours a week. Most of us were known as GFLs, which was a term we made up that stood for "guard for life." Nothing really changed at work for many years. But in the year 2001, life as we knew it would be drastically changed as a world event unraveled, which sent the United States and the rest of the world in a complete tailspin.

I was working day shift on September 11, 2001, which was a beautiful sunny clear day. I woke up in the early morning as usual, preparing myself for what was supposed to be a normal day, arriving at work at about five in the morning, getting my gear and sitting down to a normal roll call and joking with my fellow officers before we were given our duties for the day. After being at work for a couple of hours, I was assigned to a post that consisted of sitting in a small guard post designed for tactical purposes. The post had a small thirteen-inch television purchased by all the officers to occupy our time while doing our duties. The television was a controversial issue with the powers that be, but for the time being, we were allowed to have it.

I stepped in the small guard booth and relieved the officer there; as soon as he was gone, I turned on the television. What I perceived as a Bruce Willis movie was on every channel, and I called other guard posts with televisions, conversing with other officers and finding out that the event on the television was actually happening. I looked up to see my supervisor Andy Carle crossing the courtyard. I quickly called him on my radio, and he walked toward my post. We watched in horror at one of the Twin Towers in New York burning with an airplane in flames hanging high on the side of the building. Andy picked up the phone and alerted the security management team in the major building behind us.

Andy and I saw our security manager walking across the road after his daily smoke break. He entered the guard post and peered at the television, and at that time it really didn't register in his mind what was actually taking place. He left the small guard booth, seeming to be unconcerned about the event taking place. He returned in a matter of seconds asking questions and wondering what was going on, to protect the plant. By then, the post was being flooded with calls; and as I looked outside, I saw all the managers outside after their morning meeting.

Andy stayed in the booth, notifying the other security shift supervisor, Larry; and I went outside to talk to the managers. I invited them into the small booth, and they watched in complete silence looking at the Twin Tower burning, and we all stood there as the second Twin Tower was struck by another airplane. The management team exited the booth and went directly to the security manager's office for a meeting.

I sat at the post with Andy watching the entire event taking place. I picked up the phone and called the control room. I spoke to the control room shift supervisor asking him if he was aware of what was happening in New York. He was completely unaware; he went into a complete rage yelling about not being notified of the current situation. He requested me to call him every two minutes for a complete update and also wanted to speak to the security manager.

The only people in the entire nuclear power plant that knew anything were the guards with the small thirteen-inch televisions at their posts. As usual the security officers were always the first to know. We stayed well-informed and talked to each other every second of the day, notifying the powers that be of any situations that we thought would affect the power plant. That day the Internet wasn't working, and the company link to the outside world was a thirty-inch television in two major locations. The company televisions were linked into company information only; no news or current events were on that day. I stayed at the post for sixteen hours that day, providing any information or changes to the control room and the security managers. I was only relieved to go to the bathroom; I had many visitors at the post that day. I was instructed to inform the control room and my superiors of any changes. I also contacted the control room every two minutes for an update.

Later that day, we found out about another plane that crashed in Pennsylvania and had crossed over the Nuclear Power Plant. My wife called, and I told her I didn't know if I was going to be coming home that night. The plant was locked up tight with all nonessential personnel sent home. That was the day the world changed, and what used to be a fairly easy job turned into one of the most difficult jobs on the planet with a new set of rules every day.

For a couple of weeks, there were no airplanes in the skies above. As for the nuclear plant, restricted airspace would be something that would be with us forever, and we would report every airplane that got near the plant. The terrorist attack on the United States changed the world and the security industry forever, and the world we once lived in was gone. Just like all Americans, if you ask them, they can remember in detail what they were doing that day as the terrorist attack took place.

Andy Carle and I will never forget that we were with each other, and to this day we tell new officers what took place at the Nuclear Power Plant on 911 and how we helped prepare the plant. This moment in history will forever be in our memories.

The people at the nuclear power plant that took security as a joke finally realized how important we were. As people would come to work every day, they would give the officers coffee and donuts, thanking them for the job they were doing. For the first time, we were respected, and people rarely gave us any trouble as we conducted our business. They knew the value of highly trained security force, and someday we might be the determining factor between life and death. With that in mind, every officer took the business very seriously. Our training became more intense, and security at the power plant was taken up to the next level and the next level and the next level!!

That following week the country didn't know what to expect next, and the skies were still silent with no airplanes in sight. I had a couple of days off and stayed at home with my children while Rhonda went to work. Timmy was seven years old, and Victoria was about to have her third birthday. Timmy stayed close to me as we watched the news; I looked at him, wondering how much of this affected him.

One morning on the following week after 911, I was in the kitchen, and Timmy was on the couch watching television. We heard a rumble in the sky. The house was literally shaking, and things were falling off the mantel over the fireplace. I thought it was an earthquake. Timmy ran over and grabbed my leg as I looked out the glass patio doors. I saw one of the biggest black airplanes I ever saw in the sky. I had never seen a bigger airplane. It was definitely a military plane. After the plane was out of sight, I sat on the couch with Timmy tucked next to me as close as possible and Victoria in my arms.

Timmy looked up at me and said, "Dad, are we being attacked again?"

I told him no, but I really didn't know what to think as the news station gave word of more soldiers leaving the country, headed for Iraq. We joined hands at that moment, and Timmy held my hand and his baby sister's hand, saying a prayer for the soldiers and their families as we watched our fellow countrymen go off to a foreign land to war, our brothers and sisters sent to protect the lives of all Americans.

Many of my fellow officers were called back to active duty, their jobs put on hold until they returned. Also many new officers would come from the military. These were young men and women, and to them we were considered old men and women. The world would never be the same, and my job would never be the same. Airports and nuclear facilities would hire more security officers; unfortunately as the world got worse, the need for security officers was in very high demand. The pay scale never really changed, and it was very hard to find quality individuals with good training to do the job. The turnover rate throughout the industry was at an all-time high. The security force at The power plant began to see many changes, and we had a revolving-door policy with officers coming and going. I used to know who left, and soon after 911 there were too many to keep track of.

The Marine

In early December with the world still in turmoil and the war effort increasing, I prepared for Christmas as usual despite the long hours at work. I put Christmas lights on the house, and my family and I prepared for our Christmas tradition of listening to Christmas music while putting up the tree. Timmy would be celebrating his eighth birthday on December 9, and Rhonda and I made plans for his birthday party. Soon I would go on vacation until the start of the New Year.

A memory that stays vivid in my mind: Timmy and I were in the mall shopping when he pointed at a soldier walking out of a store. He was very excited and began tugging at my leg, asking me what kind of soldier was he. I looked up to see a very dark slender man walking tall and straight as an arrow with his head held high underneath his stark-white hat. I looked down at my son and said he's a marine. His uniform didn't have a ripple in it anywhere, and he looked like someone you would see in a magazine or on a recruiting poster.

The marine walked into a shoe store, my son following him closely behind as he marveled at the young officer. The marine took a seat on a bench as he waited for his shoes. Timmy took a seat right next to him, almost on top of him. Timmy looked up at him, asking the young man if he was a marine.

The soldier looked down at him and said, "Yes, I'm a marine." The young man could see the excitement in Tim's young eyes as he answered the questions of a very inquisitive eight-year-old. I stood behind both of them keeping a close eye on my son making sure that he was being respectful and not a bother.

Timmy asked him he was in the war. The officer gave him a short yes, and before he could say anything else, Tim was on his next question. "Did things blow up around you and some of your friends get hurt?" The guy had a puzzled look on his face but answered the question, telling my son he had a lot of terrible things happen to him while fighting in the war.

By then the young marine asked my son what his name was. "Tim Lowe Junior," he replied, and the conversation went on for a while; and I dared not to interfere as they seemed to enjoy talking to each other. Timmy called him "sir" and was very respectful, and I was proud of him as I watched. The young officer told Timmy his name was Troy, but my boy remained respectful as he kept calling the young officer "sir." With one swift movement, Timmy stood up and put his arms around the young marine, hugging him and thanking the young man for keeping his family safe and making it safe for everyone to sleep at night.

The young man quickly rose to his feet, taking his hat off and holding his head to the sky. He walked over to me and said, "What are you teaching this kid?"

I told him, "My son watches the news every night and knows what goes on in the world."

The young man told me he finally knew what he was fighting for and that I had a very intelligent boy as he flushed back the tears in his eyes. He took a seat next to Timmy and told him that all his fellow soldiers would know the name of Tim Lowe Junior as he told them the story of a very bright eight-year-old.

Timmy told him that he was with his mother and father every night because of soldiers like him and thanked him again for protecting his family and everyone else in the United States. The soldier hugged my son and then hugged me as he said good-bye.

As we drove home from the mall, I was quiet, and Timmy asked me why I didn't shake the soldier's hand. I looked at him and said, "Son, you made me the proudest father alive today the way you talked to the soldier and making him feel that he was loved and how important his job was."

Timmy said he probably had kids too and didn't get to see them every night like he saw his family every night. I told him about the soldiers of Vietnam and how they were spat on and called "baby killers" when they came home from the war. Timmy sat in silence, and I could see his young mind working as he tried to figure out why people would do such a thing.

I drove down the street. I realized that he was listening and watching everything that went on in the world. As a parent, I realized that my wife and I were doing a lot of right things as parents, and I would bring this story back to work, telling the Vietnam vets and the young military men I worked with. I was proud of the way my son felt about the soldiers, and I just couldn't stop talking about it. Every night before bed, we would say a prayer for the military men and women who fought so bravely to protect this country, and my eight-year-old son was very aware why we prayed for them. This was one of my proudest moments as a father.

My children were growing older, and they would make me proud of them in every sense of the word. My daughter, Victoria, was just four years old and was the apple of my eye. She had a lot of her mother's qualities, and I could tell even at a young age, she would be able to take care of herself. My son was eight years old and was everything a man could want in a son, but most of all he was very much a man for his age.

Keeping an Eye on the Teachers

As my son entered the third grade, a teacher contacted my wife and me, telling us that our son had a learning disability. We took immediate action and contacted a place to have him tested. As it turned out, the people from this place where we had him tested could find nothing wrong with him. We contacted other teachers, and they said that he didn't have any problems, and he was learning faster than any of the other children.

Later on I would find out that the schools receive money from the state for every minority child put through a learning program. I worked with the teacher, and I found out who really had the learning problem. I went to one of the special learning classes only to find all black children in the program. My son was ahead of his class and helped the other children; he was also voted president of his class.

I wonder how many more children the teacher actually held back, in the program that was supposed to help the children. For the next few years, my wife and I watched very closely, and whenever there was a problem at school, we addressed it by going to the school, straight to the source of the problem. As usual it wasn't Timmy with the problem, and we found that it was the teacher. While some teachers would tell us that he was a very good student, others would say that he had problems.

When the report card came out, there was always one teacher that would grade him below average while all the others would grade him well above the rest. I would meet with the teacher and the principal only to find out that the grade on the report card was wrong. The teacher changed the letter grade on the report card. She told me she was mistaken and gave him a grade meant for another student in the class. I made her go over every assignment and test in the class. He received nothing under a B in everything that he done in the class, and some A's. Timmy would come home and tell us what happened every day. He also never missed and assignment, always completing the work on time.

The principal actually told me that some of the staff had a diversity problem, and I was unwilling to let my son fall through the cracks, the very thing that I was a product of. My wife and I spent more time dealing with the teachers than with Timmy. I was once told to keep a close eye on the school system, and to this day, my wife and I are constantly asking our children what went on in school. We would bring Timmy to school with the teacher and the principal all in the same room, discussing any problems.

Each year there would be a new teacher for whom Rhonda and I would go to the school to discuss grades with. Timmy would get an A in the same class the year before, and the following year the letter grade would be a C or D. When I would go to the school and talk to the teacher in front of the principal, somehow the story would change; not one time was the teacher correct. I just couldn't believe the grade would change so drastically from one year to the next.

As my daughter would enter the same school system, some of the same problems would arise. Rhonda and I would go through the same process finding the same things. Later Victoria would go to a private school and never have these problems happen again. Timmy would continue to go to the same school, and Rhonda and I would continue to meet teachers head-on. We never lost a battle, and the principal would agree Timmy was a fine student, and soon he was placed in higher learning classes. This was just the beginning of the end for the school system of what was once a great place to raise a family.

Choking

One evening when my daughter was four years old, I was on night shift preparing to go to work on another twelve-hour shift. We sat down as a family; Timmy went over his schoolwork before dinner. It was a quiet evening, and Rhonda had just come home from work. We said our prayers before dinner and sat down for a chicken dinner with mashed potatoes and gravy, and corn with dinner rolls.

Rhonda was telling me how her day went, and she looked up with a panicked look on her face. Victoria was slightly colored blue, choking on a piece of chicken. I rushed over to her and performed the Heimlich maneuver used for choking victims. Pressing my fist against her tiny little abdomen with two small thrusts, forcing the piece of chicken from her throat, she began to breathe as I watched her eyes well up with tears. Rhonda picked her up and held her, calming her down and giving her something to drink. I don't know who was more panicked, Rhonda or Victoria.

Rhonda looked at me, asking me if I realized what just happened, and Timmy sat in silence with a look of total confusion. I did realize what had just happened, but being in my normal night shift funk, I told her I didn't want to think about it; and the truth was that later in the evening, I would actually think about what happened. I was at work a couple of hours later all alone. I said a prayer of thanks that I knew what to do. Every year at the plant, officers are trained in CPR and multimedia first aid, and of course we would all complain about breathing into a lifeless dummy and learning the Heimlich maneuver.

After what happened to my daughter, I never complained about the techniques that we learned. The instructor would ask, "Has anyone ever used what we learned in the class?" and I would share the experience with my fellow officers. As I explained what happened, I would also say that if it weren't for this type of training, the outcome would have been entirely different. This discussion would make a better atmosphere for learning as the class began.

In my many years at the plant, I would be involved in many first aid situations, and I used most of the things we learned in the class. Officers are assigned to first aid duties; some have had training elsewhere while the rest of us solely depended on our training we received from the first aid classes provided from the plant. Every day is a learning experience while I'm at work, and each day would be totally different from the day before. Many different life situations while on the job have taught me to deal with things that happen in day-to-day life on the outside world or at work. Not just as a security guard, but an intelligent part of society dealing with many situations that would just baffle someone not used to dealing with life situations that I faced in the normal line of duty while at work. Some would belittle the job while others would be proud of the good training and moral ethics taught in training to become a nuclear security officer. Each of my fellow officers would bring something a little different to the table, and we would all learn from their experiences in life—military, police, firemen, and just like me, the school of hard knocks.

Twenty Years of Experience

On September 10, 2004, I would receive a gift for twenty years of service as a security officer at the Nuclear Power Plant; and out of the original twenty-six officers I was hired with, only about seven of us were left. We are known as GFL, "guards for life," hoping to continue on the job until reaching retirement age. My son would be nine years old in December, and my daughter would soon have her fifth birthday in September. As for my wife Rhonda, she would be in about her twenty-third year at the phone company as a Human Resources manager. For a long time, things were pretty normal, and no major event would happen in our lives, just dealing with teachers and rotating shift work—the things that my family and I thought were normal in life.

The next major catastrophic event would come after the year of 2004, and it would be a life-changing event not only for me but all the Security Officers that worked at the Nuclear Power Plant; and September 11 would hold a double meaning for us.

Billy Moss

September 10 in the year of 2005 would be my twenty-first-year mark at work. Things were in their normal mode, with many changes along the way and many new officers. During downtimes on back shifts, officers would often talk about family and friends. I have many good memories talking to officers heart to heart as we shared the good times and the bad times together. One particular officer stands out in my mind and will be in my thoughts and prayers every day I put on my uniform. I have a constant reminder of him pinned on the left lapel of my uniform shirt, a gold-and-black metal ribbon.

Billy Moss started working at the plant in June 2002; we were from two different worlds. He was a born-and-bred country boy. I was on the opposite side of the world, born and raised in the suburban cities near Cleveland. That never stopped us as we shared a common love for weight lifting. Bill was into the world of powerlifting and ran with a group of officers that worked out together in their free time. They would often say things like, "If the bar ain't bendin', you're just pretendin'." These men of iron would do their job and go lift heavy plates of steel until it hurt. I was into more of the bodybuilding style of weight lifting and only did it in hopes of creating a perfect physique. We would often spend hours talking about the subject, and there was no one that could talk a better game than Billy. He also had the muscle to prove he actually played the game.

Billy had a lot of irons in the fire; he was a part-time police officer in Geneva on the Lake and owned a small farm in the city of Geneva, all the while trying to raise his son and living with his fiancée on the farm. For a city boy like me, this little city in northeastern Ohio was truly farm country as he talked about his acres of land. He also raised pigs and chickens. Billy was strong as an ox; he was a very impressive individual standing about five feet nine inches tall and weighing in at around 205 pounds. I would often hear the other officers talking about his tonnage on the bench press. Billy and the powerlifting officers would often compete and bring home first place trophies, proving to be some of the strongest men in the state of Ohio.

Not only was he a great weight lifter, he was also a fine officer taking on extra duties to make the shift run well. He was something I always wanted to be, a great shot. Billy would shock the security world as he demonstrated his accuracy with many different weapons. On top of all the things I just mentioned, he was a decent human being without an enemy in the world. I was told that he once saved an entire family from a burning house while on duty at the police department.

Billy was not on my shift, but I would work many overtime hours with him. We had security training classes together and did some security testing together. He was always full of laughs, and no matter what the task was, he was just what we needed to make life a little better.

On September 11, 2005, only a day after my twenty-first anniversary at the plant, I was at home, on a day off. I received a call from one of my friends and coworker that Billy Moss was in a motorcycle accident and had died at the scene, while riding with some fellow security officers doing what they do best, honoring a fallen motorcycle rider with dozens of other riders. Billy was on his big Harley Davidson and experienced some problems, colliding with a double-posted sign and then a telephone pole, suffering fatal injuries. After hanging up the phone, I sat in silence on my deck in the warm sun. As I said before, life runs in one big circle. The only thing is that not all the things that run in life's circle is always good. Years before I had lost a few other friends in motorcycle accidents.

All the security officers and many other plant employees attended the funeral a couple of days later. Billy was one of a kind; all who knew him loved him. I am not ashamed to say I cried like a baby at his funeral, and I learned a few more valuable lessons that year. We are always under the assumption that we will all be here tomorrow. Billy's death proved that's not always the case. I try to leave all of my friends and loved ones on a good note. Who knows what tomorrow will bring? Billy was made guard of the year that year, and in my opinion, he would have been the next supervisor. September 11 in 2001, the tragedy that happened in New York; on the same day in the year 2005, the loss of a fellow officer and good friend—two dates that I'm sure every officer at the Nuclear Plant will never forget.

Every day I go to work and put on my uniform, I look at the gold and black ribbon pinned on my uniform shirt. I am proud to wear that pin for all to see, and I have earned the right to say a prayer every day for not only a good security officer but a good friend. As I enter the shooting range, I look up at the picture of Billy high on the wall, saying a prayer, asking Billy the ultimate shooter to help me one more time to make it through the qualification courses. My ritual hasn't failed me yet. To some they may say it's all in my mind, to me I know I'm getting help from somewhere, and why not ask for help from a guy who was born to shoot straight? To all the officers that knew Billy, this story comes from the heart. Each day when I look at the picture on the wall, I see a man that was proud to wear the uniform, and he wore it better than any officer I know.

Olivet Institutional Baptist Church

In 2006 life ran its course, and this year was pretty much uneventful for me and my family. We would attend church on Sunday and go to breakfast after the sermon. I was still Catholic, and my wife and children were Baptist. On one fine Sunday morning, I was listening to the good Reverend Otis Moss at the Olivet Institutional Baptist Church with a few friends attending church. I listened ever Sunday to the good word and decided that I should be Baptist along with my family. As I heard Reverend Moss say, "The door is open," I made the decision to become part of the church, and Timmy also made the same decision, and my entire family walked up to the front of the church.

We were welcomed with open arms as Sheila Ashby, our lifelong friend who ran the day care at her home, sat in the front pew with all her fellow deacons. Reverend Chris and her family were lifelong friends; also her two boys were close friends of Victoria and Tim's. She sang a song that actually made you feel like the Holy Spirit was dancing right next to you. After a couple of weeks, on Easter Sunday Timmy and I were baptized, and our family became members of the Olivet Institutional Baptist Church. A few years later, Victoria would decide to join the church, and she was one of the last members to be baptized by Reverend Otis Moss. He retired shortly after that, in 2009.

When I told my mother that I was going to become a Baptist, she blessed my decision and told me that some religion was better than no religion. She also knew that a family that prays together stays together. I felt that my mother was wise beyond her years, and I am glad that she was an understanding mother.

Olivet Institutional Baptist Church was where Big John's family grew up, and I would often see his brothers in church. Often when I sit in church, I remember Big John's mother, Maggie Fryer, whom I called grandma. This was her church also. I would say a prayer in her memory. She had accepted us as her grandchildren. The church had a history with Dr. Martin Luther King Jr. when he came to Cleveland during the civil rights movement. There were pictures on the walls of Dr. Martin Luther King Jr. and Reverend Otis Moss walking hand and hand. Each Sunday as I listen to the word in church, I would often feel the power behind the words as Reverend Moss would preach from the Bible. The Holy Spirit was alive and well, and I could feel it throughout the church. I felt like my family and I were in the right place, and I thank the Lord for leading us in the right direction.

We would have powerful speakers at church, like Judge Hatchet, a famous television judge who had her own show. She would talk of her strong Baptist upbringing and tell the children there were ways to follow and trust in the Lord. There were other speakers who would come and tell the church of their struggles in life and how the Lord showed them the way.

One Sunday morning we prepared for church, and Oprah Winfrey was going to be at the church that day. As we drove around the block, looking for a parking space the police were on every corner and all around the church. That day there were so many people at church, we had to go downstairs and sit by a huge screen television. I took Victoria over to a trailer where the children had Bible school. Security was tight, and men in suits with earpieces were lined throughout the church. I stayed with Victoria. I wasn't allowed back in my own church as they prepared for Oprah.

I walked outside with the children; Oprah asked to see all the children before she entered the church. I watched a big black limousine drive up with a couple of motorcycle policemen escorting, parking it at the church parking lot. Victoria was in the middle of all the children, wearing a completely pink outfit. She looked like a model for a very expensive children's magazine without a hair out of place. As Oprah stepped out of the limo, she walked toward the crowd of little children. She walked up to Victoria and asked her what she learned in church. Victoria said, "I just got here."

The huge crowd laughed, and Oprah kissed her on the cheek and then kissed me on the cheek as the policemen cleared a path for her to enter the church. This wouldn't be the last time we would see the classy lady. She came to many of the functions of our church. She was a close and personal friend of Reverend Moss and a member of our church. Oprah attended Reverend Moss's retirement party along with Reverend Jesse Jackson and many other officials in the city of Cleveland. My family would be a part of history. We attended the black-tie affair in the heart of the city of Cleveland on a cold winter night.

The Accident

In that cold winter of 2006, the snow would pile up until the snowplows couldn't find anywhere else to put it. This was typical of the snows in Cleveland as we would experience something called "lake effect snow," which meant that if Lake Erie didn't freeze, we would get more snow than usual. That year the lake didn't freeze, and we had tons of snow.

One morning after working twelve hours, I drove home on a clear day, and the temperature was about fifteen degrees with the sun shining bright. I managed to make it to my street after a thirty-mile drive from the Nuclear Plant. I drove up my street, which was one big sheet of ice. As I turned the corner, I could see my house, and my little car started sliding. As my neighbor's wife was coming around the corner, we connected.

My little twelve-year-old Saturn was no match for her SUV. I banged in the side of her truck and my car got the worst of it. Her truck was barely damaged, and my little car had a huge chunk taken out of the front end. My whole car was made of plastic and not metal. I told her I would pay for the damages, and she drove off.

I drove my car for one more year and decided to buy a new car after about ten years without a car payment. I loved my Saturn. It had 178,000 miles on it and still drove like a champ, but after twelve years of driving, it had seen its better days. Rhonda and I would shop around, and Saturn was on the top of my list. I saw many different Saturns, but I couldn't make up my mind; I felt the prices were too high.

The Gift

That year Big John bought a Hummer H3. It was black with every special option in it, and I went to my parent's house to see his truck. The truck was everything I wanted, but I felt the price was too high. Rhonda convinced me to go to the Hummer dealer. She told me after driving that tiny car, I deserved something that I would enjoy.

We went to the Hummer dealer, and I sat with the dealer and watched my wife work the dealer until she was satisfied. The following week I drove my new royal blue Hummer H3 to work, and I did feel good, and the big blue truck was everything I ever wanted. The real point of the story is not the Hummer, but what happened to the little Saturn; for the moment it sat down at the bottom of my driveway, waiting for a buyer.

My brother Danny told me that one of my nephew's friend's grandmother needed a car. She was raising five grandchildren with no help and driving to work on a wing and a prayer. Her old car was just about to go its last mile. She contacted me and told me she wanted the car, and she asked me what I wanted for it. Knowing what she had to deal with in life, Rhonda and I decided to give her the car.

When we told her the news, she still didn't believe I was going to give her the car until Danny and I drove it up her driveway. Danny and I cleaned it up. I cleaned the interior, and he gave it a fresh wax. It looked new except for the front quarter-panel where I had the accident. I turned over the paperwork to her, and she was more than happy, but I felt truly blessed that I was able to help her in her time of need. And as I looked in her eyes, it warmed my soul as I could see the joy that filled her heart.

She reminded me of my own mother struggling to put food on the table and a roof over our heads with four children. No money in the world could make me feel the way I did that day. I still see her driving the little car today two years later, in 2009. On top of all that, the families were as if they were one. We gained friends for life. Rhonda and I explained to our children that there were some things money couldn't buy, and if you do a good deed, it comes back to you in many different ways.

My Family

In the year 2007, Rhonda would go back to school to obtain a master's degree. Victoria was eight years old and in the third grade. She was a fine student, and she brought home good grades. Timmy was twelve years old and in the sixth grade. He made us proud with grades and making the honor roll every quarter. He was voted in as class president again and was very popular in school with many friends and a first-time girlfriend. I was in my twenty-third year at the plant and trying to further my career by putting in to be the next supervisor, and I would be sent to leadership school by the company for a month, away from the plant. I felt honored for the opportunity and relished the challenge of learning something new again; not many officers were afforded this opportunity.

Before I went to the class, there were a series of tests that I would have to take on a computer, which was very trying for me as I would put in extra time at work finding the programs and dealing with the Human Resources Department with each step that I took. I was told that if I did not complete the programs, I wouldn't attend the class. I had about a week to complete the programs, and I stayed up half the night trying to complete the task. Many times I would depend on a new friend from the Human Resources Department that would guide me through the programs. Suzanne not only helped me but became a good friend as she walked me through the programs; she never let me down and was always a pleasure to work with. After spending many hours and days in her office, I finally completed the work before my deadline. Later I would find out that I was the only one in the class that completed all the programs to attend the class.

In the end of the summer, around August first, I would be sent to corporate headquarters in Akron, Ohio, to leadership school forty miles away from my home and sixty miles away from the Nuclear Plant. For the first time in my career, I would wear civilian clothes and put in a classroom full of people who were already supervisors, to learn how to deal with employees. I would learn how to deal with the union and different situations as a supervisor. I was the only one in the class of about thirty people who wasn't already a supervisor.

The class was different than any other thing that I had learned from the company before; it was basically learning how to deal with people and learning about myself. We would work in teams and put through different situations that involved employees. For the first time, I would feel very comfortable in class because we were learning a subject that I was quite familiar with, dealing with people.

After the classes were over, I would be sent back to the plant. I had learned a lot about myself. I was told that I thought with my heart and I actually cared about people, which as a supervisor could be good and bad. I felt that if I treated people the way I wanted to be treated, I wouldn't have any problems; I didn't know how wrong I was. When I was acting supervisor, the people that I considered friends were the ones that actually caused me the most problems as they thought that they should be afforded special treatment, and I felt if they were actually my friends, they would respect the position that I was in and not look for special treatment.

As of present day, no one has been promoted to supervisor, and I would remain in my current position until I was told different. This still didn't affect the way I did my job, and I would continue to do my job with a smile on my face and happy to be employed. As for my friends who were also my fellow employees, they would remain my friends as we tried to hash out the differences of Tim as a friend and Tim as an acting supervisor. I still enjoy working with them, and while learning many valuable lessons, our friendship continued to grow.

In the meantime, I dealt with school problems, and Rhonda and I kept a close eye on the school system and teachers. We would go to school and talk to Tim's teachers and Victoria's teachers; each child had a teacher or two that would see black children as inferior learning students. My children were very intelligent, and as parents our lines of communication with our children were open discussions within the family, and they never feared telling us the truth. Our children were no angels, and we both knew it, but we also knew not to take the teachers' word as gospel. If something didn't sound right, we would trust our first instincts, and we were usually not far from the truth.

School

In the fall of 2007, our family prepared for Timmy to go to Washington DC for the National Honor Society. Timmy was handpicked by some of his teachers and would spend a week with other students across the country in Washington DC. Before he went on his trip, he went to each teacher, asking for a week of schoolwork in advance so he wouldn't miss anything and stay current in his class work. Timmy was very fortunate; his best friend, Demetrius Scott, would also be going on the trip.

In the middle of October, Timmy would miss his mother's birthday because he was in Washington DC with the National Honor Society. The parents of the boys would drive to Washington, Richard and April Scott, who were the parents of Demetrius, would take them there, and we agreed to pick them up the following week. The travel plans went without a hitch despite heavy rain as we entered Georgetown in Washington for their ride home.

Timmy and Demetrius would tour Washington and learn the history of our great country. We received pictures on the Internet of a different place the group toured each day. Timmy would call late at night, exhausted from his busy day. By the time the trip was over, the boys were ready to come home, and we put all their things in the car, with Victoria asking a question every second. The boys climbed in the car, and within five minutes they were fast asleep, for almost the entire trip. It rained all the way there and back, with everyone sleeping in the SUV except Rhonda and me. We talked about when we were children and how we never did anything like this due to the lack of money; our children were fortunate, and they didn't realize it.

After the trip was over and Timmy went back to school, a week later report cards came out, and Timmy had an incomplete in one of his classes. Once again I had to go to school to talk to the teacher; I contacted the school and set up a meeting with the principal and the teacher. Timmy gave me the details and explained to me that the teacher said when he was gone, none of his classwork was done. Timmy assured me that he asked for the classwork before he left on his trip. I had no reason to doubt him because every other teacher gave him the classwork, and he had completed it before he left. I came home from a twelve-hour night shift and waited for two hours to go to the school for the meeting.

I went to the principal's office and explained to her that my son was sent by the school to Washington to represent the school for the Nation Honor Society. Why would an honor student not complete the assignments given to him by his teachers? I told her that I didn't want anything extra, just a chance for Timmy to complete the assignments like every other student. The principal knew me well from previous meetings, so she called the teacher to come to her office.

The teacher sat down with the principal and me. We discussed the problem, and I immediately knew that the teacher failed to give Timmy the assignments. As we talked, I noticed the expression on the principal's face; she wasn't pleased as we tried to come to some agreement about the classwork. The teacher tried to play hardball and refused to let Timmy do the assignments, which would change his report card grade from an incomplete to a B. This would also change his grade point average.

At first the principal asked him to let Timmy complete the work, and I watched her disposition change from pleasant to pure aggravation. Then she didn't ask, she demanded and told the teacher that he would give Timmy the work to do and change the grade, giving him the grade he earned. As he hung his head lower into his chest, he agreed but only on his terms. He wanted Timmy to complete the work in only two days; all the other students had a full week to complete the work. I told him that the assignments would be completed in two days.

After the teacher left the room, the principal and I discussed the situation a little more in detail. She was a stern but fair lady. As long as my son did the things he was supposed to, she would defend his right to receive a good education. As we talked, she apologized for the teacher and once again explained the diversity problem in the school. She didn't have to tell me, I already knew the problem well; I came from the same situation in the Wickliffe school system. This wasn't the first time the principal and I had talked, she knew my son well, and she also knew what kind of a student he was. She also knew what type of parents my wife and I were, and we weren't going to stand and watch while the teacher would use strong-arm tactics to impose his will on our son.

I went home and called Rhonda at work and explained what happened. I was careful not to leave out any of the details. My wife is a very detailed person as she asked me a ton of questions. She didn't leave out a thing, as she wanted to know everything that took place. She even asked me how the teacher responded and what the principal's reaction was. After talking to her for thirty minutes, it was close to noon; and after being awake for over twenty-four hours, I crawled into bed.

I slept for about three to four hours, just as I had done many times before I prepared myself for another twelve-hour night shift with only a couple hours of sleep. I suppose this is a common practice for all shift workers, as the world revolved on regular hours. We had to do what we needed to according to morning, noon, and night. Many of my coworkers would sometimes work on little or no sleep at all; sometimes I would drive home on a wing and a prayer as I could hear the rumble strip underneath my tires on the freeway. Thank god for the rumble strip on the freeway. I'm sure it saved more lives than I could count.

For the next few days, Rhonda would step in, making sure that Timmy completed the schoolwork that he missed while he was in Washington. A few days later, Timmy came to me telling me he had finished all the work, and he thanked me for going to the school for him. We sat down together and had a heart-to-heart conversation about teachers and schoolwork. I explained to him that as long as he did the right things, I would go to bat for him no matter what the problem was. Timmy would never let me down; and each time he had a problem, he came to my wife and me, looking for a solution. I had many more encounters with the same teacher that year, and each time Timmy told it like it was. I even went to the teacher's classroom with the principal to hash out some homework problems.

The homework in question was sitting on the teacher's desk right where Timmy said it was. The teacher took the papers from his desk and told me that Timmy didn't turn in the assignment, as he looked through the papers. In front of the principal and me, he pulled my son's paper from the stack. The problem was that the teacher wouldn't accept it because it was written too light to read. I told him that Timmy would do it over, and this time he would be able to read it. I often wondered how many of the students were being cheated by the teacher, and how many parents didn't know about how the children were being treated. How many parents were willing to accept the grades on their child's report card without question?

That year Rhonda and I watched that teacher very closely, and so did the principal. We also watched all the other teachers Timmy had classes with. Each year there would be a teacher that was similar to this one, and each year my wife and I would go to the school to deal with them. Timmy never let me down, and I explained to him that as long as he was right, I could defend him. I also told him that if he was wrong, I would reason with him to help him understand where he went wrong.

The Teachers' Strike

In 2007 as the summer months quickly approached, the school system in our community would go through many changes. In the last few months of school, the teachers of Richmond Heights public schools would go through a nasty strike. The news crews were at the school every day, and the teachers were outside in front of the school and city hall, with picket signs, protesting. With our house only a quarter mile away from the school and directly in front of it, cars would line our street with news cameras and newspaper people littered all over the small area. This made it very difficult to enter or exit the street, and with only one way in and one way out, we would see all sorts of traffic every morning in front of our home. The very thing that we moved to this small community for would become one of the biggest nightmares the good people of Richmond Heights had to deal with.

Every morning we would see camera crews and teachers with picket signs at the bottom of our street. On every corner near the school, there were teachers with picket signs and news crews, with reports taking interviews, which would be on every news channel when I entered my house. This would go on for about two weeks, and my children would get on the bus and continue to go to school as if nothing was happening. Timmy and Victoria were very aware of the situation as they would see all their teachers holding signs and marching on every street corner near the school. I would come home from work on night shift and drive them to school. The buses were still running, but Rhonda and I felt it was unsafe for them to take the bus. Just like every strike that I ever heard of, this strike would soon turn violent, separating people that didn't agree with each other. Teachers, staff members, and members of the community that were friends would soon become bitter enemies as opinions would differ.

Some parents refused to let their children go to school, saying that the substitute teachers weren't teaching the students anything. My wife and I felt the same way, but we were told that if our children didn't go to school, they would be marked as absent. After talking to my son every day about what he did in school while the strike was going on, he told me he was allowed to do whatever he wanted. The children weren't learning anything while their teachers were out on the streets picketing.

Some teachers wouldn't honor the strike not because they didn't want to, but due to money issues and health care benefits, they were unable too. There is one teacher that I often think about whenever I think about this strike. He was one of the casualties of the strike and would lose respect for many of his coworkers and damage to his personal property.

One afternoon while the strike was at a high point, I was picking my daughter up after school. I ran into one of my favorite teachers. He was sitting on a bench by the playground as the children were preparing to be let out of school. I walked over to him, noticing he wasn't his same old happy self. I could see by the expression on his face that he had plenty on his mind. He was a veteran teacher with over thirty years in the business and could most likely retire if he wanted to.

As we talked, I could see the tears forming in his eyes as he held his head low, avoiding eye contact with me. I also felt the heaviness in his heart as he explained why he could not support the strike. This teacher told me he had high medical bills for chemotherapy. He was being treated for cancer, and without his medical benefits, he would never be able to afford the cancer treatment. All of his tires were slashed on his car, and he also felt that all of his coworkers were going to hate him.

I felt real bad as I watched one of the most decent people I ever met being destroyed by the people he felt were his friends. This teacher would spend every waking moment caring for the children. He devoted most of his time even in the summer, when most teachers were enjoying a long vacation. As I watched the children coming out of the school building, I thought to myself, *how could these people kill the spirit of the old man?* I also thought that if there was ever a person that needed some prayers, it was this man. Later in the evening, before my family went to bed, we would say our prayers for a man that helped his fellowman every day.

The strike lasted about two and a half weeks, but the damages were here for a lifetime. The community of Richmond Heights would go through many changes as we saw some of the children leave the school and go to private schools. My daughter would leave the Richmond Heights school system and go to a private school at the beginning of the next year in September, leaving many of her friends behind. She would miss them a lot, and every now and then we would go to the school for sporting events where she could be with her friends. Timmy was a devoted Richmond Heights fan and vowed never to leave the school. Timmy and his friends made a pact, saying they would always be together. One of his closest friends left for a private school, and it crushed him. He didn't want to see any more of his friends leave.

Victoria's New School

While dealing with the school system of Richmond Heights, my wife and I went to the school where we wanted Victoria to go. We had a meeting with the principal of Cornerstone Christian Academy; he was a very calm and reassuring individual as he went through the rules and regulations of the school. He shook my hand as Rhonda and I sat down.

He said, "The first thing that we do here to start the day is say our prayers and the Pledge of Allegiance." And he looked us and said, "Are we all on the same page?"

I found this strange, but in today's times, this was a very valid question because God and country were taken out of the public schools a long time ago. Rhonda asked him what was the diversity ratio at the school, and he politely said he didn't know, explaining that he didn't care what color or race a child was, and plain and simple, that a child is a child no matter what, and the school system treated every student with love and respect. We are all children of God.

At that very moment, I looked out of the corner of my eye at Rhonda, and I knew she felt the same way I did; this was the right place for our daughter. We discussed tuition and many other subjects such as after-school activities. We were very pleased, but we also knew that our son, Timmy, wouldn't even consider going to this school because they didn't have a football team. Later we would try to talk to him about the school, but he wanted to stay at Richmond Heights with his friends and play football, basketball, and run track.

I knew in my heart that if it were me, I would have made the same decision. He was a very good student, and Rhonda and I agreed that if he brought good grades home, then he would stay. Timmy did that and moved into advanced classes. With a little struggle, he managed to maintain good grades and continued to play sports with his friends. He also remained class president and started a whole new career; he fell in love with singing in the choir.

Richmond Heights

The teachers' strike wasn't the only reason students were leaving. The community wouldn't support the school system, and levy after levy would fail. The taxes were higher than any other community near ours and asking for more money from the homeowners didn't sit too well with the people of Richmond Heights. We watched the new city hall building go up, and the school seemed to deteriorate more and more. After talking to many city officials, they claimed the money for city hall and the school were two separate issues.

My neighbors and I didn't understand. How could they build a new city hall and give city officials more money while our school was literally falling apart? This would break the backbone of the community and people that were willing to help at school and community functions would no longer support the failing system. For the next few years, we would watch as the devil worked his magic once again as politics and greed would separate the small community, and the future of our children were at the mercy of people who only thought of themselves. Once again the children would suffer as we watched a great community fall apart.

In the year of 2008, America was on the verge of electing the first black president, and the city of Richmond Heights would fail the school levy for the fifth time. From what I was told, the school levy failed by a margin of forty-nine votes, and Barack Obama was elected president of the United States. I went to a party that night, held in a church by the Democrats in my community. As I watched the celebration on a huge wide-screen television, I thought how far this country had come, but I also saw the school levy fail for the sixth time on the screen.

Black and white people held hands and said a prayer of thanks. I felt very proud to be a part of all this. On the downside of all the celebrating, I felt sorrow for the children that went to Richmond Heights public schools. Their future was in limbo, and more turmoil was in the balance for the people and our children in the community. I said a silent prayer for them, asking the Lord for once again just one last favor.

In the same year, we would be at the mercy of greedy oil merchants as the gas prices would soar higher than ever at around four dollars a gallon. The economy would take a turn for the worst, and America would turn on the evening news to watch the bottom fall out of the stock market. My children as well as other American children were very aware of how the world worked; they were exposed to many of the world's evils in a short period of time. Often my wife and I were explaining to our children about gas prices and the stock market. When we were growing up, these things never entered our minds as we went to school and came home to a family home-cooked meal. Life was so much simpler then, the innocence of childhood somehow got lost in our new, faster, ever-changing world.

Spartan Power

At the beginning of the school year, Victoria was very happy with her new school and met many new friends. She would also see most of her old friends when we went to Timmy's football games. The eighth grade Richmond Heights Spartans football team was unstoppable, and we traveled everywhere to see them, rain or shine. I enjoyed being part of a small group of about six to eight parents that could make more noise than an entire stadium full of the hometown crowd. Timmy and his friends lost most of their football games in 2008, but when it came to basketball, they didn't lose one single game, and the same group of parents plus a few more would cheer them on to victory. People from the opposing teams would complain about our basketball team because we had two six foot six kids playing on our team along with a few other kids who really knew how to play the game.

The seventh grade Spartans basketball team went undefeated, but due to the levy problems in the school, the boys didn't get credit for their long hard season. Once again, one of the parents stepped in and organized one of the biggest community days at the school gym, also promoting the school levy. Richard Scott and his wife April decided to rally around something positive and give the boys on the basketball team a party at the school gym, focusing on the boys and the school levy. Richard Scott, known to his friends as Zoom, had his own television show and also worked for *Fox 8 News*, a local legend and a personal friend of ours. He decided to feature the basketball team on his television show. Demetrious Scott is one of Timmy's best friends and was also a member of the basketball team. Also State Representative Kenny Yuko and his wife Pam, who are also personal friends of ours, helped organize the function and promote the school levy.

The boys were on television with Zoom talking about their basketball season, and Zoom also talked about the school levy. The next weekend, the rally at the gym was one of the biggest parties that the community ever had. The Cavalier girls and local news celebrities that lived in and near Richmond Heights helped our community celebrate the winning basketball season and the school levy. Most of the celebrities were friends and associates of Richard Zoom Scott.

With a full house, the boys were announced with their parents, receiving their trophies as they walked around the gym. The school faculty played a basketball game against the local basketball heroes. Music played on the loudspeakers and State Representative Kenny Yuko talked about the levy to promote a better school system and community. This was one of the finest days the community had, and little did we know, this would be one of the last things as a community would celebrate as we fought a never-ending battle with the school systems.

No one from any other school raised an eyebrow when the Richmond Heights eighth grade football team lost most of their games that year. Our kids were actually in the seventh grade playing sports in the eighth grade league. Soon the tables would turn in the following year, 2009, and every school would complain about our sports teams. I would come home from night shift and get some rest, waking up to pick up Victoria from her school, which was about six miles away. Victoria and I would drive down the street and pick up her best friend Savanna and head to the school or travel to other schools to watch the games.

Most of the time, I was really tired, but I wouldn't miss a game for the world as I rotated shifts from nights to days; and when I was on second shift, I had to miss some games unless they fell on my days off, which were sometimes during the weekdays. I totally despised second shift along with other security officers who had children and families. To this day, second shift is the worst shift for me because it would take me away from valuable family time. If there were some way to get out of second shift, I would be first in line to take it. Most of the time, I would schedule vacation time to avoid the horrible second shift.

World-changing Events

In the year of 2009, we would face the failing school levy along with the economy hitting its lowest point in over fifty years. People would lose their jobs by the thousands as companies would fold, leaving the employees high and dry. The housing market also took a turn for the worst as property values dipped to their lowest point in a long time. My youngest brother, Little Jonn, lost his job after thirteen years of employment with a local wholesale food company. He would return to school to learn about hospital work, with Cleveland having some of the finest hospitals in the world.

Rhonda and I worked for two utilities and were still gainfully employed while other people were hit with unemployment. The big car companies would ask for help from the government and close factories, leaving employees with over twenty years with the company seeking other means of employment. For the most part, our community would face a low, with no industry to support it. Our taxes would be one of the highest in the area.

Of course, who would suffer the most? The children, as they threatened to close the Richmond Heights schools. Timmy would deal with talk of going to a private school or bused to another local school. Many times I would watch him deal with the possibility of no sports and all his friends going to different schools. In my day, all we had to worry about was going to school and our parents taking care of everything else. I often wonder if the world we live in today is really a good thing.

At the beginning of the school year, my children would go in two different directions, Victoria to the private school and Timmy still toughing it out with all of his friends at Richmond Heights. As parents, Rhonda and I would try to keep him with his classmates as the football season began. We would attend many school meetings, and it always turned out the same—more hate, misery, and discontent between officials from the school and city officials.

The parents of the students would battle, only to be told the same things, and the newest thing would be pay to play, for each student that wanted to participate in any extra functions that the school provided. One meeting, in the early stages, Rhonda and I would get up and walk out of a meeting as it became very heated, and nothing was resolved.

Pride and Prejudice

With the school year just beginning, football took most of the heat away from the battle of the levy at the school. The eighth grade football team would literally crush every opponent it would face. As parents, we had to deal with the losing attitudes of the other team's coaches and officials as they tried to even the score by cheating and telling us we had poor unsportsmanlike conduct. Our children were even called a bunch of niggers and kids spitting in their hands before shaking hands after the game. This kind of conduct was condoned by and often directed by the coaches of the other teams themselves.

Just last year, our team took defeat from the same teams, never complaining and acting with dignity and honor, which is what we expected from the same teams that beat us last year. At the end of the football season, our boys went undefeated with one tie in the last game. Our group of about six to eight parents would go to every game, contesting every wrong call and dirty tactics done by hometown officials.

I am sorry to say that some things never change; if it weren't for my son's love of the game, I would have pulled him from the team. Even at an eighth grade football game, bigotry would rear its ugly head, and my son and his friends soon learned how to deal with unruly people and extreme prejudice. Not only because they were black but also for being better athletes as well as the better team. Soon we would put all this behind us, and basketball season would start, and the beginning of more of the same.

Directly after a winning football season for the Richmond Heights eighth graders, the basketball season started, and the team looked very promising, with two boys at six foot six and a couple of others around six foot even. The boys launched into another winning undefeated season just like the year before. The same core group of parents that followed the football team around would also be there for every basketball game. But as the season progressed, more parents and students would be there for the basketball games, and just after the first home game, you could hardly find a seat in the gym when the boys played at home.

There were also recruiters from every private school in the area, hoping to influence the parents of the two giants on the team. These two young gifted athletes were in the eighth grade dunking the basketball and doing things that colleges try to teach up-and-coming NBA stars. As the news traveled, the eighth grade Richmond Heights basketball team played in front of a packed gym everywhere they went. I watched coaches and officials from other teams try every trick in the book, but no matter what they did, the results were always the same. Our team would always win with a great margin of points. Some coaches even asked our coach not to bring the two big kids and claimed it was unfair for them to play, even trying to restrict their playing time. My son was a decent player, but he said he only played to be with his friends, and football was where he wanted to excel.

More importantly, my son Timmy's grades were topnotch as usual, although being in advanced classes would be very challenging, juggling a heavy schedule and playing sports too. Often I would see him come home from practice purely exhausted, get something to eat, followed directly with homework; he was becoming more of a man every day, being responsible in his duties.

We would often talk about sports, grades, and girls when we were alone. As a parent, I never tried to hide anything from him and always told him the truth about anything he wanted to know, including my past mistakes and how I didn't want him to do some of the same things. I also told him that not everybody could be a professional athlete making tons of money, not count on just one thing and always put maximum efforts into his grades. I would tell him about fallen heroes when I grew up, about the guys that I thought were going to play professional sports and were now still living with their parents, never leaving home because they were making minimum wage or drinking and smoking themselves to death, not earning a single penny.

I could tell he listened to every word as I watched the expression on his face change as I told him of injured athletes, drunken athletes, doped-up athletes, and homeless athletes. These were all people who never concerned themselves with grades in school or anything else because they thought they were going to be the next guy breaking records on television. My son not only listened but proved he learned from the things I told him by bringing home good grades and never getting into any trouble. My wife and I are very proud of him. He was also the perfect role model for his little sister, Victoria. She also brought home good grades.

When the basketball season ended, our eighth grade football and basketball teams were at about sixty winning games, with one tie in football and one loss in basketball due to being placed in a higher bracket with bigger schools and tougher teams. For all their hard work and efforts, the children barely got any recognition; and once again, Richard Zoom Scott would have the boys on his local television show just like the year before.

Also just like the year before, Zoom promoted the school levy; and once again, his efforts would fall on deaf ears. With Richard and April Scott and Kenny and Pam Yuko, we continued to support the school levy and battle with local officials and school board members to keep our community whole with children going to Richmond Heights schools.

Just like the Cleveland Browns, we don't know the word "defeat"; and with God on our side, we are still fighting a long hard battle for the good of our community and most of all, for the good of the children.

The Levy

Despite the winning records in sports and high achievements scholastically, the levy would still be the dark horse of our great community. The word was that all sports programs and extracurricular school actives would be cut from the program due to the school levy not passing. The cry for money from the school board would be the only thing that would be on the minds of every parent that sent their children to our schools.

Finally at one of the school board meetings, we were told that the children would have to pay to play sports, and each child would pay a sum of $350 a sport with a maximum of $1,000 for each family; and also, if your child was brilliant enough to make the honor roll, an additional fee of $100. The final kicker was taking away the school buses from the kindergartners up to the sixth grade for children within a two-mile radius of the school. Many of the school bus drivers would lose their jobs as cutbacks were made along with some of the teachers.

Speaking Up for the Community

Just a few weeks before the school board meeting that discussed pay-to-play sports and the school bus situation, my wife Rhonda would speak up for the good of the community. She made the newspapers and television news shows. Many of our friends and coworkers saw the news and saw her picture in the news papers. This was one of many heated battles, and Rhonda, just like many parents in our community, fought for the good of the children. She brought up many good points, discussing how to keep sports and extracurricular school activates for the children. She was quoted in the newspapers and shown on the news shows.

The school board members listened, and not a word was said after she spoke with authority. I could see the fire in her eyes and the passion she spoke with as she addressed the school board and members of the community. Often I would be on the receiving end of such discussions in our home, and I knew what a disadvantage it was when she spoke on something that was clearly in her heart and soul. As the news cameras panned the room and focused on the school board members that her points were taken very seriously, not a soul in the room challenged what she was saying. It was true that hell hath no fury like a woman's scorn or a mother fighting for her children and the good of the community in which we lived.

The meeting that followed, which discussed pay to play and bussing just a few weeks later, would make me the center of attention. I spoke of the harmful repercussions the city would face if the buses were taken away from the children from kindergarten to the sixth grade.

The day of the meeting, I was scheduled to go to work for another twelve-hour night shift. That day I called in at work requesting to use a vacation day. I was very tired from working twelve-hour night shifts and lack of sleep brought on by concern for my brother Danny going into the hospital for major surgery on his back. He suffered a longtime back injury for a couple of years after falling from his icy Pepsi truck, causing severe damage to his spine. That same week, I had many things that would cause me not to get enough rest; I was purely exhausted.

Calling in for a day off from work was something I never did. The night shift supervisor granted me the day off. After explaining my situation to the supervisor, I also told him about the school board meeting that I would be attending that evening; and as a joke I said, "Don't be surprised if I'm in the newspaper tomorrow fighting for school children and my community." Little did I know or anyone else that that's what would exactly happen.

Before the meeting, a paper was issued, stating that if you would like to speak, fill out the paper with your name and address. I believe this was done so that there wouldn't be any outburst or people speaking out, freely saying what was on their mind. Rhonda and I filled out the paper and turned it in; besides my wife and me, only one other person filled out the paper. Rhonda and I felt if there was something that just wasn't right, at least we would have the option to say something.

The room was filled with community members and bus drivers. As for the board members, they would be about twenty minutes late. I believe this was planned as each board member showed up with a cup of McDonald's coffee in their hand, acting as if this meeting didn't mean a thing to them or the community. I felt that the meeting was one of the most important things that happened all year; it would direct the future of our children, schools, and our city. I'm sure I wasn't alone as the crowd in the room began to air their feelings about the board members being late.

After the board members were seated, the meeting began with the only bright spot out of the whole thing—a few of the school choir members and their teacher with trophies from a national meet where they placed as being one of the finest choirs in the United States. The choir was one of the programs to be cut along with many other very special things the students do. Somehow the choir would survive the cut, and my son Timmy would be overjoyed. The school choir showed up with about ten trophies, and most of them were first place trophies. The school board somehow found it in their hearts to let the children sing, and for the time being, the choir would be left alone until further notice.

As the meeting progressed, we were informed of pay-to-play sports, which I was grateful for because we thought they were going to cut out sports totally. Everyone kind of expected that, but the next thing on the agenda would be so shocking to me that I could feel my blood boiling. The buses for children in kindergarten to the sixth grade would be cut if you lived in a two-mile radius of the school.

I held my tongue until the board called on me; restraint from immediate action was very difficult at the time. I could feel the heat from my jacket starting to rise as I pictured the little children crossing a major intersection at one of the busiest times of the day. I squirmed around in my chair trying not to explode on a bunch of self-centered, egotistical, arrogant people who reminded me of the Pharaohs when the Jews wanted to be freed of slavery in biblical days. I couldn't wait to address the board, but I held off until they called on me. The meeting was almost to a close before it was my turn.

First the board called on a woman who had questions about the hundred-dollar fee parents were supposed to pay if their child made the honor roll. The board members stood their ground, not giving an inch, never considering how the parents felt. They quickly sidestepped the issue and moved to the next name on their list. The president of the board called out, "Rhonda Lowe."

My wife sat in her chair looking at each board member as she said, "I have nothing to say." As I looked at my wife out of the corner of my eye, the board called out my name. I quickly stood up, looking the president of the board square in the eye and said, "I can't believe you are going to put the babies out on the streets. The children have to cross a major intersection. What happens when one of those babies gets splattered in the middle of the street trying to cross the street to go to school? I can't believe a community as great as Richmond Heights would take away the buses from the babies!"

I guess I stunned the board members, and the president stated he had three vehicles, and none of his children would be walking to school. With that answer, he only infuriated me more. I stood my ground, saying, "This isn't just about your children but about every child in the community who will be crossing the streets. The intersection is so dangerous, I can't even cross the street. They will be crossing the street in the peak times of traffic. One of them is bound to be hit by a car. What about the snowplows in the winter? I suggest we find the money so we don't put our children in danger!"

The president of the board began to yell, saying that the board had asked the community six times to pass the levy and six times it failed. "What do want us to do?"

I stood firmly pointing my finger at the board members, saying, "This should be a separate issue. Are we willing to sacrifice the life of a child to prove a point to the community about the levy?"

Before I sat down, everyone in the room clapped and the news reporters snapped a picture of me while I was in the heat of battle. Two news women walked over to me and started asking me questions about how I felt. I didn't hold back as I explained the seriousness of what the board was trying to do. How could they feel good about taking away the buses from innocent children who had nothing to do with failing the levy? And I'm quite sure their parents voted for the levy.

When the meeting ended, I was swarmed by the people in the room, shaking my hand and thanking me for speaking up for the good of the community. I felt like I didn't do anything great, but all I could think about was one of those kids getting hit by a car. My wife and I were one of the last people to leave the room as one of my old friends, who happened to be a news reporter, came to me and said I did a fine, just job for the community.

I told him I just did what I felt was right. Fighting for the children was something I felt was a worthy cause. Usually in such a meeting, I would sit and let other people air their concerns. But picturing a child being injured or even killed just sent me over the top.

The next day I woke up to the phone ringing. It was Rhonda telling me I was on the front page of the newspaper, pointing my finger with a stern look on my face. I took a shower and went to the grocery store. Before I went to the store, I stopped in the gas station that I regularly go to. I went inside, and the cashier handed me a newspaper telling me how proud she was to know me. She had read the article, quoting my exact words about the children. I looked down at the newspaper; and there I was on the front page in full color with my finger pointed, looking directly at the board members, stating my case. Everyone said I looked like I meant business. There was no doubt I believed in what I was saying, and my expression showed it.

The next day I went to work; and as soon I went through the checkpoint, a couple of my fellow officers held up the newspaper asking me for an autograph. I laughed as they said, "Way to stick up for the children and your community."

I entered the building and more of the same happened as I walked past my fellow officers. I went to roll call, and everyone was asking me about the meeting. As I explained, guys were saying, "Way to go," and "Nice job." I actually felt good about what I did, and everyone that knew me understood what I was trying to do.

As I walked through the plant performing my normal duties, longtime employees said they saw the picture and read the article, telling me that they liked the way I stood up for the children and my community. The newspaper article quoted the school board president talking about his three vehicles and his children, which didn't put him in a good light. For the next few weeks, I would see people that worked at the plant and everywhere I went, coming up to me, telling me they saw me in the newspaper, shaking my hand, and telling me I did a good thing standing up for my community.

As the weeks passed by, my brother Danny would go to the next school board meeting to watch my nephew Tyler receive the Buckeye Boys State Award for good grades and citizenship. Rhonda and I didn't attend the meeting due to going to see Victoria in a school play. I think this was a blessing in disguise I believe the school board had seen enough of Rhonda and me. Danny called me after the meeting to tell me that the school board decided to rethink the issue about taking away the buses from the children. Later that week I found an article in the newspaper stating that Richmond Heights school board would be reevaluating the busing issue for the community. The Lord does work in mysterious ways, and I said a prayer that night, thanking God for what was happening and asking him for that one small favor once again.

Wisdom with Age

As the school year was about to close in 2009, we prepared for a long hot summer. The small community of Richmond Heights continued to be plagued by levy issues, and the bus issue was an ongoing battle. My job and its heavy workload seemed to be ever increasing. With my children growing older, I felt I was getting wiser as I dealt with the issues of raising children on a rotating shift schedule, working days, nights, and afternoons, sometimes working twelve hours instead of the regular eight hours. My children often asked me questions about my past, and I held nothing back as I tried to educate them about the ways of the world, hoping they would not make the same mistakes as I did.

As my fourteen-year-old son and I had many moments alone, he asked me, if I did all those bad things, how come I never went to jail? I told him I really didn't know why I never went to jail; I gave him examples of being just a little smarter than the average street kid. I told him of being in a room with a group of friends, and one guy had a gun, so I didn't stick around. I knew that gun meant bad business, and as much as I wanted to stay, I decided to leave. All my friends told me the gun wasn't loaded, but somehow I didn't trust the man with the gun and decided to go home. The next day I read in the newspaper about the man with the unloaded gun killing his best friend. By the grace of God, I wasn't around, and I had the choice to make the right or wrong decision. I don't know why I didn't stay.

Another fine example was a guy with a knife sticking it in a piece of wood; again I had to make a decision, so I went home. The next day I visited a young man in the hospital with three knife wounds in his belly; his best friend had stuck him in the stomach with the knife. I told my son, when you see someone doing something wrong, just choose another path. Go home.

As we experience life together, I can always tell him things of my past that hopefully will help him make the right decisions; and as my daughter grows older, I will hold nothing back from her either, giving both of them the knowledge of experience, which is what my whole life and this book is about. Reaching a crossroad and being able to choose the right path, hopefully my life experiences will teach and help others to go down the right road.

As the hot days of summer were in full bloom, I spoke to both of my children about a new idea to help our young and not so smart. While washing my truck at a local car wash, I could hear music so loud that I could hear nothing else. A small car next to the bay I was in barely had a place for the engine or anything else, with monster speakers in the trunk and doors. The music coming from this midsized car was loud, it literally shook the ground. As I looked down, I could see the concrete and my tennis shoes vibrating from the thumping sound.

I thought of all the damage this young man and the rest of our youth was doing to their ears. By the time some of these kids reach their twenties, none of them will be able to hear anything. I think everyone by now has some experience with this because almost at every traffic light, some kid or some foolish adult is blasting music so loud that they can hear nothing else, and everyone in a five-mile radius can hear their music.

As I went home, I thought of all the damage the more-than-loud music was doing to some ears. I walked into the house, telling my wife and children about a program I would like to start, calling it B.A.L.M., which means Brothers Against Loud Music. They laughed as I told them I would like to contact Bill Cosby, who often speaks to the public about many things they don't want to hear. I joked about how I would stand onstage with two of the biggest funnels I could find, strapped to my head by my ears; and as Mr. Cosby spoke to me, I would yell "What, what, what!" with loud thumping music playing like you hear it coming from the cars on the street.

My children were laughing as I ran around the kitchen yelling, "What, what, what!" The message was well received, and all the joking was for a good cause. I asked my children what they thought of my idea. They wanted to know how soon I would contact Bill Cosby. In all seriousness, I hope Mr. Cosby would someday read my book; my wife suggested I contact Bill Cosby via email, telling him of my idea to stop our youth from ruining something I feel is very valuable in life.

As for my children, they both agreed that playing music that loud is ridiculous; but at one time, so did my nephew. But as soon as he was able to drive, he found some of the biggest speakers he could find, playing his music even louder than the kid at the car wash.

By the Grace of God

In 2010 I am experiencing a great life. By the grace of God, I am now forty-eight years old; and by his hand, I hope to see many more good years. I am currently in my twenty-fifth year of employment as a nuclear security officer at the Nuclear Power Plant. I am also in my twenty-third year of marriage to my best friend. Rhonda and I are very happy, and I could never love another the way I love her. My son Timmy is sixteen years old and more of a man than any other boy that I know. My daughter is twelve years old and is the light of my life as she sticks close to my side, and in her eyes I can do no wrong.

The Lord has truly blessed me, and I am thankful every day for the many blessings he's given me. I can't right all the wrongs that I've done in the past, and hopefully for the people who read this book, it will help them choose the right path when they come to that crossroad in their life. Hopefully with the help of God I have saved many a soul along the way; and hopefully I can save many more in the future.

Many of my fellow officers that are my age already have children who are in the working world, and I seek their advice as the younger generation of the guard force seeks mine. I often talk to guys who are twenty to twenty-five years younger than I, young officers just starting a family, seeking the knowledge of an elder who feels very much on their level.

I often give advice to young guys such as a young bright-eyed Mike Vuyanich, who has two small boys and a loving wife. We learn from each other as we share our experiences that life gives us; we often talk about growing up. Mike grew up in the Euclid school system, and he was a minority, being one of the very few white kids in school. I grew up just the opposite, going to a mostly white school in Wickliffe. It's interesting that the treatment of each individual on opposite sides of the spectrum came out of school feeling the same way. Despite all the things that happened to us, we have one thing that will make us brothers for life; we meet on common ground as we put our faith and trust in the Lord Jesus Christ.

I would like to dedicate this book to our young who are lost in the world, not finding life easy to deal with, no friends in school, living with one parent or no parents at all to guide them through life. Just when I thought I had it so bad, the Lord would always show me someone who was suffering far more than I could ever imagine. It is true about the old saying, I cried because I had no shoes until I saw a man with no feet. I see a lot of things in today's world that absolutely floor me. As an adult, I often wonder how I made it to where I am today; but as I go to church on Sunday and say my prayers every day, I find that the things that are a mystery aren't really that at all. Through God all things are possible. Trust and have faith in the Lord, for he is the guiding light.

These memories are for all to see a history of someone who through Christ changed a dark future into something so bright, and yes, I do stop and smell the roses. This book is also dedicated to my wife Rhonda and my children Tim and Victoria. Also for the misguided youth of our society, I once was lost just like you, but I'm here to tell you there is a way out—God is the answer. Also to all of those who have gone before me, I will continue to pray for your souls, hoping that you are forgiven all your sins and are seated at the right and of the Lord. Also for my fellow officers at the Nuclear Power Plant, I hope there is a place in heaven for nuclear security officers. As for now, let God be your guide as we work long hours and swing shifts. One day we will take our place with the Lord and guard the gates of heaven as we guarded our loved ones and the world. May the Lord shine his perpetual light upon you, thanks be to God.

Unsupervised Cows

If you happen to see a herd of cows standing in the rain with mud and water dripping off their hides, think about it. How much of your life have you been an unsupervised cow, or have you always been an unsupervised cow? Standing around in the cold wet rain with no direction, taking drugs, drinking, and doing all the things to make you about just as smart as a cow standing on a wet muddy hillside with no thought of what you can do to seek shelter? So do you just let things happen as I once did, contributing to crime, drugs, and alcohol, among many other things, to hurt the ones you love? Hurting some innocent family or preying on the weak, aiding them to fall into the devil's hands, taking what once was good and making it evil?

I'm calling you the unsupervised cow!

Why do we tend to gravitate toward all the wrongdoings in the world? We are truly unsupervised cows not knowing when it is time to come out of the rain. With the Lord's guidance, I came out of the rain, off the muddy hillside into his shelter. You have to make choices—will I continue to be an unsupervised cow, or will I take everything the Lord has given me and become a supervised cow? Follow God's plan, follow his supervisors, follow the Bible, get your strength from him and all his teachings. Become a supervised cow. And by the way, *brothers and sisters, I will meet you in heaven with all the Lord's supervised cows!*

Lightning Source UK Ltd.
Milton Keynes UK
UKOW03f1953110417

298900UK00001B/120/P